# The
# Monumental Impulse

# GEORGE HERSEY

# *The Monumental Impulse*

## ARCHITECTURE'S
## BIOLOGICAL
## ROOTS

THE MIT PRESS

CAMBRIDGE, MASSACHUSETTS

LONDON, ENGLAND

This book was set in Meta by Mary Reilly and was printed and bound in the United States of America.

Library of Congress Cataloging-in-Publication Data

Hersey, George L.
        The monumental impulse : architecture's biological roots / George Hersey.
            p.      cm.
        Includes bibliographical references and index.
        ISBN 0-262-08274-8 (alk. paper)
        1. Architecture—Philosophy.  2. Architectural design.  3. Nature (Aesthetics)
4. Architecture and society.  I. Title.
NA2500.H388  1999
720'. 1—dc21                                                                                    98-45657
                                                                                                      CIP

*to Rebecca Katharine Hersey and Samuel Ashton Hersey*

# Contents

# Acknowledgments

Thanks to Anders Pape Møller, the ornithologist, who read the manuscript in an earlier version and corrected many misstatements about biology. Also to Jonathan Marks, the geneticist, and Michael Frame, the mathematician, whose biological insight has been of immense help throughout the writing process and who have closely read and commented on the manuscript in nearly its finished form. I offer similar thanks to my editor at the MIT Press, Roger Conover, who was able to articulate a number of ways in which the manuscript could be given greater continuity, and to my copyeditor, Alice Falk; comparing her to other editors is like comparing Mozart to Karl Ditters von Dittersdorf. I also thank the book's resourceful designer, Jean Wilcox.

My thanks also to Joseph Connors, who has read and corrected the discussions of Borromini; to Wendy Doniger and Phillip Wagoner, whose knowledge of things Hindu was essential for my forays into that sphere; and to James P. Allen, who has usefully vetted my remarks on ancient Egypt. I finally thank Ben Diebold for introducing me to cladistics; Marty Golubitsky, Peter Richter, and George Markowsky, from whose expertise on symmetry and number series I have profited; and Paul Turner, who read and corrected me on the subject of honeycomb houses.

Others who have offered useful suggestions or essential help are Karsten Harries, Rachel and Don Hersey, Kirsi Leiman, Eve Blau, Juhani Pallasmaa, Cesar Pelli, Joseph Rykwert, Talbot Page, Andrew Stewart, Robert Steinberg, and, at Yale, Adam Griff, Dhananjana Ameresekere, Weatherly Ralph, and many other students and colleagues. I also thank my associates at the American Academy in Rome during the fall of 1994, especially its director, Caroline Bruzelius, and Malcolm Bell, professor in charge; also Sanda D. Iliescu, Karl Kirchwey, Elfriede Knauer, and other friendly fauna of that handsome habitat.

Finally, none of these people should be held responsible for whatever is still wrong with the book.

# Introduction

## Architecture and Biology

More than fifty years ago Nikolaus Pevsner, then the prince of British architectural historians, claimed: "A bicycle shed is a building; Lincoln Cathedral is a piece of architecture."[1] Such sentiments see architecture as a mandarin activity—and perhaps also as normally, though not necessarily, quite grand. Pevsner's subtext is that there is a Great Tradition in architecture, not unlike F. R. Leavis's literary Great Tradition (presented in the 1948 book of that title); for Leavis this comprises George Eliot, James, and Conrad; for Pevsner, Lincoln, King's College Chapel, and the Bank of England. For each art, there are supreme canons against which everything lesser is judged.

Yet (and I am sure many people have asked this question) why shouldn't a bicycle shed be architecture? The bicycle shed can be a symmetrical building elegantly articulated in metal and glass. It may even be said to have a nave and aisles. It is not a masterpiece like Lincoln, true enough, but to me it is just as much a "piece of architecture" as are any number of other more ambitious buildings, some of them designed by great architects. So in this book my attitude will be different from Pevsner's. Indeed I will be saying that not only a bicycle shed is architecture but so are a beehive, a bird's nest, and even certain molecules, cells, and body parts. We humans borrow from these animal "buildings"— borrow in all sorts of ways to create all sorts of human architecture.

I will look at these animal artifacts as monuments—in the sense that they are often highly elaborated, long-lasting, and colossal—that is, built at many times the scale of their individual builders and, often, destined to endure for several generations. Often, too, as with the pyramids of Egypt, the erection of these animal monuments has demanded huge investments of time and labor by large cooperating communities. My point will be that all such communities, including the human ones who build so similarly, are subject to the monumental impulse.

How else may architecture be biological? Other bioarchitectural analogies are common. The number of architectural books and articles with "evolution" in the title is almost a joke. But then so is the number of biological writings with "architecture" in the title.[2]

In a sense, any "piece of architecture" is a biological restatement by the members of the species that built it and shaped it to its users' needs. A shelter is a shell, usually made of dead tissue, for living organisms. The marble and limestone Parthenon is constructed of fossil whelk tissue. Frank Lloyd Wright's prairie houses are made mainly of defunct trees. Furthermore, both Wright's lumber and the Parthenon's stone were once shelters or homes on their own terms—the trees for any number of organisms from birds to bacteria, the shells for living members of the genus *Buccinum* or perhaps for the unrelated creatures, such as mason bees, who establish residence in abandoned snail shells.[3]

Even if we look only at architecture that is monumental in the sense that it is primarily memorial, the earliest such human structures were probably tombs; and a tomb puts biological remains in a built, excavated, or chosen container. A tomb is thus like the body of a dead whelk in its shell. And many human-built temples and shrines are simply compactions of tombs—large-scale containers or immurements for dead organisms. We will see in the stone houses from Lemba, on Cyprus, which are among the earliest of all stone-built human dwellings in Europe, that the foundation of each house served as a family tomb while the superstructure sheltered those ancestors' living descendants. This same phenomenon, the building as a compaction of dead tissue, has pervaded our human past at some of its greatest moments. When in the early years of the sixteenth century Julius II decided to pull down Old St. Peter's and build Bramante's new church, the opposition called it sacrilegious and pointed to the walls and floor of the old basilica, which were literally crammed with the sanctified bones of saints and rulers, some of them there for as long as twelve centuries.[4]

I will go on to propose that the first large multi-individual shelters that early hominids could have known were those of ants or bees, and that various shapes and techniques which later became important in human architecture were probably first observed in nonhuman societies—that, for example, the first hexagons humans ever saw could well have been in honeycombs; the first domes, birds' eggs; the first skyscrapers, termitaries (high-rise mound dwellings built by termites); the first tents, those of African weaver ants; the first gridded walls or suspension structures, those of birds or spiders.[5]

I am not the only person to have made such suggestions. Indeed the earliest architectural treatise we have, and the only one dating from antiquity, says some of these things. Vitruvius claims that architecture arose when humans began to gather into settlements. Some people, inspired by the birds, built nestlike shelters for themselves (Vitruvius, *De architectura* 2.1.1). Many of

0.1.

Woodcut from Cesare
Cesariano's edition of Vitruvius
(1521). "Building in the first
age of the human world. Many
people imitated the shelters
built by animals."

0.2.

Oriole nest, detail. From
Dunning, *Secrets of the Nest.*

EX PRIMA MVNDI HOMINVM AETATE AEDIFICATIO. MVLTI ENIM AB
ANIMALIBVS EXEMPLA VITAE CONSERVAPE OZ IMITATI SVNT & C̄

Vitruvius's army of commentators from the Middle Ages to our own time have
illustrated this thought verbally and visually.[6]

Thus the sixteenth-century Milanese commentator Cesare Cesariano says that the
wattle-and-clay houses of contemporary peasants first came into existence as
imitations of animals' buildings.[7] In Cesare's illustration (fig. 0.1) the house on
the left is composed of stripped, upright tree trunks with their upper branches
preserved. Horizontal branches and woven vines form its walls. Thus do the
humans duplicate the building processes of birds. Swallows make similar use
of withes and clay, and there are Old World orioles that weave their walls using
trees for support (though fig. 0.2 depicts a New World species). We will examine this more fully in chapter 6.

Closer to our own day, another sort of analogy between architecture and
biology provides the frontispiece of Banister Fletcher's famous survey of the
history of human architecture (fig. 0.3). Sprouting from a tapered trunk, symmetrical branches curve into an arboreal candelabrum. Each branch is wrapped
by a tendril, and each architectural style is then a nut or flower on the branch,
a flower that encases a typical building. At the base are Peruvian, Egyptian,
Assyrian, Chinese, and Japanese "flowers," while a vertical succession, beginning with Greek architecture, grows up the trunk. The trunk proceeds through
Roman and Romanesque phases to a treetop triumph: the American Style symbolized by Daniel Burnham's 1904 Flatiron Building in New York. Here there are
also several unlabeled buds. These, obviously, are the newest architectural
growths—not architecture's history but its future.

0.3.

Banister Fletcher. The Tree of

Architecture. Frontispiece of

Fletcher, *History of Architecture*.

BANISTER FLETCHER. INV.

*This Tree of Architecture shows the main growth or evolution of the various styles, but must be taken as suggestive only, for minor influences cannot be indicated on a diagram of this kind.*

# PEDIGREE OF MAN.

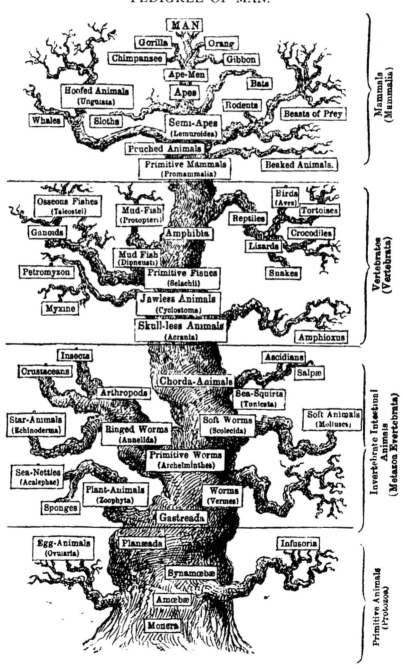

0.4.

Ernst Haeckel. The Pedigree of

Man. From Haeckel, *Evolution*

*of Man.*

Fletcher's tree almost certainly derives from what, at the turn of the century, was the best known of all such trees: Ernst Haeckel's "Pedigree of Man," which appeared in numerous editions of his works, in several languages (fig. 0.4).[8] In Haeckel's oak the main zoological taxa, from Monera (single-cell organisms without nuclei) to Man, are part of a single organism, a tree as old as life on earth. Both Haeckel's and Fletcher's trees also suggest that their own ontogeny or development as single trees is equivalent to their phylogeny—to the evolution of all trees across time. The further implication has to be that Fletcher's lowest architectures—Peruvian, Egyptian, Oriental—are equivalent to Monera, amoebas, and the like, while the Flatiron Building is equivalent to Haeckel's apex, MAN. A great and unlooked-for compliment to Daniel Burnham, this, as the American thus outranks Michelangelo. (He, poor man, languishes down among the tusked animals, below rodents.) In the last chapter of this book I will propose a better way of fashioning architectural family trees.

## THE MONUMENTAL IMPULSE: A GENETIC HOMOLOGY?

But why, in the first place, bother to build monumental structures? Why construct giant honeycombs, termitaries, cathedrals? My answer will be that it is in our genes. There are genetic homologies between us and the other species that build, no matter how distant from us they seem. This is an idea that is hardly far-fetched. It used to be thought that the notable similarities between the eyes of vertebrates and those of sharks, squid, octopuses, and so on were the result of independent evolutionary adaptations.[9] Such independent evolution of similar features is called *convergence*. Wings, for example, though they "converge" in appearance and use, were independently evolved on four different evolutionary occasions—by pterosaurs, insects, birds, and bats.

But now we know that the development of sharks' and humans' eyes did not occur as two separate episodes. Each organism, during its independent evolution, has carried with it highly elaborate, almost identical gene sequences—sequences that, at the appropriate times, expressed themselves in the form of similarly designed eyes, complete with eyelids, corneas, irises, lenses, retinas, posterior rectus muscles, and sacs of vitreous humor (fig. 0.5).[10] In this particular respect, at least, the genetics of the human and those of the dogfish are strictly related. And (I say) if we can have dogfishes' eye genes we can have bees' building genes.

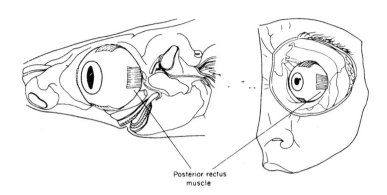

o.5.

Dissection in lateral aspect
of the eye anatomy of a spiny
dogfish; similar dissection of a
human eye. Both from Riedl,
*Order in Living Organisms*.

Posterior rectus
muscle

This and similar developments are genetic homologies. What I want to emphasize is that we humans carry gene sequences going back beyond our own origins, beyond those of mammals, beyond those of vertebrates—sequences that
may correspond almost exactly to those in otherwise very different species.

In the following pages I will be claiming something similar about our urge to
build: that *Homo sapiens* shares something that I don't yet dare call a gene
sequence for building—shares it, perhaps homologously, perhaps convergently,
with other constructing creatures such as birds, crustaceans, ants, termites, and
bees. I will also be claiming, as a corollary, that the shapes of our monumental shelters, whether bicycle sheds or cathedrals, reflect and often derive from
the shapes first created by these other species—species that, like us, are subject to the monumental impulse.

Though many people have written about animal architecture, no one, so far as
I know, has broached the question of homologous evolution in the sense given
above. Nor have others gone into the related question of architectural reproduction and evolution. Nor, finally, has anyone investigated other similarities
with human architecture—homologies, convergences, or parallels—that can be
traced from molecules to landscape and on to the cosmos. Here, I hope, lies
the freshness of my approach.[11]

But now comes a paradox: certain ants, termites, honeybees, and birds build
elaborate structures.[12] So do humans. But, as humans, we are anomalous in
doing this. Only a few other mammals build—most obviously beavers and badgers.[13] Worse still, our own closest cousins, the other primates, hardly build at

all. An African termitary might remind us of Wright, of a Gaudí spire, or of a skyscraper by Hermann Obrist. But no such thoughts come to mind when we look at the rudimentary retreats of chimps and gorillas. Thus any genetic homology that brackets us with the other builder-species will have to be very ancient and, also, will have to have bypassed our immediate ancestors and cousins. One explanation is suggested toward the end of this book when I discuss human territories and their markers. I will try to picture a humanity that was strongly territorial (like other primates) but that marked out, defended, and ornamented its territories geometrically and ultimately with architecture. Such acts can run all the way from the painting of cave interiors to the building of modern cities.

This is one reason for my guardedness about calling our monumental impulse a true genetic homology. Another reason is more basic: the idea cannot be converted from suggestion to fact until it has been scientifically proved. This hasn't happened yet. But one thing cannot be denied at this point: we humans do have an impressive instinct, whether genetic, learned, or both—an instinct shared with other species—for building.

## BUILDINGS AS EXTENDED PHENOTYPES

Animal architecture, such as anthills, termitaries, beehives, and the like, represents what Richard Dawkins calls their builders' extended phenotype.[14] The animal-created artifact is a product of the animal's genome, but one that the animal deliberately makes and that is independent of its body. And if, as Dawkins says, these artifacts may nonetheless be considered separate prolongations of, or annexes to, those bodies, then we too, since we humans also have genotypes and phenotypes, might allow ourselves to speak of our buildings as extended phenotypes. Indeed, Dawkins proposes exactly that in his book.[15]

The anthropologist Peter J. Wilson has even proposed that construction—first of shelter and then, particularly, of any shelter that is more than merely adequate—is the key adaptation in humankind's progress from the "uncivilized" life of the hunter-gatherer to that of permanent habitations, agriculture, civilization, and cities.[16] It seems very possible to me that Wilson is right (I only add that Vitruvius expressed the same idea 2,000 years ago; *De architectura* 2.1.6). Vitruvius explains further, and in a sharply proto-Darwinian way, that once the process was begun, continuous competition among the human builders resulted in architecture as we know it.

Here I must note that in many societies buildings have been thought of precisely as "extended phenotypes"—and this long before Dawkins (see chapter 6, below). Wilson shows that all over the world, buildings have been conceived by their builders and users as enlargements of the human bodies that built and used those structures. Even when their actual shape has nothing recognizably human in it, the buildings are described as having eyes, mouths, ears, teeth, bones, heads, and reproductive systems—either those of men and women or those of men's and women's animal totems, or perhaps those of giant inhabitable creatures that conjoin human, plant, and animal parts.

My book joins and weaves together the two main concepts outlined above; the bioarchitectural analogy and the notion of buildings as extended phenotypes. These are some of the reasons I will be talking about molecules, crystals, viruses, and cells, and birds' nests, beehives, and bicycle sheds—leading onward, of course, to cathedrals.

# Molecules, Viruses, and Cells

## Prebiotic Molecules

Nowadays it is frequently suggested that inanimate objects might be subject to biological processes. The idea that a piece of nonliving matter (made, say, of brick) might somehow behave biologically is not as odd as it first sounds. Many scientists claim that living molecules evolve in the Darwinian sense just as do larger organisms. And some even see reproduction and evolution among those molecules that are not considered to be living tissue at all. In this scenario, nonliving chemical molecules, carbon chief among them, originally combined together so as to form proteins, and these eventually turned into the raw material of life. In other words, it was only after the nonliving molecular combinations came into existence—after the "prebiotic" elements evolved and were subject to selection, adaptation, and mutation—that more truly living organisms came about. According to these scientists, therefore, Darwinian evolution not only dominates life, it precedes it—and perhaps lies beyond it.[1]

In short, life may be described as one facet, and one facet only, of evolution—or, at least, of reproduction plus heritable variation. And as Kevin Kelly and Claus Emmeche remind us, there can be post- as well as prebiotic selection and reproduction.[2] Darwinian evolution with its various kinds of selection seems to work for things like computer programs and robots.[3] Julius Rebek has shown that laboratory-made nonliving molecules create copies of themselves, "mutate," and form themselves into assemblages of look-alike molecules that then compete for resources. All of these things, of course, reinforce the idea of nonbiotic Darwinian paradigms in nature.[4]

I will note further that this pre- or nonbiotic evolution accords with precise reciprocal likenesses in the geometry of certain molecules. The likenesses, their mutual fit (portrayed only as a graphic demonstration in figure 1.1, not literally), cause the molecules to be attracted to each other. They join up in a process I will call "shape-mating." And, in the nonbiotic realm as in the biotic, some shapes are more mateable than others. In other words, there can be sexual or at least shape selection on this geometric level.[5] Figure 1.1 diagrams such a mating. Molecule A and molecule B, which have complementary geometries (and complementary electrochemical properties) "dock" into each other along a snaky joint, with the protuberances of the right-hand form penetrating precisely apposite indentations in the left-hand form, so as to unite into a disk or sphere. Thus do two fragments become a whole. These same principles apply

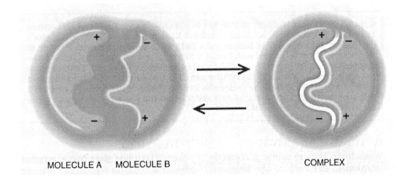

MOLECULE A    MOLECULE B                            COMPLEX

1.1.

Diagram of molecular shape
recognition. Adapted from
Rebek, "Synthetic Self-
Replicating Molecules."

1.2.

The molecular distribution of a
liquid colloidal solution of silver bromide. Author.

1.3.

Hypostyle hall plan. Author.

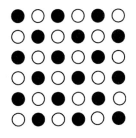

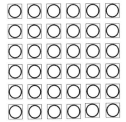

even when the two shapes are far more complicated. They are still negative and positive toward each other, and capable of perfect juncture.

A. Lima-de-Faria has proposed that the evolution of life itself has to do with shape—or, as biologists call it, morphology.[6] Certain mathematico-geometric shapes can engender such varied molecules as a virus (sometimes considered a living organism)[7] or as a piece of opal or a ball of latex—the latter two being not "pre" but simply nonbiotic.

And let it be said that such nonbiotic molecular matings can have more than two partners—there can be billions of avid self-assemblers, to use the biological term, in a single such conjunction. This brings up another aspect of shape-mating, known to mathematicians as *tight packing*. One notable shape that tight packs is the sphere. In colloidal crystals, for example (fig. 1.2), spheres are stacked together like piles of billiard balls.[8] This is tight packing proper; but another type of packing, called *standard proximity*, establishes a set amount of space around each ball or disk. When the balls actually touch, by the way, mathematicians speak of them as kissing.[9]

Here there are many architectural analogies. Notable similarities exist between one of the commonest types of ancient hall plan, the hypostyle, and the arrangement of colloid spheres into molecules (fig. 1.3). (We must note, though, that the rows of disks in the hypostyle plan are sections through columns, while the disks in the silver bromide molecule are sections through spheres.) The bisected columns reproduced are arranged in standard proximity packing.[10]

Hypostyle halls are among the commonest and most impressive achievements in ancient Near Eastern, Egyptian, and Hellenistic architecture. So, one asks,

1.4.

Buckminster Fuller. U.S. Pavilion
at the Montreal World's Fair,
1967. From Kultermann,
*Architecture in the Twentieth
Century.*

1.5. Model of a buckminsterfullerene: a truncated icosahe-
dral cage formed by 60 carbon
atoms. From Cohen and
Stewart, *Collapse of Chaos.*

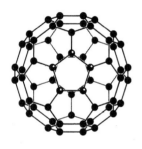

does our delight in a plan like the one here illustrated have anything to do with the fact that much of nature—including ourselves, our bodies, and our bodies' molecular components—is shot through with similar aggregates? The builders of ancient hypostyles clearly could not have known about modern molecular architecture, let alone the graphic conventions by which it is expressed. But that is not the point. What is important is that this is how we are all made.

Throughout this book I will attempt to show that in architecture and ornament, we design forms that homologously reflect those that constitute our bodies, from the molecular level on up.[11] One designer who has expressed these ideas is Buckminster Fuller. His concept of *tensegrity* involves a larger form composed of self-similar (in the mathematical sense) nested smaller forms, progressing downward in size, like Chinese boxes, to the atomic level.[12]

At the moment, the most famous molecule/building analogy involving Fuller is the buckminsterfullerene, or buckyball. Fuller's U.S. Pavilion at the 1967 Montreal Exposition (fig. 1.4) illustrated the architecture of this carbon molecule (fig. 1.5).[13] Like many molecules, and like so many Fuller structures, the buckyball is an Archimedean sphere made out of the frames of pentagonal and hexagonal surfaces. The normal fullerene consists of five hexagons surrounding a pentagon. When enough of these shapes are assembled with all edges touching, the result will be a faceted spherical surface like that of the Montreal Pavilion.[14]

In the 1920s Frank Lloyd Wright too was experimenting with concentric three-dimensional domical constructs made out of hexagons, pentagons, and the like. The Wright plans or cross-sections mix spheres and cylinders—domes and columns or towers. The plan of a 1926 proposed Steel Cathedral for New York City, intended to be 1,500 feet high, consists of a hexagon core with identical symmetrical polygons rotated out from the center in fivefold rotational symmetry (fig. 1.6). The whole is inscribed into an outer hexagon. While several of these forms do not have equal sides and are to that extent irregular, their rotations around the building's center are nonetheless perfectly symmetrical and obey the principles of tight packing and exact fit—principles we also find in molecular and crystal structures.[15]

## DNA AND OTHER SPIRAL COMMUNICATORS

As to molecules that are unquestionably biotic, the most famous is of course deoxyribonucleic acid. DNA contains most of the genes of all plants and animals and inhabits the nucleus of every tissue cell. These molecules, therefore, are among the most widespread of all shapes in nature.[16] And their shape, as everyone now knows, is almost always a double helix.

1.6.

Frank Lloyd Wright. Plan of the Steel Cathedral, project, 1926. From Alofsin, *Frank Lloyd Wright: The Lost Years*.

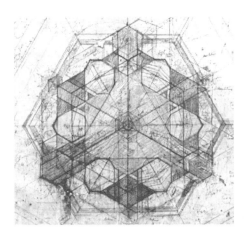

MOLECULES, VIRUSES, AND CELLS

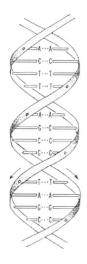

1.7.

DNA molecule with like base

pairs and opposed helices.

From Watson, *Double Helix*.

The normal DNA double helix consists of two concentrically twisted chains or ribbons of sugar-phosphate nucleotides (molecules with nitrogen bases; fig. 1.7). In scientific publications the spirals are usually drawn to look like plaits of hair or spiral ramps. They either have two opposed spirals—one left-handed (counterclockwise) and the other right-handed (clockwise), as in figure 1.7—or two nested right-handed ones (handedness is determined by starting at the bottom and moving up). As normally illustrated, DNA spirals also have steplike hydrogen bondings between the "ramps," making them all the more resemble spiral staircases in their explanatory diagrams. There is also a triple-helix form of DNA.[17]

As the Belgian physicist David Ruelle points out, what DNA spirals mainly do is process information.[18] They copy, edit, and transfer. The letters by which the base pairs are identified are, as it were, words, and the strings of base pairs that constitute actual genes are sentences. Mutations alter the sentences' "meaning." The creation of new life, then—reproduction—involves the passing-on of information. It is nowadays commonplace for DNA biologists to speak of "misspellings" in genetic transcriptions.

Just as, recognized or not, double-helix genes have always been with us, and inside us, so helices—single and double, left- and right-handed—have long been common in architecture. Staircases and columns in particular have exploited the form. Double helices also occur in steeples, finials, and the like, not to mention the countless ornaments that imitate the wide and intricate variations among helical shells.

Helices fascinated Leonardo. A simple architectural double helix (fig. 1.8) appears on the next page. Leonardo's stair is labeled *lumaca doppia*, which means "double snail." Note that two separate upper corridors, each with its own arched opening, lead to the two nested left-handed ramps wrapping a central pier. Leonardo's stairs are unlike DNA in that they have this pier. The most famous of double-helix staircases, which also has a central pier, is that at the French Renaissance palace of Chambord. This is occasionally attributed to Leonardo. It is a double concentric stair composed of two right-handed spirals.[19] We'll see more of these central piers and spiral outworks in chapter 3, which considers shells.

A much more stylish double helix, however, and one built without the central pier, was designed by Nicolas Le Camus de Mézières for his Halle au Blé, Paris,

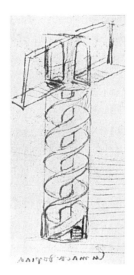

1.8.

Leonardo da Vinci. Drawing of a double-helix staircase with nested left-hand spirals, c1487–1488 or earlier. Paris, Bibliothèque Nationale. Ms B, fol. 69v.

published in 1769 (fig. 1.9).[20] This structure was all in vaulted masonry, the two magnificent whorls anchored inside a cylinder. The stairs led through two lower floors up to a tall barrel-vaulted attic. At the base, each flight separated into a Y-shape, with each branch of the Y forming a set of approach steps.

In function, and not just appearance, these spiral stairs may be likened to DNA. In the Middle Ages and Renaissance such corkscrew architectural communicators were principal ways of transmitting people, food, and other goods, as well as messages, commands, and the like. Like DNA, the stairs copied, translated, reproduced, and edited information; and they still do.

Just as both DNA and spiral staircases communicate, so do columns. First of all, in a classical columnar order, a column speaks of that order's geographical and social origin. Doric, Ionic, and Corinthian are geographical designations. Different types of columns, furthermore, were said to be statues of different types of people—matrons, maidens, soldiers, Ionians, Dorians, Corinthians, and so on. This makes them informational. Indeed, in the Hermetic tradition columns were the first, most venerable modes of communication. It was said that Hermes Trismegistus, in legend the founder of philosophy, inscribed his ideas on columns, and that his pupils (including Socrates, Moses, and Zoroaster) first learned their art by reading and interpreting Hermes' columns. Nor did the idea ever really die out. All throughout northern Europe, especially in the baroque period, there were cults of *Säulenlehre* and *Säulenphilosophie*. Eager students learned the intricacies of the five orders, along with many old and new subsets of them, so as to quicken their minds

1.9.

Nicolas Le Camus de Mézières. Halle au Blé, Paris. Double spiral stairs, 1762–1766. Now demolished. From Neufforge, *Receuil elementaire.*

and improve their stock of culture. Extraordinary philosophical digressions were read into the rules for designing the orders, their numerical proportions, and their legendary meanings. The architectural orders thus became constitutive metaphors for order in general. These ideas were passed on from the Hermeticists to the Freemasons, the Rosicrucians, and other early modern mystical sects.

Much has been written on *Saülenphilosophie*, so I will not pursue it further here.[21] But I will discuss one of its key aspects, one that is even now unjustly neglected. Among all types of columns, the one most like DNA is the kind that has a twisted, spiral, or "Solomonic" shaft. One of the very first Roman honorific columns, that of Minucius Augurinus at the foot of the Aventine (c439 BCE), seems in contemporary coin reliefs to have had such a shaft. The much more famous columns of Trajan (113 CE) and Marcus Aurelius (180–196 CE) are also wound with spiral figure reliefs detailing military episodes in their builders' careers. Here, then, are two major instances of information stored and transmitted in spiral form, DNA-wise, along column shafts.[22] One might even add that the information on these columns is genetic as well as cultural: it encapsulates the phenotypic traits of a hero and embeds the information in later populations. It instills the prowess of their ancestors in future generations.

But this classical background for twisted shafts pales beside the biblical tradition. Spiral columns were held to have been used, perhaps even invented, by Solomon (or by his architect Hiram of Tyre) for his temple. Now the preeminent, if almost completely imaginary *modello* for the Christian church, both East and West, has ever been the Jerusalem Temple, especially as described by Ezekiel in his vision (Ezekiel 40–41); so in the Christian context Solomon's spiral columns might well be called the most important, most sacred, of all column-types. In Old St. Peter's, for example, the apostle's shrine was supported by a four-whorled Solomonic order with Corinthian or composite capitals.[23] One such column is still present in St. Peter's, where it is venerated in the Cappella della Colonna as the very one that Christ leaned against while discoursing with the temple doctors (Luke 2.46).[24] In one of his Sistine Chapel tapestries (*The Healing of the Lame Man*) Raphael projects the interior of Solomon's temple as a hypostyle hall glistening with these bronze tortile columns.

The great age of the twisted column was the baroque. The immense impact of Bernini's four colossal Solomonic shafts for the Baldacchino in St. Peter's,

1624–1633 (fig. 1.10), can be mapped all over Europe and throughout the Catholic empires of the New World. Such columns are also found in Protestant countries. Baroque treatises on architecture almost always devoted plates to them. These whorled baroque shafts are powerfully biotic. Their twists suggest that their shafts are elastic, muscular, capable of sinuous effort—of reach and retraction. They are the best illustration I can think of for Joseph Rykwert's title, *The Dancing Column*—the dance in this case being a rhumba with lots of rambunctious rump-work, or, better yet, the twist.[25]

Similar hyperwhorls, leading through degrees of order eventually to chaos, can be made with a leather band or piece of cloth. You can twist it into single, double, even triple whorls. Up to a point, it all looks very organized. But if you twist far enough, you simply get a hopeless mess of knotted fibers (chaos). Above all, the stems and tendrils of many plants form these single and double

1.10.

Gianlorenzo Bernini.

Baldacchino, St. Peter's, before

1624–1633. Courtesy Art and

Architecture Library, Yale

University. Slides and

Photographs Collection.

1.11.

Molecule of the protein keratin.

From Goodsell, *Our Molecular

Nature*.

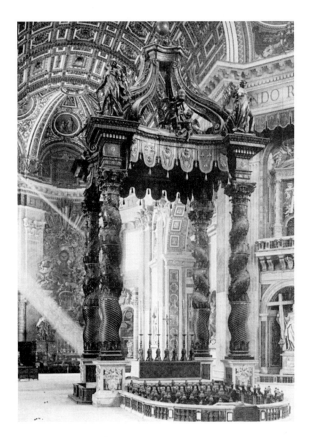

(and sometimes triple) helices. And they too can achieve a fully chaotic state, with windings and plaitings that become more and more random as they build up beyond the regular original inner helices.

Once again: we ourselves, at the microlevel, are partly composed of these forms, complete with hyperwhorls. An example is the molecule in figure 1.11. Keratin is known as an "intermediate filament" and, like a grid of columns across a facade, it forms a strengthening network that weaves all through our cells.

Column shafts, then, may be said to have developed from straight-up-and-down striations to twisted ones. Students of chaos theory have found that fluids, fabrics, and plants, and even air (e.g., tornadoes), clouds, and a host of other substances, transmitted under sufficient pressures, follow the same pattern.[26] In the chaoticians' language, the forms go from the straitly laminar, through degrees of helical turbulence, to chaos proper.[27]

Let us turn from spiral columns to spiral buildings. These too, after all, process information. A celebrated early modernist example is provided by the Russian revolutionary architect Vladimir Tatlin (fig. 1.12). Tatlin spent much of his life refining this design as a monument to the Third International. It is a huge steel double helix with opposed coils. And, as with the DNA helix, communication was to be paramount. Indeed, the program was wild: apparently, motorcycles were to travel up and down the ramps, and the structure's hollow core was to be hung with glass rooms for propaganda broadcasts, meetings, and the like. The rooms are shown as colossal latticed polyhedra. A continuous barrage of news and slogans, in the form of large signs and booming voices, would emanate from the monument night and day.[28]

One could create a model of Tatlin's tower by curving a long piece of spring-wire into the requisite loops. The loops were to be supported by an inclined vertical girder-truss (on the right in the illustration). Here Tatlin may have been making visual Trotsky's paraphrase of Lenin: "a powerful steel spiral, surrounded by a strong band, which in the future will expand, spread out, and embrace ideologically the entire meaning of the revolution."[29] The proposed size of Tatlin's monument has not been sufficiently noted: it would have been 1,300 feet high. (Note the scale given by the background buildings in the illustration.) This would make it taller than any then-existing (c1920) skyscraper;

1.12.

Vladimir Tatlin. Design for

Monument to the Third

International, begun 1919.

From Conrads and Sperlich,

*Architecture of Fantasy.*


1.13.

Hermann Obrist. Design

for a monument, c1902.

From Conrads and Sperlich,

*Architecture of Fantasy.*

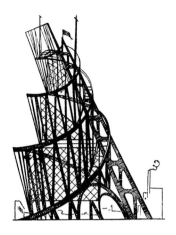

indeed, it is comparable to Wright's contemporaneous Steel Cathedral or, among executed buildings, to the World Trade Center in New York.

As to sources, Tatlin was undoubtedly thinking partly of the Eiffel Tower and, much more, of Hermann Obrist's project (c1902) for a similar leaning helical tower-monument—though that is only a single helix (fig. 1.13). But while Tatlin's monument is purely industrial in style, Obrist, trained as a naturalist, creates a biological tower concocted, seemingly, from the mouthparts of a micro-animal or a mollusk's spicules (the tiny spears that support the tissues of inverte- brates).[30]

## CRYSTALS

Perhaps of all natural objects the most geometric and hence most architec- tural are crystals. These may be single or multiple molecules. A crystal is formed when a chemical element, compound, or mixture solidifies.[31] As D'Arcy Thompson pointed out long ago, crystals and crystalline structures pervade nature well beyond the realm of crystallography proper.[32] Calcium carbonate appears everywhere in plant cells, for example, as well as in limestone and shells. We can see the exquisite geometries of this substance, which is a salt, under polarized light. Similar crystal structures show up in the skeletons of ver- tebrates and in bony growths such as spicules. However large an organism may be, indeed, crystalline infusions can turn it into a cluster of three-dimensional polygons—much on the order of Buckminster Fuller's tensegral trusses.

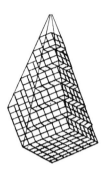

1.14.

A scalenohedron crystal of
calcite built up of rhombohe-
dra. Author.

1.15.

Gustave Eiffel. Eiffel Tower,
Paris, 1887–1889. Courtesy Art
and Architecture Library, Yale
University. Slides and
Photographs Collection.

Crystals provide a case history for the early phases of evolution. If a small crystal is dropped into a solution of the chemical it's made of, it begins to repli-
cate and grow as a self-assembling aggregate of itself. Eventually, after reaching
a certain threshold, the enlarged crystal will break in two. Two things have happened: first, tight packing (i.e., shape-mating) and, second, reproduction.
Graham Cairns-Smith has proposed that the mating and reproduction of crystals in this manner was a model for the evolution of DNA.[33]

The geometry of crystals is a subject unto itself. "The three-dimensional pattern of a crystal has two component parts, the motif and the scheme of repetition," writes Noel F. Kennon.[34] In crystals the motif might be, say, a tetragon,
and the scheme of repetition would be what an architect would call its distribution—for example, into rows and columns, along horizontal and vertical
axes, or according to some other kind of lattice. For the crystallographer there
can be two-dimensional or plane lattices, and three-dimensional or space lattices. Theoretically, these extend to infinity.

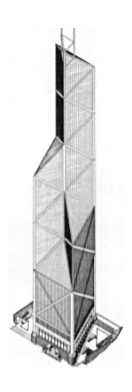

The calcite crystal I compare to the Eiffel Tower (figs. 1.14, 1.15) is of the long, inclined cubic type—that is, having four triple axes at 70° angles to each other. The tower's four uprights are based on a cluster of large scalene triangles assembled in three dimensions; their smaller constitutive units are parallelepipeds, also tight-packed along 70° axes. Note too that just this same "crystalline" principle characterizes the tight-packed lattices (not rectangular but triangular) of the Eiffel Tower itself. Of course, Gustave Eiffel may not have thought consciously about crystals nor, as Buckminster Fuller was to do, about the geometry of steel molecules. But the one shape, the traditional engineering truss, does not exclude the other, the crystal, as a "source."[35] On the contrary: the point is that nature works with similar building blocks (or perhaps I should say with similar regular polyhedra) and that nature and art can produce similar final shapes nested at micro and macro scales.[36] Buildings, indeed, might be defined as giga-molecules. But there are in fact crystals that are much bigger than buildings: some scientists have claimed that the whole solid inner core of the Earth is an iron crystal 1,500 miles wide, formed into a shape-mated hexagonal composite of spherical atoms.[37]

1.16.

I. M. Pei. Bank of China, Hong Kong, 1982–1990.

From Kultermann, *Architecture of the Twentieth Century.*

Any number of other crystals have architectural aspects. In fluorite, crystals can be, among other things, cubes, regular octahedra, and rhombododecahedra (twelve-sided shapes with rhombic or slanted edges). I. M. Pei's faceted carapace for the Bank of China in Hong Kong shape-mates several such clustered crystal forms (fig. 1.16).[38] Indeed the bank resembles a hemimorphic crystal (fig. 1.17). Notably, too, hemimorphic crystals are often transparent, making them much like the crystalline glass cladding of this and other office blocks.

1.17.

A crystal of hemimorphite.

Author.

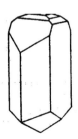

Crystals would seem to have a bewildering array of possible structures. But in fact there is a limit. For crystals of the more "architectural" type, formed on space lattices, there are only fourteen possibilities. These, known as the Bravais lattices, can in turn be occupied by only seven different motifs. The seven motifs are defined in terms of the number of their axes and their type of rotational symmetry.[39] All existing 3-D crystal patterns apparently abide by these limitations.

The science of crystallography, and particularly the Bravais lattice, can help us discern underlying order in what is seemingly chaotic or at least hopelessly complex. For example, Daniel Libeskind's 1996 winning project for an addition to the Victoria and Albert Museum, London (known as the Boilerhouse Project),

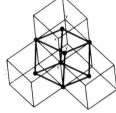

1.18.

Daniel Libeskind. Winning

entry for the Boilerhouse

Project, an addition to the

Victoria and Albert Museum,

London. Adapted from the

*New York Times,* 3 July 1996.

1.19.

A rhombohedral Bravais

lattice. From Kennon, *Patterns*

*in Crystals.*

has caused outrage (fig. 1.18). Its overlapping trapezoids and "deviations from the geometrical norm" have been considered offensive. The design represents "disorder," we read, and "an absurd jumble of broken and collapsing boxes dumped at random and crushed into space."[40]

But must we think of it this way? Are the angles and orientations of Libeskind's boxes really all that chaotic? (And anyway, what's wrong with chaos?) I, at least, see in the proposed building something like a Bravais lattice (fig. 1.19).[41] Many Bravais-type crystals stand at crazy angles inside a three-dimensional grid of regular cubical cells. When a crystal formation involves a cell that is similar but angled within its cage, the Bravais lattice projects the angled cell from well-defined points in an outlying ortholinear grid, as in the illustration. The heavy lines represent the angled cell and the light ones the outer lattice. Note that three of the angled cell's corners conjoin with corners in the outer lattice. The other junctures of the tilted cell can then be generated from these three common corners because the tilted cell is cubical and the same size as the ortholinear cells.

A comparable ortholinear grid could be constructed around Libeskind's facade, though this is more complicated and has more than one tilted "cell." Moreover, the Boilerhouse cells are not all cubes: some are rhombic, and interpenetrate. But the Bravais principle, extended to architecture, can absorb these complications—though they force us beyond the canon of fourteen grids and seven motifs.

## Viruses

Viruses can be defined both as huge molecules and as the simplest of living organisms. Manfred Eigen makes them one of his steps from nonbiotic forms toward the evolution of true life.[42] They thus provide a good transition from a discussion of molecules proper to the rest of this book, which deals with multicellular organisms.

Viruses first became visible in the earliest microscopes. Antoni van Leeuwenhoek, a seventeenth-century Dutch merchant and optician, made lenses that magnified objects up to 300 times. Through them he saw whole bestiaries, "wee animalcules," in drops of water.[43] Today we know Leeuwenhoek's discoveries as bacteria, protozoa, algae, yeasts, sperm, eggs, red blood cells, and more.

1.20. Diagram of a virus.
From A. Levine, *Viruses*.

1.21.
Konrad Wachsmann.
Tetrahedral truss forms for modular construction,
1951–1953. From Conrads and Sperlich, *Architecture of Fantasy*.

Many viruses have an extraordinarily high-tech appearance, both as diagrammed and as micrographed. Seeing them, one thinks of robots and lunar modules. In figure 1.20 I illustrate a T4 bacteriophage virus, which is parasitic on certain bacteria. Its DNA is kept in the hexagonal container on top, called the *head*. This head, let us note, is a strict geometrical elongated 32-hedron encased in a protein coat. The creature's long angular "legs" are actually tail fibers, but it uses them for walking.

In terms of human architecture this virus well exemplifies interwar modernism (fig. 1.21). Konrad Wachsmann's clunky, robotoid tetrahedral truss element is

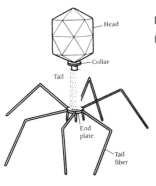

Head
Collar
Tail
End plate
Tail fiber

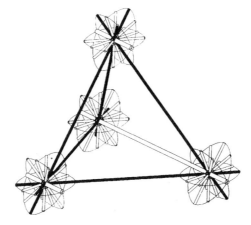

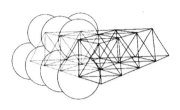

1.22.

Computer graphic image of a

rhinovirus particle. From

Levine, *Viruses.*


1.23.

Buckminster Fuller. How a

space frame is generated from

the centers of tight-packed

spheres. From Fuller

(in collaboration with

Applewhite), *Synergetics.*


1.24.

Antoni Gaudí. Upper part of

finial on the Sagrada Familia,

Barcelona, 1920s. From Conrads

and Sperlich, *Architecture of

Fantasy.*

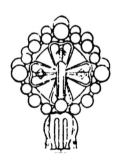

the virus's spiritual kin—pipelike supports with cylindrical sockets at the ends that culminate in "heads" or polygonal vertices where all elements of the truss component are joined.[44]

Viruses are capable of other kinds of geometric regularity. The rhinovirus particle in figure 1.22 is more like something designed by Buckminster Fuller than by Wachsmann. It generally resembles Fuller's geodesic domes and, more particularly, the tight-packed spheres with which he generates his space-frames and other kinds of trusses (fig. 1.23).[45]

If we look at what might be called the pseudo-icosahedra forming the rhinovirus, we note that these are not tight-packed rigid spheres, like billiard balls, but are squeezed like balloons. We also note that the outer surface of the virus is subdivided into two groupings, with fivefold and threefold radial symmetry. Thus the surface of this particle has forty different component stages (in geometric jargon, it's tetracontahedral).

Rhinovirus particles, especially when color-coded, resemble the gaudy crockets with which Gaudí topped off the finials on the Sagrada Familia (fig. 1.24). Note that his spheres are also divided geometrically—but into three sizes rather than into tight-packed radial symmetries. I should add that I do not know that Gaudí was consciously associating these crockets with viruses. Indeed, any number of molecules and atomic models, the so-called space-filling types (clustered colored spheres of different sizes), look like Gaudí's finials. But viruses were known to be so shaped, and were illustrated with models made of colored clustered spheres, at least from 1872 (the finials date from the 1920s). In the 1870s, in fact, the architect's brother Francisco was a medical student, so Gaudí would have had access to such images—for example, in Marc-Antoine Gaudin's *L'Architecture du monde des atomes* (1873).[46]

## Cells

We move up from molecules. Cells have frequently been called architectural—and they are (figs. 1.25, 1.26, 1.27). David S. Goodsell, a molecular biologist, even makes them into practicing architects—nay, city builders:

*Cells are inventive architects. . . . To build these elaborate structures . . . one can find examples of any engineering principle in use today. Fences are built, railways are laid, reservoirs are filled, and houses are constructed complete with rooms, doors, windows, and even decorated in attractive colors. Lap joints, buttresses, waterproofing, reinforcing rods, valves, concrete, adhesive— each has a molecular counterpart.[47]*

1.25.

Generalized diagram of a cell. After Staski and Marks, *Evolutionary Anthropology.*

There is even more to the analogy. The word "cell" was first used in something like its biological sense by Robert Hooke (*Cosmographia*, 1665). He was describing the rows of tiny cavities in a slice of cork. But the primary meaning of *cella* is "small room." Hooke's conception ties in, too, with our notion of tight packing, since that is how cells are arrayed.

1.26.

Lemba-Lakkous, Cyprus. Detail from 1980 plan of excavated remains of Chalcolithic I (c3900 BCE) settlement. From Karageorghis, *Cyprus.*

Now look at some post-Neolithic Cypriote house-plans (fig. 1.26). They are among the oldest remains, anywhere, of human habitations.[48] The people of Lemba-Lakkous organized their houses in a cell-like way, with an outer membrane, a nucleus-hearth, various "organelles" or household elements such as

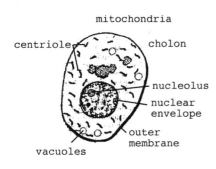

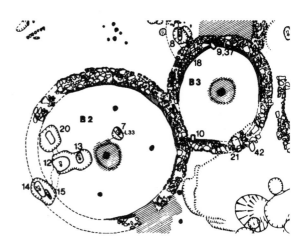

fireplaces, and sleeping and cooking equipment in between. All these elements are essential devices for survival and reproduction—reproduction, of course, being the ultimate form of survival. The house plans are in fact sections through spheroids—prolate, oblate, or otherwise stretched—much like body cells. (This is true only of the plans, however: as for the houses' elevations, masts draped with vines or hides were raised in the central socket as protection against the weather.)

Certainly the builders of these dwellings would have known similar forms in their immediate surroundings—things that, unlike true body cells, were visible to the naked eye. One prototype would be the egg, which begins as a container for a single-cell embryo embedded in the nourishing matter it will need in order to reproduce and grow. Also, eggs are usually surrounded by an outer shell (see chapter 8). And then there are cell-like beehives, birds' nests, and plants. To the Greeks, moreover, and therefore maybe even to the Chalcolithic residents of Lemba, the word for cell (κυτός) also meant uterus, and even the whole human body. So we must not relinquish the thought that the Lemba cells are the extended phenotypes of builders whose own bodies, though they did not consciously know this, were put together similarly.

The idea has continued down the centuries. One architect who felt it strongly was the German expressionist Hermann Finsterlin. Around 1919 he was to write:

*Tell me, have you never regarded your holy body as a building composed of the tiniest, most emancipated single-cell structures? What if we are only living architectural cells, Lilliputian elements that build themselves into the giant proliferation of their organic machinery? . . . [W]e could follow the thousand-times-more beautiful example of lice and beetles when they build their breeding-palaces directly out of the bodies of living plants—greenly glittering, sap-swollen domes in which the chorus of the world rings out no less beautifully than in the columned halls of a solar system.*[49]

In this sense the Cypriote village is another instance of humans creating their architecture as body parts or clusters of such parts writ large. The village's site plan, indeed, particularly recalls modern diagrams of cell division and aggregation—meiosis, mitosis, and so on. Thus we see a fractal or tensegral chain leading from tissue cell to natural cell-like entities created by animals to human

1.27.

Francesco di Giorgio Martini.

Plan of church. From the

*Trattato di architettura,* c1485.

Turin, Biblioteca Nazionale.

Codice Torinese Saluzziano 148.

body parts, all of them rather similar in form, and in several cases with the smaller forms composing the larger.

Cellular architecture is not limited to monasteries, prisons, and prehistoric villages. I illustrate (see fig. 1.27) a plan for a domed cylindrical church by the Renaissance architect Francesco di Giorgio Martini. Here, an outer colonnade with large columns containing pairs of smaller columns acts as the cell's outer sheath. Within that, and concentric to it, is the wall proper, articulated with clustered pilasters matching the outer column-pairs. Inside this is the space, labeled nave, for the congregation. It is screened from the altar area or tribuna by further column-pairs.

Like the Lemba house plans, Francesco's "cell" has its interior "organelles" of furniture (including, no doubt, one or more organs), its outer membrane—the masonry and architectural equivalents of the real cell's outer plasma membrane—and a nucleus in the form of a central lantern. Other organelles in the church would be the cornices, entablatures, windows, steps, and so on. In cellular language, the dome's inner surface of coffers could even be given the cytological name of "endoplasmic reticulum": a reticulum is a net or grid, and dome interiors normally are reticulated on their inner skin into coffers. That the church was to consist of four identical versions of this cell—in other words, that it was to be a tight-packed array—reinforces its cellular nature.

Houses, churches, and cells, then, can resemble each other; but so can whole cities. As James E. Rothman and Lelio Orci recently put it: "All nucleated cells— whether in colonies of yeast or in plants and people—have a complex internal organization resembling that of a well-run city."[50] In their drawing, the long, densely folded interior wrappings constitute the endoplasmic reticulum. The Golgi apparatus is a series of globules, a kind of industrial zone connected by channels where proteins are processed. Small, independent globes near the front of the drawing are vesicles that transport proteins from place to place inside the cell. The lysosome is a lobed chamber in which worn-out component molecules are recycled. Thus the whole organism is an urban industrial complex.

The drawing in figure 1.28 is a cutaway view through a cell that in completed form would resemble a soft, irregular blob. Only by cutting it open (and using a microscope) can you actually see the concentric walls, the central rounded

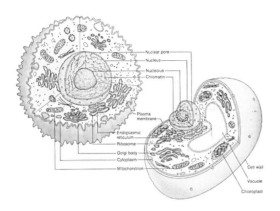

1.28.

Cross-section of a typical cell.

From Rothman and Orci,

"Budding Vesicles in Living

Cells." Drawing by Tomo

Narashima.

1.29.

Pieter Bruegel the Elder.

*The Tower of Babel,* 1563.

Vienna, Kunsthistorisches

Museum.

keep or citadel with its battered bank of ear-shaped battlements, the walled streets, the outer gardens (i.e., the area filled with cytosol or fluid in the cyto-plasm surrounding the cell's nucleus), the semi-independent suburbs (upper right), and the bastions on the perimeter. Rothman and Orci liken all these ele-ments to the gated fortifications of an ancient city. The whole setup controls the entry, distribution, and exit of food and other supplies to and from the "city." The authors point out, by the way, that the outer coatings of the vesi-cles are made of fullerenes.

Though the elder Pieter Bruegel could never have seen such a view of a cell, this whole cross-section does resemble that artist's famous vision of the Tower of Babel (fig. 1.29; Genesis 11.1–9). The rising walls of Bruegel's city have the same curved concentric structure as the cell's endoplasmic reticula; and the city itself, though clearly made of masonry, has the rounded elasticity that we see in cells. These, I hold, would impose their form and organization directly, from the actuality of the artist's living tissues. The hand, brain, and eye that imag-ined and painted the *Tower of Babel* themselves consisted of invisible but omnipresent tight packings of that city's shape: a man made up of cells has painted a cell.

But I should also allow for feedback—for the possibility that in drawing out his image of the cell, the *Scientific American* artist, Tomo Narashima, was influ-enced by Bruegel's image or something similar. Note that he has pushed the cell's perspective upward and pulled the nearer parts of it downward to display as much as possible of its interior. As a result, the cell's urban configuration—its concentric walling, the cisternlike vesicles, and the spiraling orientation of the whole toward its nuclear center—are given special focus. Four hundred years earlier, Bruegel had given Babel the same flowering thrusts, and for the same reason. But if Narashima was influenced by Bruegel or one of his imitators, so what? That only reinforces what binds the images together. And of course the cells of Narashima's own hand, brain, and body are just as Babel-like as Bruegel's were.

## SINGLE-CELLED ORGANISMS

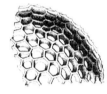

1.30.

*Ceriosphaera.* From Haeckel, *Die Radiolarien.*

1.31.

Gianlorenzo Bernini. Dome of Santa Maria dell'Assunzione, Ariccia, commissioned 1624. From Pinto, *Italian Baroque Architecture.*

Compared to ordinary tissue cells in multicellular organisms, the one-celled organisms called *protozoans* exist at a slightly larger scale of size and complexity. Protozoans have fascinated artists and architects ever since Leeuwenhoek began looking at them. Their bodies, though consisting of a single cell, may develop parts and articulations that approximate the separate organs of metazoans, or multicelled animals. Just as a virus is a single molecule with head, tail, and legs, so a one-celled organism gestates its means of locomotion, its stomach, its reproductive system, and all its other functioning parts from its single cell. Paradoxically, and in contrast to the orderly, tight-packed arrays of metazoans' cells, protozoans can be among the most flamboyantly ornate of nature's shapes.[51]

I have noted what I call Buckminster Fuller's tensegrity principle, which multiplies tiny shapes and aggregates them into successively larger ones, suggesting self-similarity. We see something comparable when we look at the way protozoans reappear in human architecture. The *Ceriosphaera* in figure 1.30, with its reticulated hexagonal spherical surface, can become the coffering of a dome.

The grids of hexagons in Bernini's dome interiors (fig. 1.31) are often compared to the "coffers" of honeycombs, which they do indeed resemble.[52] Here again we see a considerable boost in scale as well as the imitation of forms found in nature. And let us note that honeycomb structures seldom map out spherical surfaces like that of the Ariccia dome. Because they are spheroid, many such domes are in fact closer to the spherical hexagonal grids of marine animals like the *Ceriosphaera* than to any honeycomb. Bernini's generation already knew about the marine microanimals that Leeuwenhoek had been discovering and publishing a quarter century before Bernini designed his dome. (Hooke, who printed comparable protozoan grids, did not publish until 1665.)

But while Bernini's coffers are more radiolarian than hivelike, there are still differences between the natural objects and the artificial ones. Unlike those of the sea creature and the beehive, the hexagons of Bernini's coffers shrink in accordance with a regular progression as they rise toward the dome's summit. This, too, is a biological phenomenon. Known as *vertical condensation*, it is found especially in the plant world. Bernini could have known it from something as common as the broccoli flower (though the broccoli species we see nowadays in supermarkets doesn't have it). Vertical condensation exists for the simple reason that in plants, newer leaves and florets are similar and closer together than more mature ones.

Hence, more like botanists than beekeepers, we might think of Bernini's dome as having grown gradually, with its upper hexagons being newer or younger than the lower ones. Note that the dome is also divided into vertical zones by upright pilaster strips. These emphasize the coffers' vertical condensation. They also proclaim, and even stipulate, that the number of coffers per row does not increase. There are further botanical motifs; note the blossoms in the center of each coffer and the leaf garlands that sculptured angels have draped around the dome's base. Meanwhile the entablature below, consisting as it does of foliaged modillions, dentils, and other floral moldings, carries on the botanical analogies. But I am anticipating the next chapter.

As sources of architectural inspiration, the protozoans' heyday came during what I will call the age of Haeckel, from about 1890 to 1920. His drawings of microscopic sea creatures greatly affected the art nouveau. They were published between 1899 and 1904 in an influential work that was translated into many languages (in English, it is called *Art Forms in Nature* and is still in print).[53] As a result, the years around 1900—the years of art nouveau in France, Jugendstil in Austria, floreale in Italy, and Louis Sullivan in the United States, with all their floral extravagance—saw any number of buildings and other artifacts take their flamboyant forms and colors from oceanic and other microorganisms.

1.32.

Ernst Haeckel's drawing of a
*Dictyopodium scaphodium,*
1862. Jena. Ernst Haeckel Haus.
From Krause, "L'Influence de
Ernst Haeckel sur l'art nou-
veau."

1.33.

René Binet. Porte Monumentale
for the Paris Exposition of
1900. From Borsi and Godoli,
*Paris 1900.*

A splendid article by Erika Krause, in the catalogue to the 1993–1994 French
exhibition *L'Ame au corps: Arts et sciences 1793-1993,* shows off this side of
Haeckel. Krause tells of his influence on the French architect René Binet.[54] She
reproduces a drawing by Haeckel (fig. 1.32) for his monograph on the
Radiolaria. Haeckel's image represents a *Dictyopodium scaphodium* (*scaphé* =
bowl; dictyopodia = "net-feet"). Like the dictyopodium itself, Binet's triumphal
gateway (fig. 1.33) is a tightly swollen lattice curved into a huge, three-legged
truss, with two legs in front and one behind. The gate, again like the animal,
forms an open, webbed dome. As a further bow to Oceania, Binet's structure is
outlined with arrays of light bulbs beaming light to the world in the manner of
a sea creature's organs of luminescence. As Krause shows, Binet explicitly
acknowledged his debts to Haeckel in letters and annotated drawings now collected at the Haeckel-haus in Jena.[55]

Note, too, that perhaps influenced by, or influencing, the decorative style of his
time, Haeckel has given the upper part of his animal a coffered pear-shaped
dome whose spicules and orifices strongly suspect a then-popular type of metal
lampshade. And the animal's opened legs have the erotic compound curves of
a fin de siècle arch. The arch, moreover, looks a bit like the base of the Eiffel
Tower, built for an earlier Paris exposition of 1889. Note, finally, that the gate-

way's suggestion of a great domed church or mosque—for example, Hagia Sophia—is augmented by the four obelisks at each corner, which match the four minarets the Muslims erected when they seized the Christian basilica and dedicated it to Allah. The exposition's entrance arch is a trophy of science and exploration just as Hagia Sophia, turned mosque, is a trophy of Islam's triumph.

So, perhaps, the idea that a metal, stone, or brick building may somehow behave biologically seems less odd than it might have done at the beginning of this chapter. The marriages of molecules and similar things not only form the beginning of our tale, but they also create the busy substance of what is to come.

# LEAVES AND FLOWERS

2

## PHYLLOTAXIS

One cannot hope to discuss the architectural use of plant ornament in a single chapter or even in a single book. It is universal. Here, therefore, I will limit myself to a few offbeat but telling aspects of the subject. The first of these has to do with the geometry of flower and leaf arrangement—phyllotaxis—which, we will find, can transform the way we see and think about plant ornament.

Architecturally, phyllotaxis is particularly important when it involves spiral symmetry and the spiral lattice. It is thus an adjunct to our earliest discussion, at the molecular level, of informational spirals. We will also be looking at four representative earlier attempts—by John Ruskin, Alois Riegl, Jurgis Baltrušaitis, and Elizabeth Lawrence Mendell—to discern biological principles in the development, the evolution, of plant ornament in architecture.

First, a few definitions. Among flowers and leaves, spiral phyllotaxis usually appears in the form of overlapping rows that radiate from a center to an outer rim. In figure 2.1(a), we see a strawberry flower (genus *Fragaria*) with five petals and five sepals (modified leaves) arranged in alternating order. A student of phyllotactic symmetry would call this a double $C_5$ spiral, C being the center around which the petals and sepals are rotated, and 5 their frequency. Figure 2.1(b) is sweet woodruff (*Asperula odorata*), with rotated phyllotaxis of leaves and flowers in several stages or whorls along the stem; (c) is a *Nerium oleander* with tricussate phyllotaxis (each three-leaf whorl is twisted spirally to the left at a uniform distance with respect to the whorl below); (d) is a mint plant, *Urtica urens*, with what is called decussate phyllotaxis (leaves arranged in pairs that, rising up the stem from one whorl to the next, are at right angles to each other).[1]

2.1.

Four patterns of spiral phyllotaxis. From Friedman, "Spiral Symmetry in Plants and Polymers."

a          b          c          d

2.2.

Capital by Polykleitos the
Younger. From Gruben, *Die
Tempel der Griechen*.

These and other comparable arrangements show up over and over again in architectural ornament. Historians and critics would sharpen their normally vague descriptions of leaf and petal ornament if they could talk about phyllotaxis. Often architectural carvers and stuccoists copied the plants quite accurately. But many other examples of plant ornament in architecture represent arrangements that are nonexistent in nature. Nevertheless, even these can be described phyllotactically.

Let's test this. Probably the commonest botanical specimens in all of Western building are Corinthian capitals. They have been known, repeated, and studied from ancient Greece down to the present. Yet those who write about them can be unexpectedly diffident. Gottfried Gruben, for example, discussing and illustrating a capital from Epidauros, only says it was "carefully carved."[2] Other experts are equally unhelpful. Why not look harder? For example, one could say that Gruben's capital (fig. 2.2) consists of two layers of leaves, the upper being eagle fern tendrils (a thin coil of leaf, stipule, or stem that attaches a plant to its support) with Archimedean spirals (see next chapter), formed into distychous (i.e., with doubling) mirrored pairs; one tendril, the longer, faces out, and the other faces inward toward the center of the capital.

2.3.

A young leaf shoot of the
eagle fern (*Pteridium aquilum*).
From Baumann, *Die griechische
Pflanzenwelt*.

Hellmut Baumann tells us that in their mature form these fern blades (fig. 2.3), which are put forth in the spring and which can reach almost three feet in height, were seen by the ancients as symbols of the sun.[3] The most striking thing about them in the compacted form of their earliest appearance, as primordia, is their tight spirals. Does this mean that other spirals could have such a meaning? The trope of helix/helios suggests the possibility. And that in turn would give a possible solar significance both to Corinthian and Ionic capitals—as well as to composite capitals, which combine coiled Ionic volutes with Corinthian acanthus crowns.

In addition, the cluster of acanthus leaves (figs. 2.2, 2.4) at the bottom of the capital is also in two layers, with a higher set and a lower, both in a double $C_8$ rotation around the capital's base. In architecture (but not usually in nature) the leaves of *Acanthus spinosus* curve or are folded sharply downward just before their apex. Vitruvius says the Corinthian capital was first fabricated by the architect Callimachos, who based its form on a basket of cups that had been set on a tomb. An acanthus bush (bear's-foot) had grown up around this basket, surrounding it with a sheath of leaves (*De architectura* 4.1ff.). See also Virgil,

*Eclogues* 3.45, where ritual cups are girded around their handles with acanthus ornament. The Greek adjective *akanthinos* ("thorny") had associations of protection and defense: thorns keep predators at bay. In the New Testament St. Mark calls Christ's crown of thorns an acanthus crown (ἀκάνθινος στέφανος, Mark 15.17), which of course gives the Crucifixion, described in Greek, an irony it doesn't have in languages that speak merely of a crown of thorns. Christ, crowned with acanthus, becomes a Corinthian column defended by its capital. Or, putting it the other way around, a Greek-speaking Christian could see a Corinthian capital as a head (capital) crowned with thorns. Thus do a capital's botanical aspects suggest further sacred meanings for it.

From the column as leaf arrangement to the column as stem: Hellmut Baumann's *Die griechische Pflanzenwelt* invokes the stem of the forest angelica (*Angelica silvestris*) as a possible inspiration for the Doric column (figs. 2.5, 2.6). Note that the strong, even, vertical veins, known as *phloems*, barely visible within the cortex and epidermis of the plant's stem, are placed, sized, and distributed just like the flutes of a Doric column's shaft. Note also that the base of the angelica's umbel, as here broken off, resembles the echinoi of the columns' capitals. It has been commonplace to trace the Doric order to Egyptian floral prototypes such as the lotus and papyrus column. Here, as supplemen-

2.5.

Stem of the forest angelica.

2.6.

Doric columns of the Hieron of Apollo, Delos. Both 2.5 and 2.6 from Baumann, *Die griechische Pflanzenwelt.*

tary inspiration, is a plant native to Greece. And here, too, we can see in the columns' flutes the notion of a vascular system for fluids—fluids that would nourish the capital at the top, which thus becomes a sort of flower. And, as noted, the very word capital, *capitulum*, is itself a word for flower.

## RUSKIN, RIEGL, BALTRUŠAITIS, AND MENDELL

But now let us look at four earlier attempts to deal with architectural phyllotaxis. The first is in John Ruskin. He, after all, is by all odds the most important voice in favor of botanical naturalism in architectural ornament. It is everywhere in his work; here I will cite only The *Seven Lamps of Architecture* (1849). Ruskin writes: "Unnatural arrangements [of plants] are just as ugly as unnatural forms; and architecture, in borrowing the objects of Nature, is bound to place them, as far as may be in her power, in such associations as may befit and express their origin." He adds, however, that nature's irregularities and deformities should be regularized, and he is also willing to accept a considerable degree of fantasy—or at least of what might be called virtuoso horticulture. He commends the Corinthian capital because it makes its impossibly varied cluster of plants look as if they had all grown from the same root: "And the flamboyant [Gothic] leaf moldings are beautiful, because they nestle and run up the hollows, and fill the angles, and clasp the shafts which natural leaves would have delighted to fill and to clasp." No nonsense here about the pathetic fallacy (i.e., attributing human emotion to nonhuman things, a practice Ruskin elsewhere famously deplored). "They are no mere cast of natural leaves: they are counted, orderly, and architectural: but they are naturally, and therefore beautifully, placed."[4] In other words, shafts and other architectural features should look as if they had been overgrown with plant forms: the look of botanic parasitism, of an ivy-haunted ruin.

Some of Ruskin's examples of proper plant ornament are illustrated here (fig. 2.7). Note—speaking of ruins—that contorted, even broken column shafts, which twist like tangoing tendrils, are not considered antinatural.[5] Indeed, throughout Ruskin's books, in his illustrations (almost all from existing monuments), paired colonettes dance together, wrap each other, intersect, and in a hundred ways suggest various fantasized human or reptilian playfulness—as well as, to be sure, the interactions that one sees in climbing plants. Ruskin's plates are an architectural dance of the flowers. One is also brought back to

2.7.

John Ruskin. Lithographs of
details from an arcade on the
south side of the cathedral at
Ferrara, twelfth century. From
Ruskin, *Seven Lamps of
Architecture.*

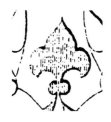

2.8.

Painted arabesque wall decoration from the palace of Sultan
Abdul Aziz, Istanbul, nineteenth
century. An "Islamic Trefoil."

2.9.

Detail of frame ornament from
the Koran of the Mamluk Sultan
Mou'ayyed, 1411.

our discussion of the twisted shafts of DNA molecules. And note that the foliage is not limited to capitals or moldings. A large sprig of leaves and stems is laid directly over one pair of colonettes. This could make them an Adam and Eve hiding their pudenda with leaves.

But let us turn to a more "scientific" investigator. In 1893 Alois Riegl published his book *Stilfragen: Grundlegungen zu einer Geschichte der Ornamentik.*[6] In it he several times remarks that the descent of ornament, like the descent of man, has been genetic. Genetic descent, for example, marks the transformation of what he calls the naturalistic tendril and palmette ornaments of Greece, Rome, and Byzantium into the Islamic arabesque. Thus the arabesque, though apparently abstract, in reality consists of mutated and adapted plant-forms found in ancient Western art.[7] He adds, however, that Islamic abstraction is decadent while Greek naturalism is progressive (his English translator renders Riegl's characterization as Islam's "advanced retrograde tendency" toward stylization).[8] Thus, too, says Riegl, in progressive, evolutionary Western antiquity blossoms were attached to their stems in a way that imitates nature; in backward Islam, not.[9]

Yet, curiously, there is no illustrated example in Riegl's book of a naturalistic antique flower or leaf that has been "abstracted" (presumably in two senses of the word) by Islam. Furthermore, many of his supposedly naturalistic Western motifs, such as the palmette and the anthemion, defy botanical classification. However, Riegl does seem to illustrate progressive abstraction within Islam.

CHAPTER 2

2.10.

Detail of ornament from
Mycenaean vase. All (2.8–2.10)
from Riegl, *Problems of Style.*

2.11.

Three types of
romanesque architectural
phyllotaxis: 1. repeated,
2. confronted, 3. rotated.
After Mendell, *Romanesque*
*Sculpture at Saintonge,*
and Baltrušaitis,
*Stylistique ornementale.*

2.12.

Jurgis Baltrušaitis. Romanesque
frieze motifs: (top) basic formula; (middle) Maillezais; (bottom)
Toulouse. From Baltrušaitis,
*Stylistique ornementale.*

Thus one can call the nineteenth-century blossom in figure 2.8, from the palace of Sultan Aziz, more abstract than that from Sultan Mou'ayyed's 1411 Koran (fig. 2.9). The earlier motif has details of the calix, flower, and what may be a stigma or anther. These botanic essentials are lacking in the later example. But the only specimen from antiquity itself that is even vaguely comparable, in Riegl's book, is the Mycenaean ivy-leaf in figure 2.10. This is as abstract as any of his earlier or later Islamic examples. Riegl remains painfully Grecocentric.

Riegl also has a freewheeling way with terminology (for example, he continually misuses the term *tendril*). But this is only one of the ways in which art historians have gone off on their own in describing architectural vegetation. Jurgis Baltrušaitis represents another. Baltrušaitis has analyzed the French Romanesque architectural phyllotaxis that turns leaves into what, playing with botanical jargon, we might call odd-pinnate animals. By this I mean that a given leaf is provided with an S-shaped stalk or petiole that then is reflected vertically at the bottom end of that stalk. Such a figure could be repeated in successive horizontal mirrorings along an axis, as in figure 2.11. Or the adossed leaf-pairs could turn into perching dragons and birds holding worms in their beaks, as in the second and third rows in figure 2.12. A botanist would call this setup distychous. Thus, at least in Romanesque architecture, there is a phyllotaxis of dragons and birds as well as of leaves. (Think of the animals as perching among the leaves.) Note also the pinnate distychous plants growing up between the pairs of birds in the example from Toulouse (right, bottom row).[10]

The Romanesque era in France was a great period for architectural flora. Elizabeth Lawrence Mendell demonstrated her own system for studying it in her 1940 book, *Romanesque Sculpture in Santonge*.[11] While acknowledging her debts to Baltrušaitis, she claims that although some of the ornament she studies was copied from other architecture, and is highly abstract (though she does not say that it is therefore decadent), much of it came from the actual leaves and flowers of the Santonge region in France—daisies, fleurs-de-lis, bellflowers, morning glories, poppies, and various vines. Thus for all their stiff sturdiness, the plant carvings of these Romanesque craftsmen are usually recognizable. Moreover, and more important for us, they follow the phyllotactic principles of the plants they portray. In other words, the Romanesque ornamentists were not interested simply in a leaf-by-leaf and blossom-by-blossom study of plants, or, like classical ornamentists, in plants woven into bouquets, wreaths, and garlands. Instead, the craftsmen of Santonge studied the ways that leaves and blossoms grew and interacted in nature (fig. 2.11). Here, indeed, perfectly valid phyllotactic principles apply even when the carvers create generalized leaves and blossoms of no particular species. In row 1 of Mendell's example we see a simple repetition known to botanists as odd-pinnate; in row 2 vertically reflected pairing ("adossed," in Mendell's language), a setup known to science as abruptly pinnate; and, in row 3, a $C_3$ clockwise rotation with abruptly pinnate distychy. This latter border could also be a series of top views of a plant with decussate phyllotaxis, much like the mint plant illustrated in figure 2.1(d).

## Spiral Symmetry

Much phyllotaxis can be understood as one form or another of spiral symmetry. The theoretical biologist Roger V. Jean tells us that the spiral symmetry found in flowers, leaves, pinecones, and shells is the result of genetic homologies. And these homologies, in turn, "reveal fundamental mechanisms beyond the gene." Jean is thinking at the level of the individual molecule as it participated in shape-mating, self-assembly, and so on.[12]

As so often, we can find precedents for these ideas in Leonardo, though he found his homologies not in molecules, viruses, and the like but in water, hair, plants, and storms—as well as in his extraordinary foreshadowings of the science of chaos. Like the modern student, Leonardo sensed strong common currents in all flowing, curving, twisting, and turbulent things. These were linked

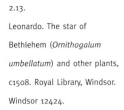

2.13.

Leonardo. The star of
Bethlehem (*Ornithogalum
umbellatum*) and other plants,
c1508. Royal Library, Windsor.
Windsor 12424.

2.14.

Leonardo. Deluge study, c1515.
Royal Library, Windsor.
Windsor 12380.

manifestations of common energies that obeyed as-yet-unknown, but perhaps knowable, common rules.[13]

Leonardo's study of a plant in figure 2.13 was made for the lost Leda (the picture seems to have been a hymn to spiral symmetry).[14] Note that the *Ornithagalum*'s petals are arranged in radial groups of six or three, with like arrangements of the sepals. But the most spectacular part of the plant is its ring of tendril-like leaves.[15] These form themselves into a disheveled, spiral space-lattice, wherein they resemble both hair and water.

How does all this play in architecture? Leonardo's tornadoes (and the very name means "twisted," "spiraled") might better be called anti-architectural (fig. 2.14). Masonry walls explode into thick showers of heavy blocks; forces carry the blocks off into the sky or twist them into cascading whorls. Everything—water, earth, stone, wind—is coiled into a unified destructive spiral.

Similar long, tightly coiled flat spirals are found also in Leonardo's large building and sculptural projects (fig. 2.15). One such is for a lighthouse at a harbor mouth, probably intended for the Roman port of Civitavecchia. Here the quay spirals left-handedly (counting the center as its origin, as mathematicians and biologists do) from a lighthouse past curved buildings that form part of the whorls, to end in a rounded pier. A more recent spiral, also "grown" left-handedly, was Robert Smithson's 1970 earthwork known as *Spiral Jetty* (fig. 2.16). Both images fully possess the dynamic curling energy of a tendril or stamen.

2.15.

Teofilo Galluccini, after

Leonardo, c1515–1516. Spiral

port. Biblioteca Comunale di

Siena ms. L.iv.3. From Pedretti,

*Leonardo Architetto*.

2.16.

Robert Smithson. *Spiral Jetty*,

Great Salt Lake, Utah, 1970.

Leonardo's spirals are usually three-dimensional, but in plant ornament the two-dimensional kind also exist. We see this in a Roman mosaic pavement (fig. 2.17), and in the chrysanthemum beside it (fig. 2.18). Note that here we have a different sort of spiraling than any discussed so far: not two concentrically intertwined three-dimensional strands but, as with Leonardo's star of Bethlehem, a spiral lattice. Two sets of curved axes twist out from the center, one turned clockwise and the other counterclockwise. The two sets of whorls are superimposed.

In figure 2.19 I illustrate a similar but incomplete spiral lattice in which the two sets of whorls (known as *sigmoids*) have begun to be generated but have not

2.17.

A Roman mosaic pavement.

Rome, Museo Nazionale.

Both 2.16 and 2.17 from

Field and Golubitsky,

*Symmetry in Chaos*.

2.18.

The capitulum of a

chrysanthemum. From Field and

Golubitsky, *Symmetry in Chaos*.

2.19.

An incomplete spiral lattice
(author). The two sets of
whorls would continue to
rotate so as eventually to
overlap completely.

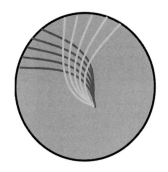

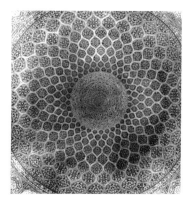

2.20.

Sunflower (botanical
description: disk phyllotaxis
with sigmoidal growth).
Author.

2.21.

Cupola of mosque, Isfahan.
Painted decoration, 1602–1619.
From Papadopoulo, *Islam and
Muslim Art.*

yet crossed each other. The interstices between the spirals that are thus
formed—that is, the holes in the lattice—are called *parastichies* ("marks
beside"). By outlining the parastichies and erasing the actual whorls, we can
generate panels or coffers. Another way to describe the sunflower capitulum in
figure 2.20, and the mosque dome beside it in figure 2.21, is to say that they
have vertical (i.e., moving toward the center) condensation. Bernini's dome in
Santa Maria dell'Assunzione, Ariccia (see fig. 1.31), we observed, also had this.
Note that both domes, also, preserve and develop this floral idea, as each
parastichy surrounds clustered blossoms.

## Fibonacci Distributions

Now here is something important: the number of curved axes in spiral symmetry is significant, for these numbers frequently correspond to what is known
as the Fibonacci sequence. In this sequence, each new number is the sum of
its two immediate predecessors (table 2.1). Leonardo Fibonacci, a medical

merchant and accountant, developed his sequence by speculating on the (highly biological) topic of increases in the fertility rate of a population of rabbits bred over many generations from a highly theoretical single original pair.[16]

Many kinds of phyllotaxis—for example, in the chrysanthemum (fig. 2.18; 34 lefts, 34 rights) and sunflower (fig. 2.20; 34 lefts, 21 rights) capitula we just looked at—have Fibonacci values. In contrast, the artificial spirals—the pavement (fig. 2.17; 48 lefts, 48 rights) and dome (fig. 21; 32 of each)—do not. Note also the distribution of the Fibonacci sequence vis-à-vis the cardinal numbers: between 0 and 10 there are 4 Fibonacci values; between 10 and 20 only one, and only two between 30 and 70. The sequence gets sparser and sparser but never dies out. This means that a Fibonacci correspondence between 0 and 10 has only moderate significance—40 percent of all the numbers in this group are Fibonacci. But between 50 and 100 the correspondence between the sequence and some outside count, such as the number of leaves on a bush (consistently finding, say, either 89 or 144 per branch), is pretty significant. The Fibonacci sequence has a huge literature—indeed, there is a *Fibonacci Quarterly*.[17] The object both of serious mathematical inquiry and numerological fantasy, the sequence has had a particularly long life in architecture. Le Corbusier's Modulor system of proportioning is based on it. Adepts discover the series in many aspects of art, life, science, and nature.[18] Like chaos theory and complexity, and for that matter like the Golden Section (which is related to the Fibonacci sequence), Fibonacci values are found in election returns, the stock market, the weather, and in literary analyses (e.g., word counts) of the Bible, Dante, and Shakespeare. Thus does it move off gradually (but not at all reluctantly) from the mathematically valid into the country of the mad.

TABLE 2.1 THE FIRST TWELVE NUMBERS IN THE FIBONACCI SEQUENCE

| | | | | |
|---|---|---|---|---|
| 1 + 1 | = 2 | | 13 + 21 | = 34 |
| 1 + 2 | = 3 | | 21 + 34 | = 55 |
| 2 + 3 | = 5 | | 34 + 55 | = 89 |
| 3 + 5 | = 8 | | 55 + 89 | = 144 |
| 5 + 8 | = 13 | | 89 + 144 | = 233 |
| 8 + 13 | = 21 | | 144 + 233 | = 377 |

2.22.

Rome, Vatican, Cortile
del Belvedere. Pinecone.
From Fagiolo dell'Arco,
*The Art of the Popes.*

2.23.

A cone from a California cedar.
Author.

Some of these applications are trivial, others not. If you count the numbers of petals on common wildflowers you will find that they reflect Fibonacci numbers, though admittedly these values are generally low. But botanists have maintained that in almost any leafed stalk the number of buds per revolution, as well as the number of revolutions per stalk, fall within the series; and these numbers, furthermore, either are consecutive or alternate in the series depending on whether one is revolving the branch to the left or to the right. It has been claimed that 95 percent of the spiraling bracts of pinecones and similar growths have Fibonacci distributions.[19]

The reason for all this has to do with what, in botany, is called *morphogenesis* — the birth of forms. Primordia (fresh buds) branch out from the growing ends, or apical rings, of plants. The growth of the primordia is controlled—prevented or permitted—by hormones in these rings. And this control follows the pattern of Fibonacci distributions. The hormones are thus like gatekeepers who admit a line of waiting spectators in groups of five or ten. Only instead of letting people through five or ten at a time, they let primordia through in groups of 8, 13, 21, 34, and so forth—Fibonacci groups. I admit that this only shows how Fibonacci distributions come about, not why. Roger Jean thinks the prominence of these distributions in the plant world is a property of all lattices built of soft objects that are subjected to environmental deformation.[20] But at present, little more is known about the adaptive benefits of Fibonacci quantities and their close cousins, the Golden Section or Golden Mean.[21]

Are Fibonacci growths in nature more beautiful than the non-Fibonacci arrangements we mostly get in art? I mentioned pinecones. Probably the most famous pinecone in Western art is the colossal bronze now in the Cortile della Pigna at the Vatican (fig. 2.22). Its spines or bracts were designed as waterjets. They are arranged in 24 right-hand whorls overlapping with 16 left-handed ones; and neither 24 nor 16 is a Fibonacci number. A real pinecone of this density would almost certainly have, respectively, 13 and 21 spirals. (In defense of the Vatican artist, Publius Cincius Salvius, I should add that Leonardo Fibonacci did not arrive on the scene until about 1175 CE, and that people do not seem to have started counting bracts until centuries after that. The artist who designed the Roman mosaic pavement in figure 2.17 also gets off the hook; but not the designer of the Isfahan dome, figure 2.21, which dates from 1602 to 1619 CE.) In contrast, the real pinecone illustrated (fig. 2.23) does have the proper totals of 13 left-hand spirals and 8 right-hand ones.

Am I wrong, or does the real pinecone pack its spines together more hand-somely than the bronze ones? Isn't the real pinecone smoother, more pleasantly dense, more streamlined? Isn't the Vatican cone's packing amateurish and inse-cure, reflecting shape-matings that look as if they're ready for divorce? If you agree, and decide to design something based on a pinecone, you might keep Fibonacci in mind. But of course it's not just a question of number. You must also deal with the angles of the spirals and their degree of equiangularism — that is, the slight but constantly maintained degree to which they curve out and away from each other. We will examine this in the next chapter.

## TRANS-SPECIFIC MORPHOLOGIES

Let us return to evolutionary homologies. Some geneticists claim that these play a role in an organism's body design or, as the Germans say, bauplan. I will now declare body design, furthermore, to be proto-architectural.

A. Lima-de-Faria, a geneticist, illustrates branching baupläner that are extraor-dinarily similar in such insects as the *Samia* (a genus of moths; fig. 2.24), and in prehistoric reptile skeletons like those of *Captorhinus* (fig. 2.25).[22] Thus the genetic codes for these shapes (though the codes themselves might differ) pro-duce similar morphologies. The result, in widely different species, is this par-ticular form, which Lima-de-Faria calls "athyrial," or fernlike.[23] Now look at the roof of a building also based on this shape, Eero Saarinen's Yale hockey rink (fig. 2.26.)[24] This too may be said to consist of a central spine with regular, densely branched ribs growing symmetrically outward to a caliper-shaped perimeter. In terms of morphogenesis, then, Saarinen's "athyrial" building would be another instance of homologous reproduction.

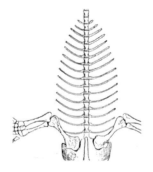

2.24.

Antenna of the insect

*Samia californica.*

2.25.

Part of the skeleton of

the reptile *Captorhinus.*

From Lima-de-Faria,

*Evolution without Selection.*

2.26.

Eero Saarinen. Ingalls Hockey

Rink, Yale University, 1957.

Courtesy Art and Architecture

Library, Yale University. Slides

and Photographs Collection.

Yet Saarinen was not, here, growing his own ribcage or watching his fingers put forth leaves. With pencil and paper he was consciously mimicking structures found in nonhuman nature. Some might argue that this was a uniquely human thing to do, thus proving our special self-conscious role in the scheme of things. But there are plenty of nonhuman organisms that borrow or mimic the structures of other species. As noted, the mason bee builds its nests by borrowing an abandoned snail shell and walling up pebbles in it.[25] As to mimicry, many predatory birds and spiders create nests and webs, traps that mimic the structures of harmless species. Of course, as I said, the insects and birds borrow and imitate instinctively; Saarinen acted self-consciously. But so what?

At the beginning of this chapter I expressed the hope that by studying phyllotaxis we could transform the way we see and think about architectural foliage. The same hope, we have seen, applies to foliage's subsets of spirals and Fibonacci sequences, and to formal homologies between the artifacts and baupläner of very different species. Our look at spirals and the recursive sequences we see in the Fibonacci sequence now leads logically on to the next set of events in our drama, and the even more extravagant world, baroque and rococo, of seashells.

# SHELLS

3

It is more than appropriate to link seashells to architecture. Most such shells are rigid dwellings made of dead tissue within which living creatures dwell. In this sense seashells are architecture. And then, too, as noted in the introduction, most limestone (including marble) was formed from carbon originally deposited on ocean beds by these same animals. So the very substance of much monumental human architecture is shell-derived.

The molecular structure of most seashells consists of roughly hexagonal calcium carbonate crystals. At the intermediate level between the molecules and the finished phenotype, many mollusk shells also consist of prismatic crystalline aggregates. The teredo or shipworm, for example, has a shell identical in design to crystals found in building stone.[1] And while the shapes of the completed seashells do not often reflect the shapes of their molecular and crystal components, they do adhere to various other geometrical formulas. In particular, they exhibit several kinds of spiral symmetry.

The very word *shell* is frequently architectural. We humans build band shells, shell vaults, shell plating, shell roofs, and more. Domes have single, double, or triple shells. Other languages have these and other analogies. *Conca*, "shell" in Italian, also means "niche" in that language; *coquille*, "shell" in French, also means "house" and "den"; and, in German, a snail shell is a *Schneckenhaus*.

## MOLLUSCA AND SPIRALS

The type of shell that most concerns us is the commonest one in nature—that of the phylum Mollusca. (All the animals just named are Mollusca.) Apart from their shells, most mollusks consist of a fleshy lower part, the foot, or else of a foot combined with a head (cephalopodium), which moves the animal and contains its sensory organs. Then there is an upper part, the mantle, that—except in those few mollusk species, like the slugs, that don't have shells—secretes the shell. Mollusks are divided into two types, bivalves and univalves. The "valves," by the way, are the actual shells, so called because they control the inflow of food and outflow of waste. So let us note that in architecture a valve is the leaf of a double door (the word comes from the Latin *volvere*, to roll or swing). When you operate the great bronze door of a cathedral, you control outflow and inflow by opening or closing a valve. You could even think of entering visitors as food and exiting visitors as waste—or, if not "waste," exactly, then matter that the cathedral no longer needs.

There are five classes of mollusk: the Amphineura (with chitons or coat-of-mail shells), the Gastropoda (limpets, whelks, snails, and slugs), the Scaphopoda (turk shells) the Lamellibranchia (oysters, mussels, and scallops), and the Cephalopoda (squids, cuttlefish, octopods). In all there are more than 60,000 species among these five classes. Mollusks can live in the ocean, in freshwater, and on land. They can be as large as the Atlantic's giant squid, often fifty feet in length, or so small as to be more or less microscopic.[2]

The shapes of mollusk shells, often so weird and splendid, have long fascinated humans. Aristotle discusses them in *De partibus animalium*, and the elder Pliny in his *Historia naturalis*. The ages of the baroque and the rococo, with their relish for extravagant shell-derived shapes, appropriately saw the beginnings of modern scientific shell study.[3] Piranesi, in the eighteenth century, etched several plates in which he compared and contrasted marine shells and classical architectural ornament. Indeed it was only just after the shell-saturated architecture and decoration of the rococo age that Georges Cuvier first systematically described and categorized the Mollusca (1799).

But, all along, shells were present in architecture. The Romans used real cockle-shells (family: Cardiidae), or casts from them, in their plaster, terracotta, and mosaic moldings (fig. 3.1). In the Middle Ages these shells, with their radiating flutes rising into oval silhouettes, became the *coquilles Saint-Jacques* of those who made the pilgrimage to Santiago de Compostela. The commonest shells in classical architecture are those forming the upper vaults of niches. I have just noted that in traditional Italian terminology, a niche or vaulted recess is a *conca*. Conversely, *nicchio* is an Italian word for a bivalve mollusk.

Note also that the architect of this particular niche (fig. 3.2), Francisco Xavier Pedraxas, has both copied the mollusk's corrugations and enhanced the lunular

3.1.

The true cockle, species *Cardium costatum*. From Abbott, *Kingdom of the Seashell*.

3.2.

Francisco Xavier Pedraxas. Portal of the Church of the Carmen, Estepa, Spain, 1768. Detail of niche. From Bottineau, *L'Art Baroque*.

44

3.3.

Drawing the (left-handed)

equiangular spiral of an Ionic

capital from a whelk shell.

From Fletcher, *History of

Architecture.*

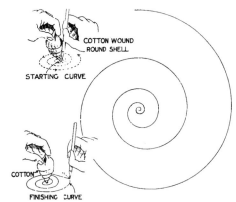

3.4.

An Archimedean spiral.

Adapted from Thompson,

*On Growth and Form.*

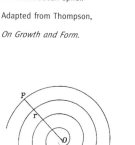

3.5.

Ionic capital with Archimedean

spiral from crypt of St. Michael,

Fulda, 820–822. From Onians,

*Bearers of Meaning.*

segments that form each corrugation's cross-section. More arbitrarily, he has swept the flutes into a coil just behind the Madonna's head. I do not claim that for his basic shell Pedraxas went only to nature; he was also relying on generations of artistic adaptations of the shell-niche motif—adaptations that had much elaborated, abstracted, and varied the originals. And those very originals, of course, had always been subject to variations. Let us recall, too, that mollusk shells have always sheltered other organisms as well. The graceful curved vaults of these shells are equally appropriate as shelters (note the trope) for statues. A niche is a nidus, a nest, for the figure within.

The more deeply wound spirals that we find in whelk shells are equally important in architecture. Worldwide, there are millions of cockleshell niches, but there are also millions of Ionic, Corinthian, and composite capitals, almost all of which have spiral volutes drawn from the shapes of the Buccinidae family. (The word *whelk* means "twist.") Traditionally, Ionic capitals have been drawn out using a whelk shell as a pantograph (fig. 3.3).

There are two types of spirals in these capitals, the Archimedean and the equiangular. The Archimedean spiral (fig. 3.4) is made by a point, $P$, that moves outward from the center, $O$ (for origin or source-point), in constant distances. That is, when you measure the distance from $O$ to $P$ or, along that same axis, to any other point on the spiral, the distance increases in an arithmetical sequence according to the number of whorls that have been crossed. In the illustration, those values are 0, 2, 4, 6, and 8. The volutes on the Ionic capitals in the crypt of St. Michael, Fulda (3.5), are also Archimedean.

3.6.

Leone Battista Alberti.

Capital on the facade of the

Tempio Malatestiano, Rimini,

1450s. From Rykwert et al.,

*Leone Battista Alberti.*

3.7.

Equiangular spiral.

From Thompson,

*On Growth and Form.*

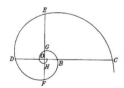

But we see these same Archimedean coils in Ionic, Corinthian, and composite capitals from ancient Greece and from Rome, throughout the Middle Ages, and into modern times. They appear on Alberti's composite capitals on the main facade of the Tempio Malatestiano, Rimini (fig. 3.6). This eccentric invention sets a crown of Ionic volutes on a Roman Doric capital rimmed with ovolos and acanthus palmettes. It has been particularly popular.

Unlike the Archimedean, the second type of spiral, the equiangular (fig. 3.7), seems not to have been discussed mathematically before Descartes did so in 1638.[4] Yet it is, I think, the only type of spiral found in mollusks. It had always existed in nature and, indeed, in architecture. (It would be interesting, however, to investigate the architectural use of this spiral with Descartes's definition as a guide.) Where, in the Archimedean spiral, the whorls are all separated from each other by a uniform distance, in the equiangular spiral—those distances increase, at some constant—that is, equal—angle, as the coils move outward. Starting at $O$ the spiral grows differentially with each new coil as it moves through $G$, $B$, $F$, $D$, $E$, and $C$, as measured along $DC$ and $EF$. These latter points are known as the *radius vectors*. But even though the angle actually does change, it does so recursively, at set ratios. Reading from $O$ respectively to $H$, $G$, $F$, and $E$, we get 6, 12, 36, 72—a pseudo-geometric series ("pseudo" because all the values double except the second, which triples). To put it more mathematically, successive crossings of the spiral with a radius are all in a fixed ratio. Thus in fig. 3.7, $H$ and $F$ are on the same radius from $O$. If $OH = 6$ and $OF = 36$, then $OF/OH = 36/6 = 6$. $E$ and $G$ are also on the same radius from $O$, and $OG = 12$, $OE = 72$. $OE/OG = 72/12 = 6$.[5]

46

3.8.

Corinthian capital with

equiangular volutes from

the temple of Apollo Epikurios,

Bassae (begun c429 BCE),

reconstructed by G. Roux.

From Gruben, *Die Tempel der

Griechen.*

3.9.

Torquate Turban

(*Turbo torquatus* Gmelin) with

equiangular spiral. From

Conklin, *Nature's Art.*

3.10.

Section of a nautilus shell

(*Nautilus pompilius*). From

Conklin, *Nature's Art.*

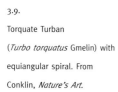

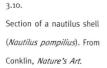

The inner tendrils on the Corinthian capitals from the adyton of the Apollo temple at Bassae (fig. 3.8) are equiangular spirals. And, in nature, the torquate turban grows outward in this fashion (fig. 3.9). But the most lovely, most perfect, most smoothly streamlined of all equiangular spirals are those of the chambered nautilus (fig. 3.10). The interior view illustrated shows the recursive growth of the chambers within the outer spiral. These follow the values of the radius vector established by that outer spiral.

Most mollusk shells do not have flat coils but wind downward from the starting apex known (architecturally, be it noted) as the *spire*. The growth process thus thrusts the spire outward, extrudes it. In the capital from the New England church (fig. 3.11), note that the carver has created a flat, leatherlike, cross-fluted plane whose spiral pulls back toward the shaft face on both sides of the volute, just as in a real shell. Such flutings might even portray the lateral growth marks—the folds, tubercles, or varices—on the shell, though the actual shell model for this capital, if there was one, had probably been sawn open so as to create the hollow section we see. As far as I know, the closest American mollusk to this capital is the *Busycon canaliculatum*, as illustrated (fig. 3.12), which is commonly found on the Connecticut shore.[6]

Finally, there is the question of handedness in spirals. All spirals, natural and artificial, are either left-handed (counterclockwise from the spire or center, i.e., the point of origin) or right-handed (clockwise ditto), with the latter overwhelmingly predominant. (In conchological lingo, spirals are either dextrally or sinistrally coiled.) But note that in architecture the situation has to be different. An Ionic, Corinthian, or composite capital must have both left- and right-handed spirals. Hence left-handed spirals are much more common in architecture than in nature. (The *Busycon contrarium*, found in Florida and South Carolina and on the Gulf Coast, is so named for being, contrarily, left-

3.11.

Ira Atwater and William Booth.
First Congregational Church,
Guilford, Connecticut,
1829–1830. Ionic capital, left-
handed volute, from inner
facade. Author.

3.12.

The exterior of a right-handed
channeled whelk shell *Busycon
canaliculatum*. Author.

handed.) The shells illustrated in the preceding discussion are all right-handed.[7] In contrast, Banister Fletcher's draftsman draws his volute from a rare whelk that is sinistrally coiled (see fig. 3.3).

To my knowledge, classical architecture has used only the Archimedean and equiangular spirals. But an unusual spiral that doesn't fit these formulas is endemic in the Near East. For it I have to return to the world of vegetation. We see this eccentric vegetal spiral inlaid on a dome that was hewn from solid rock in Turkey—the Byzantine church at Karanlik Kilise (fig. 3.13). These whorls have angles that vary both inwardly and outwardly along the path of the vine stem's growth. Measuring the radius vector across the whole of an Islamic spiral would produce a rising, then falling—or, simply, an irregular—number series.

3.13.

Church at Karanlik Kilise,
Cappadocia. Dome, left- and
right-handed spirals. From
Mainstone, *Developments in
Structural Form*.

## Seashells and Stairs

We have looked at spiral staircases as enlarged versions of DNA molecules. But seashells are also forms of spiral stairs, a fact long acknowledged in both the architectural and conchological vocabularies. Even the key word *helix* itself means, among other things, "snail" (Pliny, *Historia naturalis* 32.147). Theodore Cook claims that the *escalier à jour* at Blois (see fig. 3.15) is based on a specific shell, that of the *Scalaria scalaris* (and that name means "stairlike stairs").[8] That shells form one of the ornamental motifs along this famous staircase's central post or (in the language of shells) *columella* is also significant.

But spiral stairs, unlike most shells and unlike column volutes, do not follow either the Archimedean or equiangular formats. They do not enlarge or decrease in diameter with the addition of whorls. Instead, they are twisted into uniform cylinders whose whorls rise upward, one exactly on top of the other as in a coiled metal spring. Spiral stairs can be called equiangular, to be sure, but it is not the angle of departure from the origin point that is equal—this would produce a spiral that widened as it rose, like the one in Wright's Guggenheim Museum. Rather, in most spiral staircases, the only angle that is equal or continuous is that of the tilt as the ramps rise upward.

One of the most beautiful and best-known spiral staircases is the Scala del Bovolo in the Palazzo Contarini del Bovolo, Venice (fig. 3.14).[9] And here we can deepen the analogy between crustaceans and staircases. In Italian, spiral stairs are known as *lumache*, "snails," it is true, but in Venetian dialect a *bovolo* is another type of gastropod, *Helix pomatia*—a particularly delicious species. Moreover, still another (non-Venetian) Italian name for spiral stairs is *chiocciola*—a different name for *Helix pomatia*.

Leonardo was fascinated by stair spirals, often drawing them and linking their shapes to those of shells as he did so. Though we noted the DNA-like aspects of these stairs, clearly Leonardo's conscious thought (as opposed to his genetic impulse) was not about molecules but about shells. Thus he called one of his double-helix stairs a *lumaca doppia*, a double snail (see fig. 1.8). It is an illuminating phrase, for it suggests two interlocked, colossal snail shells. But more common than the double snail in architecture is the single *scala a lumaca*. These were the norm, for stairs, all throughout medieval and early Renaissance architecture. Almost every multistory structure in this period had a seashell-shaped communications spiral.

3.14.

The left-handed Scala del Bovolo, Palazzo Contarini del Bovolo, Venice. Photo Mimmo Jodice.

3.15.

Blois. The right-handed *escalier à jour,* 1508. Courtesy Art and Architecture Library, Yale University. Slides and Photographs Collection.

The *escalier à jour* at Blois is probably the most famous French example of a single-helix stair (fig. 3.15). This is a whimsical concatenation of pilasters, parapets, and ramps, with an inconstant pitch, in a courtyard corner. It is sometimes attributed to Leonardo, who was living nearby in his manor house of Cloux when it was built;[10] but I doubt that he would have designed anything so ugly. Compare it with the Venetian stair's elegant swoop.

It is not overly fanciful to suppose that the builders of snail-stairs, in the sea city of Venice and at Blois as well, knew that those animals' shells had a double purpose: shells and stairs alike afforded circulation for incoming supplies and outgoing detritus. Anyone would have known, also, that both spirals pro-

3.16.

Saint-Etienne-du-Mont, Paris,

interior, *jubé*, with right-handed

spirals, 1517–1620.

From Fletcher, *History of*

*Architecture.*

3.17.

Giovanni Battista Piranesi.

Plate from the *Carceri* (1761),

with left-handed spiral stairs.

tected against predators. The upper parts of the staircases can be fortified against invaders just as a mollusk's shell with its compartments forestalls advancing foes. Note, particularly, the abandoned chambers of the nautilus's shell (see fig. 3.10), which the animal once occupied but outgrew as it matured. The disused chambers act as buffers against unwelcome guests.[11] They are equivalent to the so-called enceintes or peripheral walled spaces of a medieval fortress, erected between its outer walls and the more impregnable keep containing the residential quarters. Observe, in the Venetian staircase, the open arcades through which defenders can shoot at human predators, and the narrowness of the stair interior, which would tend to stymie intruders. These same advantages would apply to Blois, with the added benefit that intruders could be got at through the open architectural bays. Viollet-le-Duc describes medieval wooden spiral stairs that, as a further measure to "éviter les importuns," you could rotate.[12]

The two great right-handed helical staircases on either end of the *jubé* or choir screen in Saint-Etienne-du-Mont, Paris (fig. 3.16), are not defensive. But they are perhaps France's most flamboyant architectural spirals. Steeply wrapping their columellas, and of symmetrically reflective handedness, they circle upward to a horizontal bridge across the church's nave. Then they move on to other aerial causeways, proleptically invoking the Piranesi of the Carceri (fig. 3.17). Note that Piranesi, too, will combine similar (but usually left-handed) spiral stairs wrapping circular pier-shafts with linking lateral bridges.[13] And, with Piranesi, security is once more clearly a theme, for some of the bridges are drawbridges. Indeed, any fugitives or intruders in this flimsy helical world would, like the potential invaders at Blois or Palazzo Contarini, be particularly vulnerable due to their visibility. But one is also reminded of S. T. Coleridge's description of a Piranesi dream-prison filled with numberless spiral stairs disappearing into the distance. Each stair led to emptiness; and at the top of each, a tiny Piranesi stepped off into the void.[14]

## MALACOLOGICAL MAPPING

In figure 3.18 I illustrate the shells of several gastropod mollusks. As diagrammed, their compound curvatures exemplify the branch of mathematics known as *topology*. Topology maps a flat plane lattice, or else one that curves like the lines of latitude and longitude on the globe. It is thus related to, but not the same as, crystallography. Topologies can have all sorts of hills and valleys, high points, abysses, and subsidiary rotundities. By using similar curving topological grids, architects are able to achieve spectacular condensations and

3.18.

Various gastropod shells.

(a) *Planorbis,*

(b) *Haliotis,*

(c) *Epitonium,*

(d) *Oxystele,*

(e) *Turritela,*

(f) *Lyria,*

(g) *Conus,*

(h) *Terebra,*

(i) *Gulella,*

(j) *Achatina.*

From Cortis,

"The Molluskan Shell."

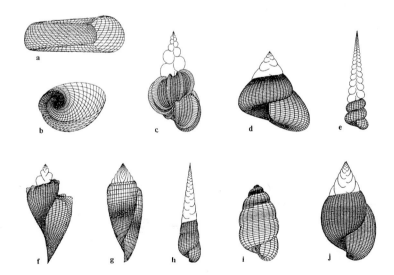

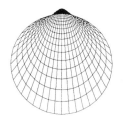

3.19.

Geometric mapping with lattice

of a *Codakia* shell.


3.20.

Same lattice used to map a

detail from Borromini's dome

coffers in San Carlo alle Quattro

Fontane.


3.21.

Francesco Borromini. Dome

interior coffering of San Carlo

alle Quattro Fontane, Rome,

begun 1638.

expansions in the interiors of vaults and domes. Such undulant planes exist throughout nature: in the shapes of various fruits, for example, and in mammalian bone structures—not to mention mountain ranges. But perhaps nowhere are they more fascinatingly architectural than in seashells.

We should recall, also, that such undulating shells would be found not only at the seaside but in and around quarries, often embedded in the very blocks an architect or sculptor was selecting. Such fossil shells almost all consist of what are called invaginated spiral lattices.[15] We saw similar things when we looked at crystals. Not just domes but many steeples, amphitheaters, finials, and other architectural forms can be thought of and mapped as topologies.

In figure 3.19 the valve lattice of the *Codakia* provides the bunched coordinates that also map out the Greek crosses, octagons, and other shapes that Borromini uses for the coffering of the dome of San Carlo alle Quattro Fontane (figs. 3.20, 3.21). Only coordinates that condense in accordance both with horizontal concentric curves and straight radiant verticals (the circles and straight axes in gray lines in fig. 3.20) will properly lay out the coffers. In other words, the ends of each lozenge or rhomb are unequal, the upper half of each octagon is smaller than the lower half, and the top of the upright in each Greek cross is shorter than the bottom of the lower part of the cross's upright.

Between this and Bernini's coffering in the Ariccia church (see fig. 1.31), the contrast is particularly striking. There, as we recall, the hexagons are uniform. There is one-directional compression of horizontal arrays across a dished plane.

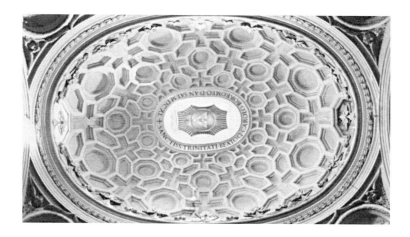

In Borromini we have two-directional compression, horizontal and vertical at the same time, over a (much shallower) dished plane.

Borromini probably achieved this by the same method later used by Giovanni Battista Gaulli, better known as Baciccia, who was famous for his deep perspective paintings on shallow concave ceilings in Rome (e.g., the Gesù, 1672–1685). The technique involved using a single-source light to project the shadow of a full-scale, ortholinear grid, made of ropes, onto the curved vault surface. Then the preparatory cartoon with its corresponding grid could be redrawn onto the vault, but obeying the projected coordinates that were now properly curved—swollen and contracted—by the vault's curved surfaces. As the coordinates were curved, so then would be the figure drawings constructed from them. I assume that Borromini used the same projection system to map out his coffers at San Carlino. The method is described in a contemporaneous treatise.[16]

Seashell terminology—the lingo of malacology (mollusks) and conchology (seashells generally)—is an architectural historian's feast. Gastropod shell shapes, for example, may be patelliform (pan-shaped), conic, tubulous, discoid, planorbic (like a flat ring), oval, pyriform (pear-shaped), globulous, turbinate (shaped like a top), cylindrical, fusiform (spindle-shaped), turriculate (turreted), auriform (ear-shaped), clipeiform (shield-shaped), trochiform (cap-shaped), or agglutinate (several of these forms combined). Moreover, the numerical value of the angle of twist, in a shell or in a spiral staircase, can be measured with a device called a *helicometer*.

Armed with this vocabulary we can proceed to say that the Archimedean spire of Sant'Ivo (fig. 3.22) is dextrally coiled and crowns a petallated belfry stage. The spire as a whole is trochiform, conic, and turriculate, using an Archimedean spiral with a constantly changing tilt that moves from about 8° at the bottom to about 40° at the top.[17] Borromini's turret is particularly like the upper (equiangular) spire of a spiny crown conch (fig. 3.23; the illustrated specimen comes from Florida but there are similar species in the Mediterranean). Some of these tropical whelklike animals develop double rows of spines, too, like those lining the whorls of Borromini's structure. Beyond this Borromini's spire is fusiform, with solcated (furrowed) or scrobiculate (trenched) whorls, and slightly planorbic, beginning from a spinous spire.

3.22.

Francesco Borromini. Right-handed (measuring from the top, shell-fashion) spire of Sant'Ivo alla Sapienza, Rome, 1642–1660.

3.23.

Right-handed crown conch (*Melangea corona* Gmelin). From Conklin, *Nature's Art*.

Looking back, and still keeping in mind our new conchological vocabulary, let us note that the Ionic capital derived from the whelk shell (see fig. 3.3) is turbinate and corniform; that the *scala del bovolo* (see fig. 3.14), as well as being scalariform, is liscid and decollate (no apex), with a clearly and regularly plicate columella. And the spiral on the Guilford capital (see fig. 3.11) is scrobiculate, acute, incurvate, and decollate, with open whorls. (The real-life shell next to it is, in contrast, striate, solcate, and pappilous.)

## ROCAILLE

But all this, much as it is, is as nothing when we confront the importance of shells in the eighteenth century. A whole style, the rococo, of French origin and in French called *rocaille* ("rock work," but with the idea that fossil shells are embedded in the rock), was named for shell-impregnated caves.[18] The idea goes back to antiquity, when shell-lined grottoes paid homage to a family's ancestors. And Leonardo, I have noted, was fascinated by fossil shells and their relations to the movements of earth and sea.[19] To him they spoke of deep time. A generation later, the main figure in shell aesthetics was Bernard Palissy, a French potter. He was commissioned by the Connétable de Montmorency to decorate the gardens of the Château of Ecouen in 1548 with rocky, shell-strewn ornaments—a preview of eighteenth-century rocaille. Like Leonardo, Palissy was interested in the natural history of his fossils, on which he lectured and which he explored also in his ceramics.[20]

In the eighteenth century the rococo spread over much of Europe. Some of its most extravagant aspects developed in Germany and Austria. If we look at an advanced rococo interior in Germany by Dominikus Zimmermann (fig. 3.24), we see that any sense of the classic, columnar vaulted interior has been overlaid with frothing waves of shell-like forms. Being inside it is like inhabiting a huge conch (fig. 3.25), through whose upper opening we gaze upward through the waters to the blue air of heaven.[21]

One advantage of shells is their variable suggestiveness of form. Their voluted helical shapes, as well as being those of mollusks, can be read as tendrils, blossoms, and leaves, or as the wavy undulations of foaming spindrift. Especially rococo, in this sense, is the shell of the murex (fig. 3.25), which, as adapted by rococo designers, fully retains the invaginated spiraling, the swellings and shrinkings, the spikes, spicules, and mottlings, the rotundities,

3.24.

Dominikus Zimmermann. Upper

part of interior, Church of Die

Wies, Upper Bavaria,

1745–1754. From Janson,

*History of Art.*


3.25.

Löbbeke's murex,

*Pterynotus loebbeckei*

Kobelt. From Abbott,

*Kingdom of the Seashell.*

inflections, convolutions, flares, and twists, that it had developed as a marine animal.

## TEREBRA

While mollusks in general provide the architect with shapes and formal vocabularies, the gastropod known as *Terebra maculata lam* (see fig. 3.18[h]) is particularly rich in possibilities. The marks on terebra shells may be liscid (smooth), lineate, scrobiculate, striate, solcate, digitate (dotted), varicose (warted, pimpled), and spinous. The apex of such a shell can be acute, pappilous (nippled), incurvate, umbellicate (with clustered bells), or decollate (point sheared off). The lip can be extire, dentated, undulate, digitate, saw-toothed, inspissate (thickened), revolved or reflex, involuted, or introflexed. The columella may be caudate (tailed), retorted, spiral, plicate (with folds), or callose (calloused). Scalariform (staircase-shaped) shells have open whorls, or they can be corniform (horn-shaped), that is to say with whorls that are smoothly melded into a continuous surface; or the whorls can be planorbic (depressed). One could therefore call the volutes in figure 3.11, the Guilford church, planorbic—though I also called them scrobiculate, acute, incurvate, and decollate, with open whorls. But different people have different takes on terminology. And in architecture as in conchology, categories and terms may overlap.

3.26.

Right-handed shell of *Terebra maculata*. From Pickover and Hargittai, *Spiral Symmetry*.

3.27.

Copenhagen, Børsen (Stock Exchange). Right-handed Dragon Spire. Ludvig Heidtrider, 1624–1625. Photo author.

By means of architecture, mollusk shells can translate into other species. Look again at *Terebra maculata lam* (fig. 3.26). It is quite orthodox. But on one occasion when it was borrowed architecturally, it unexpectedly invaded the realm of fantastic reptiles. (Once more we are in the world of Lima-de-Faria and homologous baupläner.) I am thinking of a Copenhagen landmark by the seventeenth-century Danish architect and fireworks designer Ludvig Heidtrider.[22] In 1624 he designed a terebra-shaped spire for the Stock Exchange (fig. 3.27), but one in which the familiar shell was morphed into the tails of four dragons. Their spread-eagled bodies grasp the cupola's roof as they do a joint handstand. This metamorphosis entails (pun intended) others: the terebra's single spiral becomes a quadruple set of nested whorls and the shell's equiangular helix now gradually straightens until, at the top, the tails are almost vertical. (One cannot help but notice, too, how tight, how anal-retentive, the spire is compared to the shell's robuster coils.)

Gaudí often documented his interest in terebra shells.[23] The evidence includes a photo, formerly in the possession of his friend Juan Matamala, of a cluster of them.[24] It has every appearance of being the inspiration for the architect's famous project for a mission house in Tangier (figs. 3.28, 3.29). However, Gaudí's extraordinary biographer, Tokutoshi Torii, claims that the shell photo

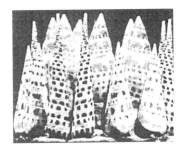

3.28.

Antoni Gaudí. Project for
Franciscan Mission at Tangier,
1893, with left- and right-handed spirals. From Torii, *Gaudí.*

3.29.

*Terebra maculata* shells, both
left-handed and right-handed
types, in Matamala's photo.
From Torii, *Gaudí.*

came after the project, "imitating its typology." One can only reply that while this particular photograph may have followed the project, that claim can hardly be extended to Gaudí's knowledge of such shells, any more than it is true of the shells themselves. *Terebra maculata* (*terebra* means "drill," "auger," and *maculata* means "spotted" or "marked") has been around for millions of years, and the architect presumably knew about them from boyhood.

And let us emphasize that of all the other sources proposed for this project,[25] only terebra has the helical "fenestration" (its maculae) that we also see in the mission towers. Note also that to make his "city" bilaterally symmetrical, Gaudí has put left-handed shells on the left and right-handed ones on the right. There are left-handed shells, too, in the photo, though they are not set up symmetrically. This means that Gaudí (or a friend) went to considerable trouble to find left-handed terebra shells. Similar helices reappear in those glorious descendants of the Franciscan project, the spires of the Sagrada Familia, even though in execution (and with their molecular-model tops) these towers came to lose the overtly terebra qualities that we see in the Tangier project.

Gaudí's contemporaries were well aware of his interest in mollusks. Juan García Junceda's caricature of the Casa Milá (fig. 3.30) shows it as a cartoonish essay in rocaille (a rocaille, let us note, that is appropriately varicose, turriculated, spinous, and filled with many varieties of shell shapes and shell textures)—a

3.30.

Juan García Junceda. Caricature
of Gaudí's Casa Milá, Barcelona,
c1911. From Torii, *Gaudí.*

rocaille, too, in which the (fossil?) marine animals swarm monstrously about
their concave entrance.

## SEASHELL MONOLITHS

The architectural shells we have been looking at were made of masonry, brick,
and plaster. They are thus exceedingly frangible. Real shells, in contrast, are
monolithic. Their geometric molecules and spicular crystals are woven into single rigid planar piece of matter called *conchiolin*.[26]

So I will briefly mention a significant early modern building that was originally
intended to be built monolithically of concrete—the human version of conchiolin. Unhappily, the monolithic concrete ended up as a suspended ceiling
intended—only intended—to look monolithic. I refer to one of Hans Poelzig's
several shell-like projects for concert halls (fig. 3.31). Not only is its concave
shape seashell-like, but the horizontal arrays of corbels articulating the interior
can be likened to the growth rings and studded rows of spines we find in so
many marine shells, such as the triumphant star (fig. 3.32). But the main point
is that Poelzig's dome looks like a single self-supporting span, a vast tiered
scrobiculate valve.[27]

Yet even (or especially) as a fake, Poelzig's hall is one more landmark in the
history of our human desire to build and inhabit huge seashells—to copy their
forms, fabrics, and functions into our buildings. In doing so, we make seashells,
for ourselves, into what they have always been for their original dwellers—

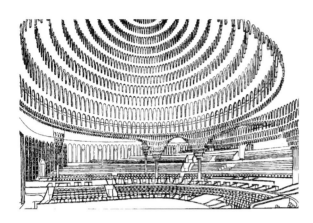

3.31.

Hans Poelzig. Project for

Grosses Schauspielhaus, Berlin,

1910? 1919? From Kultermann,

*Architecture in the Twentieth*

*Century.*


3.32.

Triumphant star shell,

*Guilfordia triumphans.*

Central part. From Abbott,

*Kingdom of the Seashell.*

protective shelters and means of communication, as well as objects that are often willful, ornate, and filled with gorgeous spiral symmetries. Along the way, therefore, shells have taught us much about the nature of spirals, about topology, and even, as rock-embedded fossils, about the earliest ages of life.

# INSECTS

Insects are the first truly monumental builders that we encounter in these pages. We will look at anthills and at the galleried pyramids that ants create inside and under them. And we will look at the strange high-rise cities built by African and Australian termites. But bees, above all, have inspired architects, and poets too—so colossal (in bee-scale), elaborate, and geometrical are their dwellings; and so often has the bees' polity been proposed as a model for our own.

My main points are going to be about scale and shape. Any representation of tiny organisms plays games with scale. The tradition has flourished with the growth of the illustrated book. Larger-than-life bugs are often depicted on the pages of manuscripts. In 1602 Ulisse Aldrovandi published a treatise on insects; in its illustrations we see a multitude of nature's tiniest but, as magnified on the page, now suddenly monstrous creatures. Even more monstrous are the magnifications of flies, beetles, and such, printed later in the century by Robert Hooke and Antoni van Leeuwenhoek.[1] The illustrated book and the loose print or drawing, along with the optical microscope and its electronic offspring, have contributed much to our interest in such dramatic scale shifting. When we build three-dimensional architectural fantasies that imitate the work, or the bodies, of insects, we continue with this process.

## THE MONUMENTAL IMPULSE OF THE BEES

The bees' exquisite modular architecture has existed far longer than anything made by humans. Honeycombs, indeed, have probably influenced our architecture ever since the occasion I proposed in the introduction, when, on first seeing a honeycomb, we discovered the hexagonal grid. Perhaps on a similar occasion we first saw the possibilities of large-scale group building activity. I will turn to these questions in a moment.

First, however, let us consider honeycombs, beehives, and their associations, which just by themselves are rich with thoughts of harmony, sweetness, and happy social business. The name of the honeybee, *melissa*, has been troped with *meli*, honey, sweetness, and hence with melody, *melisma* (one syllable sung over several notes), and the like. Honey was said to be the special food of Apollo's priestesses, for whom such bee banquets preserved their fleshly immortality.[2] And honey's sweetness was equated with that of words: *mel* is the Latin for lyric poetry. And since honey is proof against most bacteria it stays fresh practically forever; archaeologists have excavated bodies embalmed in it. After centuries, the honey was still sweet and clear.[3]

Aside from their honey, bees have other associations: the more doubtful ones of hierarchy and territoriality. In the *Politics* 1.2, Aristotle uses the analogy of the beehive to explain and partly justify the human lord's dominion over his household, and by extension the notion of one-man rule in the state. Bees also helped him justify slavery. As with bees, he says, so with men: some are born to rule and some to be ruled.

All these ideas come together most significantly in book 4 of Virgil's *Georgics*. In the very first lines is the notion of scale shifting. Virgil calls the hive an *aula*, palace hall (90), and describes its builders smearing its entrances with their wax and with paste taken from flowers. It is better than the mortar men make, says the poet. He describes the division of labor inside the palace (158ff.) and compares the bees' work to that of the cyclopes who assist Vulcan in his miraculous metalwork. But unlike Vulcan's assistants, bees are garden dwellers: they love to build their hives where there are sweet waters and leafy coverts.[4] Set Priapus with his sickle, guardian of gardens and ready fount of seed, to watch over them. Thus does the honeycomb become an element in a garden city whose sculptural expression identifies it as a breeding territory.[5]

Even more architectural, and indeed urbanist, are the bees of *Aeneid* 1.430–436, who are likened to the builders of Carthage. The workers erect harbors and theaters, rear the citadel, roll great stones, and hew columns out of cliffs "even as bees in early summer, amid flowery fields, ply their task in sunshine, when they lead forth the full-grown young of their race, or pack the fluid honey and strain their cells to bursting with sweet nectar, or receive the burdens of incomers, or in martial array drive from their folds the drones, a lazy herd; all aglow is the work." It is an irony that Virgil thought the workers and their ruler were males. Or you might say that he wrote better than he knew when he described the erection of Carthage (under a queen's direction, we recall) as beelike.[6]

Ever since these lines were written, Virgil's thoughts on bees and their palaces have been with us. It is in this Virgilian mode that Origen (*Contra Celsum*, iv) refers to bees as having cities and suburbs, πρόπολις, for their hives.[7] Indeed, zoologists call the sticky paste that bees spread around the outskirts of their hives propolis—"suburb" (it traps predators). In Shakespeare's *Henry V*

(1.2.187ff.) bees build a kingdom whose emperor lives in a royal tent and watches his "singing masons building roofs of gold" (198).

## THE BEE'S BODY'S BAUPLAN

The supreme moment for another sort of apian enthusiasm—its apex—was in the age of the Roman baroque, particularly in the iconography of the Barberini family. This was a family abounding in art-minded princes and prelates. Their pope (Maffeo Barberini, Urban VIII, 1623–1644) was a consummate patron. Their palace off the Via Quattro Fontane, Bernini's baldacchino in St. Peter's, and the Borromini church designed and begun in Urban's reign, Sant'Ivo alla Sapienza, as well as other commissions, are iconographically bee-driven, with *Apis mellifera ligustica* as the star.[8]

Let's look at the plan of Sant'Ivo (fig. 4.1). With its six lobes, alternately round and segmented, and rotated at 120° and 60° intervals around a center point, this plan has suggested, to some, the body plan of a honeybee. Joseph Connors, however, who has recently written brilliantly on this church, maintains that a true bee plan would have to have four lobes, two on each side, for each pair of wings, along with a central upper head and lower tail.[9] And indeed that is the silhouette honeybees unquestionably create when they are flying. But when they are at rest, they fold their large forewings over their smaller hindwings to create the configuration we see in Bernini's relief (fig. 4.2). I have superimposed the silhouette of Sant'Ivo's basic layout (keeping its proportions) on Bernini's bee, which shows how the two forms do in fact reflect each other.

4.1.

Francesco Borromini. Plan of Sant'Ivo alla Sapienza, Rome, 1642. Vienna, Albertina. From Connors, "Sant'Ivo alla Sapienza."

4.2.

Gianlorenzo Bernini. Bee from a pedestal of the baldacchino, St. Peter's. Completed 1633. Courtesy Art and Architecture Library, Yale University. Slides and Photographs Collection.

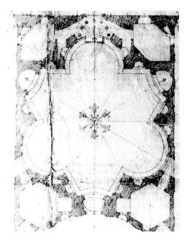

4.3.

Patterns of comb cells.

From von Frisch, *Aus dem*

*Leben der Bienen.*

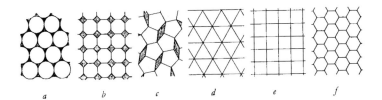

a      b      c      d      e      f

## HONEYCOMBS

In a more direct and practical way, the most important architectural influence that bees have exerted on humans has been that of their hives and honey-combs. The geometrical arrays of hexagons in honeycombs have frequently absorbed the interest of mathematicians and others concerned with structure.[10]

Karl von Frisch, for example, demonstrates the design advantages of the hexag-onal cell in figure 4.3 at (f), though some bumblebees build round cells (a) that waste space—as in the dark solids shown. Octagons and pentagons (b and c) would be even more wasteful and would also need independent as well as common walls for each cell, hence increasing the amount of construction nec-essary. These problems are all averted by triangular, square, or hexagonal cells (d, e, f). And the capacities of all three of these latter shapes would be the same. We can recognize all these lattices, by the way, as further examples of tight packing.

But of the three most tightly packed cell-shapes, the hexagon (f) has by a slight margin the smallest circumference. Thus, of all six shapes illustrated, the hexag-onal is indeed the most efficient—it yields the greatest volume with the least constructive energy. This parsimony has further advantages. Freshly built combs have a beautiful precision. All the angles are exactly 60° and 120°. And they are extraordinarily efficient. One kilogram of wax, turned into comb, can support 22 kilograms of honey.[11] The more economical the lattice, the lighter the space frame it forms, and the more efficiently it distributes its weight equally in all directions. And then, like all space frames, a honeycomb requires a minimum of support. I hardly need say that the advantages von Frisch sees in the honey-comb's hexagonal module apply equally well to human structures.

4.4.

A garden plan from

Ferrari, *Flora*.

4.5.

Ferrari plan:

detail of "bee."

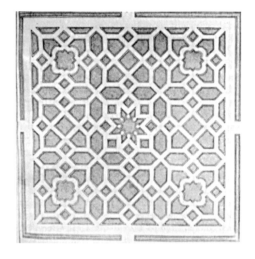

A honeycomb suggests a pattern of flowerbeds. In this spirit, and that of Virgil's *Georgics*, Giovanni Battista Ferrari, in *Flos, seu De florum cultura* (1633), designed ornamental gardens that were honeycombed with flowerbeds and topiary displays.[12] One of his techniques is to structure a square with a nine-square grid formed of chains of 45° hexagons (fig. 4.4). As an integrated overlap of the nine squares, following the diagonals of the hexagons, diagonal chains of quincunxes come into being, some with elaborated central features. Each combination of paired, angled 45° hexagons, plus the quincunx element between them, makes a tripartite geometrical design. The resulting shape is that of an abstract flying bee (fig. 4.5). And these too are quincunxes. Ferrari's geometric "bees" rotate busily throughout the garden, creating a lovely maze.

Ferrari uses 45° hexagons, not the 60° kind that is considered canonical. So here we note that there are variations among hexagons and hexagonal grids. A number are shown below, along with the ways in which they can be latticed or tight-packed, as I deal with some of these more wayward hexagons (fig. 4.6). And still others are possible—for instance, there can be multiple irregularities

4.6.

From left to right, above: a normal 60°/120° regular hexagon; a 60°/120° hexagon rotated 30°; the same hexagon stretched vertically; the first hexagon stretched horizontally; a regular hexagon with 45° offsets; an irregular hexagon (unequal sides). Author.

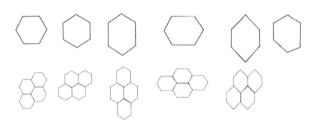

4.7.

A 1951 *Vogue* photograph.

From Weyl, *Symmetry.*

in the length of sides, lattices with more than one type of hexagon, or that combine hexagons with other shapes, and so on. (A good example, both of irregular hexagons and of hexagons combined with other shapes, is the lattice in Borromini's dome of San Carlo alle Quattro Fontane, figure 3.21.) We see these altered hexagons in worn-out honeycombs—and elsewhere (fig. 4.7). Note that the elastic veil maps out the three-dimensional sculpture of the woman's face, a beautiful effect achieved entirely by a grid of distorted hexagons. We see the same principles here that we see in the topographically curved grid in Borromini's dome—though, as we recall, that mixes its hexagons with crosses and octagons.

Our own time has perhaps been richer than any other in its architectural use of the honeycomb lattice. Many of Frank Lloyd Wright's Usonian house plans are based on it. In constructing these houses the workers set out sections of prefabricated walling directly on the cells marked out by the concrete floor tiles, so the lattice served as a practical built-in template.[13]

Indeed, Wright was fascinated by the hexagon and its variants. That interest shows not only in buildings and furniture but also in the delicate interpenetrating hexagon patterns of tiles, bricks, window detailing, and other ornamental devices. One thinks of the leaded glass in the Harley Bradley house, Kankakee, Illinois (1900); the dining room windows of the Robie house, Chicago (1909–1910); or of the many irregular but symmetrical hexagons, of several sizes, thoughout the Coonley house, Riverside, Illinois (1908).

But above all one thinks of the Hanna house in Stanford, California, originally built from 1935 to 1937 (fig. 4.8).[14] The house is laid out on a hexagonal grid, all of its cells being 60° and 120° hexagons with 26-inch sides, incised into its

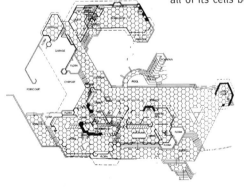

4.8.

Frank Lloyd Wright. Hanna house, Stanford, California, 1935–1937. Plan after Wright's additions of 1950 and 1957. From Storrer, *Frank Lloyd Wright Companion.*

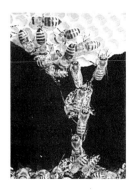

concrete floor. Everything is based on this grid or its subset, a hexagonal 13-inch module. Walls and roof elements, and even the built-in furniture, grow out of it; for example, the foyer (center left on the plan), the living and dining rooms (bottom), the central dominant library, kitchen, master bedroom, and other spaces. It is worth noting that Vitruvius also advocates honeycomb pavement grids (but with real tiles, and of marble), in *De architectura* 7.1.4. He even speaks of pavements made of "honeycombs."

But the grid is not the only sign of the Hanna house's beelike nature: Mrs. Hanna was called its Queen Bee. Wright in fact associated the whole Hanna family with "those master builders, the bees." Much as worker bees build, clean, and add to a comb (fig. 4.9), the Hannas added many details and touches, most of them hexagonal, to their honeycomb.[15]

4.9.

Worker honeybees building a new comb. From Teräs, "Bee and Wasp Cells."

Wright's grandest honeycomb structure was his unbuilt 1957 project for the Arizona State Capitol (fig. 4.10), which was to have been crowned with an immense quasi–space frame formed into a hexahedral solid and cladded with a comblike concrete grid. The hexahedron is the top half of a double hexahedron, that is, a dodecahedron. The basic idea for such a roof may have come from Buckminster Fuller's models of hexagonal Dymaxion houses (fig. 4.11), in which prefabricated elements, including the roof hexagon, were to be slung from a central mast—not, by the way, unlike the Stone Age houses on Cyprus in figure 1.26.[16]

4.10.

Frank Lloyd Wright. Project for the Arizona State Capitol, 1957. Detail of perspective. From Riley, *Frank Lloyd Wright, Architect.*

4.11.

R. Buckminster Fuller. Model of a Dymaxion house, 1930. From Henderson, *The Fourth Dimension and Non-Euclidean Geometry in Modern Art.*

But Wright's roof is truly a "comb," unlike Fuller's, which is merely a smooth-planed hexagon. And in Wright there is far greater play with hexagons generally. Each visible plane of the hexahedron is punctured by a hexagonal opening framing a small garden. Hex-plan turrets articulate the building's rear. There are two spires, one at the hexahedron's vertex (as with Fuller's house) and the other, much taller and off-center, composed of rhombic facets and zigzags.[17] In addition to being an artificial honeycomb, the whole building, with its gardens, would have been worthy of Flash Gordon. We note that the project dates from the same year in which Wright made his final additions to the house in Stanford.

## Honeycomb Cells

The great biologist D'Arcy Wentworth Thompson points out that there is more to the geometry of honeycomb cells than simple hexagonality. Each cell is in fact an essay in complex solid geometry.[18] "My house is constructed according to the laws of a severe architecture, and Euclid himself would learn, admiring the geometry of its hive," Thompson adds, quoting the *Arabian Nights*.[19] Though they are usually thought of as hexagonal tubes, he shows that bees' cells are in fact incomplete rhombic dodecahedra: twelve-sided solids.[20] But the bees' dodecahedra are special. They are hexagonal tubes, sure enough, but the ends of the cells facing inward (toward the center of the comb) consist of three rhombuses formed into a pyramidal tip. The other end of the tube is left open to make an entrance (fig. 4.12). In a normal dodecahedron, this end would receive a rhombic pyramid like the one on the tube's other end. So in fact you have to call this shape, as the bees build it, a rhombic decahedron; a ten-sided structure with one side open.

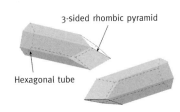

3-sided rhombic pyramid

Hexagonal tube

4.12.

Honeybee comb cells: lengthened rhombic dodecahedra with one end removed. Author.

*Mellifera* honeycombs consist of two banks of these cells, adossed so that the entrances all face outward. I have drawn two cells much as they would be built into the comb. Each plane of the three-sided pyramid at one end of the cell meets a corresponding plane of the pyramid on a cell facing the opposite way. The cells are angled upward, away from the opening, at approximately 7°, which prevents the honey and wax, and maybe even the pupae who lodge there, from falling out.

The shape of honeybees' comb cells is also eminently architectural and, in particular, Germanic. In figure 4.13 I have lengthened the form and stood it upright.

4.13.

A honeybee cell lengthened
into a skyscraper. Author.

4.14.

West towers of Limburg
Cathedral, Germany, 1213–1242,
as lengthened by the author.
From Fletcher, *History of
Architecture.*

4.15.

Helmut Jahn. Project for the
Bank of the Southwest Tower,
Houston, Texas, 1982.

The rhombic pyramid on top serves as an elegant water-shedding, sky-piercing roof whose angular base penetrates sharply downward into the hexagonal tower tube. If only the twin west towers of Limburg Cathedral (1213–1242, here slenderized for the sake of the comparison; fig. 4.14), or Helmut Jahn's unbuilt 1982 project for the Bank of the Southwest in Houston (fig. 4.15), had had hexagonal rather than square plans! Then they could then have been called architectural imitations of the cells built by *Apis mellifera ligustica*. Perhaps some enterprising architect will remedy this lack.

## Beehives

In architectural history the term *beehive* is possibly most familiar from Sir Arthur Evans's "beehive tombs," which are certain Mycenaean monuments; for instance, the so-called Treasury of Atreus (fig. 4.16) and Tomb of Clytemnestra.[21] Geometrically these buildings are convex conoids and, like many actual beehives, are partially supported by a hollowed slope of ground.

As a somewhat comparable form I illustrate Brunelleschi's similarly profiled dome in Florence (fig. 4.17). Brunelleschi, of course, could not have known about the Mycenaean tombs, and anyway we have no idea whether their builders referred to them as *melisseia*, "beehives," or whether that term is entirely modern. (To be sure, a thing that seemed beehive-shaped in the 1920s could also have seemed so in the Bronze Age.)

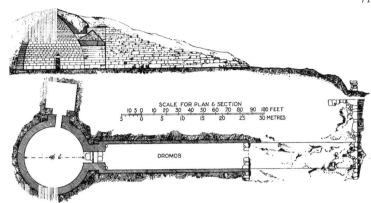

4.16.

Treasury of Atreus, Mycenae,

c1340–1190 BCE. From Fletcher,

*History of Architecture.*

But actually Brunelleschi's similarly shaped dome for Santa Maria del Fiore is more like a real beehive than are the beehive tombs. The latter are made of large stone blocks, especially around the base of the wall. The dome, in contrast, like a beehive, is and must be as light as possible. The dome fabric is girdled by chainlike tension rings bonded into its shells. The beehive illustrated (fig. 4.18) consists of similar elements. Indeed the hive, like the dome, is actually a ribbed vault, with the tree branches functioning as the ribs (I reproduce the beehive upside down to push the likeness). Beyond this, both hive and dome are convex cones built around concentric three-dimensional geometric latticeworks with hollow centers. In both cases, too, the lattices are cladded with layered outer shells filled with perforations. The bees make their shells of a paperlike fabric and mortar that they create. Brunelleschi's builders

4.17.

Filippo Brunelleschi. Conjectural

scheme for the frame of the

dome of the Florence

Cathedral, 1420–1436.

From Kostof, *History of

Architecture.*

4.18.

Nest of a stingless bee

(*Melipona*). From von Frisch,

*Aus dem Leben der Bienen.*

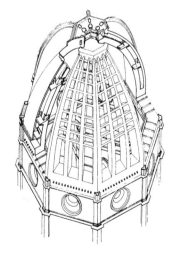

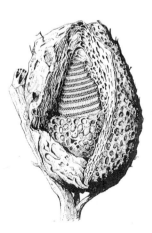

made their shells, not that differently, out of brick and pumice, or from spiraling interlocked courses of brick set on end, with an outer cladding of tile and an inner one of plaster.[22] The open eye at the dome's apex, and the corresponding "eye" in the beehive, are other common factors. And the profiles of the two domes are also similar. This profile was specified in Brunelleschi's contract as being that of the *quinto acuto*, which seems to mean that the radius of the arc of each rib should be equal to 9/10 of the octagonal base's inside diameter.[23]

Finally, when one reads Vasari's account of the construction of Brunelleschi's dome, with its squads of workers buzzing through the spaces between the shells and all over the dome's interior and exterior, climbing the stairs built between the shells and even being fed on high, the beelike nature of Brunelleschi's masterpiece is deepened.[24] One thinks also of Virgil's hive-building analogy for the construction of Carthage, discussed above.

## Ants' Pyramids

Ants, like bees, have elaborate social organizations and monumental structures, though perhaps they have been somewhat less popular as cynosures for humans. Ants are not generally considered handsome, while bees—some bees, anyway—can be extremely so. The Barberini bee, the Italian *mellifera*, with its two plump body-lobes, narrow waist, elegant legs and antennae, diaphanous wings, and brilliant black-and-gold military striping, is a particularly good-looking animal.

Some ants, however, make up for their lack of beauty by their ability to construct (at their own scale) much larger habitations than bees do. At the same time the social arrangements in many ant colonies have the same "imperial" categories of royalty, slaves, and colonizers we find among the bees. Many ants, like the dusky ant in Britain (*Formica fusca*), are burrowers who dwell in underground galleries and tunnels. But the dusky ant also raises many-storied palaces of mud. "This task is accomplished," writes the Rev. J. G. Wood, whose book on animal architecture was popular with the Victorians, "by covering the former roof with a layer of fresh and moist clay, and converting it into a floor for the next story." The interiors of the anthills erected by the brown ant (*Formica brunnea*), as observed by a Mr. Rennie (quoted in Wood's book), are two stories high, "composed of large chambers, irregularly oval, communicating with each other by arched galleries, the walls of which were as smooth as if they had been passed over by a plasterer's trowel."[25]

Ants, say Bert Hölldobler and E. O. Wilson in a recent review of the subject, not only build elaborate communal habitations, they also set out and claim territories by laying chemical trails (leading to their mounds or underground chambers), and in some species by means of bushes and rocks, which they somehow recognize as landmarks similar to those that (prehistorians have supposed) led to the development of human territoriality. Moreover some ant species—for example, *Prionopelta amabilis*—"wallpaper" the interior chambers of their nests to protect their pupae, who need a dry environment, with fragments of discarded pupal cocoons.[26] One thinks here of our own practice of putting human remains in wall tombs.

I will propose that the ancients might first have caught the idea of huge communally constructed solids, penetrated by chambers and passageways, from the termitaries and anthills of Africa. Pre-architectural humans might well have noted, for example, that teams of the red wood ant, *Formica polyctena*, could construct a five-foot-high mound made of twigs and such. For ants, this is a Giza-scaled pyramid (figs. 4.19, 4.20). And, like the pyramid, the anthill is filled with galleries and chambers, some within the pyramid itself and some below-ground. Similar ant pyramids are found throughout North Africa and the Nile region.[27]

4.19.

A five-foot-high mound created by the red wood ant, *Formica polyctena,* in Finland. From Hölldobler and Wilson, *Journey to the Ants.*

4.20.

Pyramid of Ammenemes III, Hawara. From James, *Ancient Egypt.* Photo Diana James.

## Termites' Villes Radieuses

Perhaps even less attractive than ants are termites (sometimes known as "white ants"). Yet, more than any species we have looked at, termites are subject to the monumental impulse. The animals who made the termitaries in figure 4.21 have created rounded, central tower shapes buttressed with smaller, thinner towers—a practice frequently found in human architecture. Perhaps most similar to these insect structures are the towers of Hindu temples (see chapters 8 and 9). As the illustration also shows, the hollow interiors of these termitaries—they can be 12 feet high or more—contain great halls as well as smaller chambers.

Many termitaries are covered with an outer shell that, says Karl von Frisch, functions like a layer of concrete. It is a strengthening armature or cladding and helps control the interior temperature. Von Frisch calculates that some termitaries, if rebuilt at human scale, would be four times the height of the Empire State Building (5,000 feet; in other words, pretty much the height of Wright's proposed mile-high skyscraper, fig. 4.23).[28] That Africa should be the home of these colossal structures, as well as of the pyramids, is only one more piece of evidence that ancient civilization is indebted to the indigenous buildings, animal and human, of that continent.

4.21.

Engraving of African termitaries from Henry Smeathman, "Account of African Termites," 1781. From Hancocks, *Master Builders.*

With superb anthropomorphism, Jules Michelet wrote in the mid-nineteenth century about termite architecture, basing his visions on Henry Smeathman's still-unsurpassed eighteenth-century views (fig. 4.21):

*[The termitary's] curious form is that of a pointed dome; or, if you like, of an obtuse and preponderant obelisk. For support, the dome or obelisk has four, five, or six cupolas from five to six feet high; and against these are propped up below some small bell-like structures, nearly two feet in elevation. The whole might well be taken for a kind of Oriental cathedral, the principal spire of which had a double cincture of minarets, decreasing in height. . . . Not only may several men stand on it without injury, but even wild bulls station themselves on its summit as sentinels to watch, through the high grasses of the plain, that the lion or partner does not surprise the herd.*

*Nevertheless, this dome is hollow, and the inferior platform which supports it is itself supported by a semi-hollow construction formed by the junction of four arches (two to three feet in span),—arches of a very substantial design, being pointed, ogival, and in a kind of Gothic style. Lower still extend a number of passages or corridors, plastered spaces which one might call saloons, and finally, convenient, spacious, and healthy lodgings, capable of receiving a large population; in brief, quite a subterranean city.*

*A broad spiral passage winds and rises gradually in the thickness of the edifice, which has no opening, no door, no window; the vomitories [corridor-entrances] are disguised and at a distance, terminating afar in the plain.*

*It is the most considerable and important work which displays the genius of insects; a labour of infinite patience and daring art.*

Michelet even likens these termitary domes to Brunelleschi's, so my own earlier comparison of that dome with a beehive is not so strange. Yet Michelet strongly sees the irony: "The Memphis, the Babylon, the true Capitol of the insects is built—by whom? by lice!"[29] Finally, with their bulbous organic shapes and wattle-like towers and turrets, the African termitaries probably also share in the parentage of Gaudí's projects for Tangier (see fig. 3.28) and the Sagrada Familia.

The termitaries of Australia rise like tower blocks in open countryside (fig. 4.22). In this they resemble Le Corbusier's ideas for skyscraper cities set in wide

4.22.

Termitaries of Australian

compass termites.

From von Frisch,

*Animal Architecture.*

4.23.

Frank Lloyd Wright. Project

for a mile-high skyscraper,

the Mile High Illinois, 1956.

From Conrads and Sperlich,

*Architecture of Fantasy.*

grassy spaces, except that the termitaries are more spaciously arranged, have lower densities of inhabitants, and instead of being slabs achieve fanglike shapes. These forms would resonate more with Haeckel's generation than they do with ours. Yet it ought to be a sobering thought that in all nature, termites and ants are the main beneficiaries of high-rise architecture. As suggested earlier, Australian termitaries, particularly, resemble Wright's notorious skyscraping tusk for Chicago (fig. 4.23), just mentioned, which also has shaped, deep-slanted offsets and a piercing, faceted silhouette.[30]

Michelet mentions freestanding arches built by termites—surely one of the most formidable feats of insect design and construction. And von Frisch illustrates one of these as it is being constructed by *Macrotermes natalensis* (fig. 4.24). The workers are divided into two teams. A member of one team will bring a soil particle to the site. A member of the other will orient his anus on the spot where the soil particle is to be set into the arch. Then he excretes a tiny blob of special shit that serves as mortar (arrow). The first termite then sets the particle in place. (Sometimes they use spit as glue.)[31] Such procedures, along with the *Prionopelta amabilis*'s use of pupal remains as wall paneling, enlarge our conception of arthropods' buildings as extended phenotypes.

Each new soil particle in the arch is placed so as to corbel each pier out toward its mate. In other words, the end result is a type of arch building, or vault build-

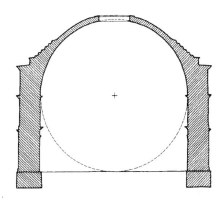

4.24.

Arch being built by

*Macrotermes natalensis.* From

von Frisch, *Animal Architecture.*

4.25.

Section through the Pantheon,

Rome, 118–128 CE. From Mark,

*Architectural Technology up to*

*the Scientific Revolution.*

ing (a vault is simply a rotated arch) that reflects human building practices—for example, in the Mycenaean beehive tombs (see fig. 4.16). One cannot say that the termites' arch has the geometric perfection of, say, the Pantheon (fig. 4.25). But the similarity of formal sensibility and even structural techniques, as well as the final shape of the termite arch compared with the Pantheon's vertical section, are worth noting. Observe also, in both, the progressive thinning of the building fabric from lower wall to upper wall, and thence to arched vault and on to the central opening, which in both cases is empty—a so-called eye.

It seems that Nature's more fantastic morphologies, her more compelling and beautiful insect body-plans, and the extraordinary buildings that these insects can create have always been in the background, and often in the foreground, of our human architectural consciousness. It is fitting that as we have borrowed and adapted over the centuries, we look back at our origins, at the energetic actions of the insect builders, and trace their effects on our life and culture.

# BIRDS

## Dinosaurs and Bridges

Scientists claim that dinosaurs, though reptiles, are descended from ancestors like the archaeopteryx—a flying reptile of the Upper Jurassic. And archaeopteryxes were also the ancestors of the birds. Moreover, certain other birdlike dinosaurs—for example, the oviraptorids of the Late Cretaceous—seem to have raised their young in nests not unlike those built by modern birds.[1] This will be my justification for beginning a chapter on birds with a look at dinosaurs.

But it is the bridgelike, not the birdlike, qualities of dinosaurs I want to examine. The relevant writer is once more D'Arcy Thompson. He prints a diagram of a stegosaurus skeleton that he discusses in terms of bridge engineering (fig. 5.1).[2] Note that the animal's relatively small forelegs sustain its smallish head and anchor one end of the main arch of its anatomy. This latter curves up and over to the animal's tall hind legs. A second span is created when the backbone continues as the animal's tail. The two spans represent the most rigid and economical method of bridging the distance between the arch's three springing points—forelegs, hindlegs, and tip of tail, the last being also a support.

The stegosaurus's bones, which are all that is visible in the diagram, supplied the structure's compressive forces. But in a living animal this compression would have to have been counteracted by muscles and ligaments. These provide the tension needed to keep a bone-built arch or truss erect and taut.

5.1.

The skeleton of a stegosaurus.
From Thompson, *On Growth and Form.*

I have converted Thompson's animal into a real bridge (fig. 5.2). This diagram shows that when you translate a dinosaur into a practical bridge, there is an

5.2.

Diagram of a "dinosaur" bridge.
Author.

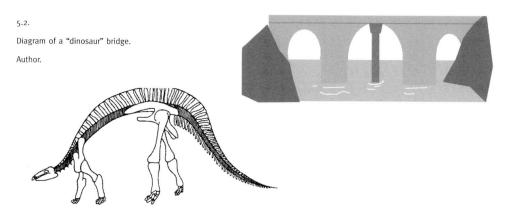

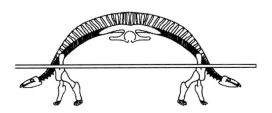

ugly and obstructive pier right in the middle of the river: those massive hind legs. Water traffic would be incommoded. So most bridges resemble a somewhat different dinosaur (fig. 5.3). I have redesigned this animal so that its head and forelegs on either end can be the abutments. It is called the bicephalous gephirosaur (two-headed bridge lizard). The roadway, which I have also added, will of course help hold the main vertebral arch in tension as well as reinforce the abutments.

A human-built bridge is not all that dissimilar (fig. 5.4).[3] The Bayonne Bridge, for example, between Staten Island and New Jersey, proves that the dinosaur design permits wide spans that are fit to carry immense loads, at the same time allowing river traffic to flow freely. The Bayonne arch spans 1,675 feet and supports a roadway, suspended from the arch, more than three times that length. The bridge's skeleton, its bones, are its steel frame. Its ligaments and muscles are the cables that hang the roadway from the arch.

My gephirosaur also complies with Thompson's diagram of the compression and tension in a normal dinosaur spine (fig. 5.5). Indeed, exactly Thompson's structures—arches, piers, and roadway—appear in another dinosaur bridge, the Quebec Steel Bridge, with its wide, clear central arch and twin abutments (fig. 5.6).

Tail          B     A     Head

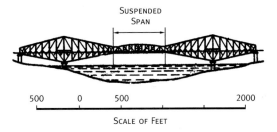

SUSPENDED
SPAN

500        0      500                    2000

SCALE OF FEET

## Weaverbirds

5.7.

Two weaverbird nests. From

Hancocks, *Master Builders.*

As we knew them today, birds have forfeited several of the bridgelike qualities in their skeletons, not to mention the bridgelike size, that their dinosaur ancestors enjoyed. But birds are builders. Some—for example, the bowerbirds—even build bridges (see fig. 5.10)! And most birds build nests for raising their young, nests that can be extraordinary. Another architectural point about birds is their bodily ornament. Their patterns and colors, and even their bodily shapes (their baupläner), have frequently been appropriated by human designers.

Birds' nests can have a great deal of beauty and craftsmanship. The handsome teardrop nests of African weaverbirds (family Ploceidae) are tightly and smoothly woven of thin vines and spiderweb (fig. 5.7). Much time and energy go into their construction—and equally into the judgments that female weaverbirds make about the final products. As an artifact, the weaverbird nest is subject to what evolutionists call sexually selective pressure: the male builder uses the nest to show off his qualities as a potential mate. When a female is present he flutters and dances around his masterpiece—incidentally pointing up his agility and attractiveness. The females are often slow to make a decision. If, despite his best efforts, a male goes for as much as a week without attracting a mate, he demolishes his work and starts over. He then tries again, harder, aiming for a tighter weave, a smoother surface, a neater silhouette. Once his work has satisfied a female, she agrees to mate and even does the interior decorating, strewing the inside of the nest with feathers and such.[4]

Thus, of the two nests in figure 5.7 the upper, by a beginner, is indeed amateurish. And it has failed as a sexual attractor. Its builder waited and waited, we are told, all in vain.[5] If he wants to pass on his genes he must build better. Here again, by the way, we recall Vitruvius and his notion that early humans, after getting the idea of architecture (partly) from birds, competed in the refinement and attractiveness of their house building (*De architectura* 2.1.6). Weaverbirds do the same: the lower nest in figure 5.7 is by a mature adult who has built many nests in his time.

The weaverbird is a craftsman whose handiwork was available to early humans in parts of Africa. Gottfried Semper, the mid-nineteenth-century German theorist, followed Vitruvius and investigated architecture's primitive debts to the art of weaving[6]—though he does not speak of weaving by birds. Feminist scholars today often theorize that the primacy of weaving, fabric making, and tent construction in early civilizations (and in some traditional societies today) is evidence that humankind was at first ruled by matriarchies—and that women, who were the builders in these early societies, were the first human architects.[7] A possible corollary to Semper's thesis, even more au courant, would be that males, having seized power from the ruling females, continued with an architecture that, in contrast to the flexible encompassing world of the females' supple tents, was inert, arrogant, defensive, and hence phallic (i.e., built of brick or stone). But, Semper would say, human architecture was still derived from weaving. Indeed he illustrates the claim with comparisons between woven textures and similar ones in patterned stone and brick.

Maybe so. But I want to make a different point: though Semper pays no attention to birds, the samples of different knots and weaves that he provides for his human ur-architecture are extraordinarily similar to those of the weaverbirds (figs. 5.8, 5.9). Note, in particular, the birds' use of loop tucks and interlocking loops (top left and right; compare with Semper's [a] and [f]), spiral coils (middle left; compare with Semper's [i] and [j]), the simple weave (middle middle; compare with Semper's [h]), and the half-hitch (bottom left; compare with Semper's [e]). Such weaverbird knots are almost exactly those that Semper proposes as first steps toward human architecture.

5.8.
Weaves and knots used in nest construction by weaverbirds. From Hancocks, *Master Builders*.

5.9.
Gottfried Semper. Knots used in ur-architecture. From Semper, *Four Elements of Architecture* (1863).

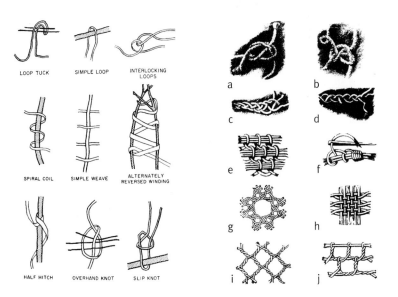

## BOWERBIRDS

Now for another architecturally minded bird family, the Australian and New Guinean bowerbirds (Ptilonorynchidae). The name covers several genera and many species. But almost all of them build what ornithologists call bowers. According to Merriam-Webster's dictionary (which orders its definitions historically), a *bower* is, first, an "attractive dwelling or retreat"; second, a lady's private apartment; and third, a garden shelter made of boughs and vines. Human bowers are frequently places for trysts—that is, like the weaverbirds' creations, they are theaters for sexual selection.

Here is Jared Diamond's description of the first bird bower he ever saw:

*Suddenly, in the jungle, I came across a beautifully woven circular hut eight feet in diameter and four feet high, with a doorway large enough for a child to enter and sit inside. In front of the hut was a lawn of green moss, clean of debris except for hundreds of natural objects of various colors that had obviously been placed there intentionally for decorations. They mainly consisted of flowers and fruits and leaves, but also some butterfly wings and fungi. Objects of similar color were grouped together, such as red fruits next to a group of red leaves. The largest decorations were a tall pile of black fungi facing the door, with another pile of orange fungi a few yards further from the door. All blue objects were grouped inside the hut, red ones outside, and yellow, purple, black, and a few green ones in other locations.*[8]

Bowers represent enormous investments of time, skill, and energy. Weeks, indeed months, can be spent on them. They are erected on a piece of breeding territory the male builder has staked out. Many are even waterproof; but since they are made of perishable materials like fruits and twigs, they must be constantly refurbished. Bowerbirds' retreats are often decorated with borrowed attractors—flowers, shiny objects, shells, snake skins, feathers, and even beer cans and other human detritus. Shiny dead beetles laid out in geometric patterns are popular.[9] Thus, human-fashion, does a bowerbird's extended phenotype make use of the (nonextended) phenotype of another species. This notion is borne out by the builder's preference, in selecting ornaments, for colors matching his own; for example, for the satin bowerbird, a bright satiny blue. Well-maintained bowers may last as long as thirty years, passing through several generations.[10]

It is important to note that authentic, bird-originated design is very much present. If a human observer rearranges a bower's display, the builder will put everything back the way it was.[11] The birds also clear away the foliage above the bower so that rays of sunlight can dramatically illuminate the building and its builder. Nor does the decoration consist solely of found objects. Many bowerbirds create a paint out of blueberry juice and, holding the crushed berry in their beak, paint the bower interior a dense blue. "Sometimes," remarks von Frisch, the bird "even uses a tool for this purpose. He picks up a piece of fibrous bark simultaneously with a squashed berry and proceeds to use the bark, soaked in the juice of the berry, like a brush or sponge."[12] Other plant juices provide black, gray, green, yellow, and reddish-brown interior decors.[13] Some of this painting is done by the female after she has chosen the builder as her partner. The bowers known as maypoles are probably the most ornamented of all nonhuman structures.[14] I will add that shells, leaves, acorns, and fruits are also among the commonest subjects in human-designed architectural ornament.

The bower is a theater. In it, or in front of it, the prospective groom does a mating dance. There is a specially cleared floor where he capers and flutters in order to attract female attention and point out the beauties of his shrine. Darwin quotes a description of the process from an Australian observer, a Mr. Strange: "At times the male will chase the female all over the aviary; then go at the bower, pick up a gay feather or a large leaf, utter a curious kind of note, set all his feathers erect, run round the bower and become so excited that his eyes appear ready to start from his head; he continues opening first one wing then the other, uttering a low, whistling note . . . until at last the female goes gently towards him."[15]

It is useful to have this instance of an avian link between dance and architecture. Indra McEwen has written brilliantly about the origins in dance of Greek temple layouts, showing how the temple plan with its rows of columns recalls aboriginal rows of dancers in their precise arrays, dancers whose patterned distributions established the χώρα or dancing floor. From this, directly or by trope, we get the chora or columnar array of the chorus, that of the phalanx (for dances were military as well as sacred or sexual), and then that of the temple whose columns are soldiers or dancers—or both.[16]

86

5.10.

Bowers constructed by different
species of Australian bowerbirds. From Cronin,
*The Ant and the Peacock*.
Drawing by Melissa Bateson.

All unknown to its human counterparts elsewhere in the world, the bowerbird
has proleptically built such human garden ornaments as the grotto, the mount,
the gate, the obelisk, and, among urban amenities, the piazza (fig. 5.10). Note
also the bridge (second row center). For this latter, the golden bowerbird constructs two twig-wrought towers around saplings while a third sapling becomes
the bridge's roadway. Each species has a distinctive style. The toothbilled
bowerbird (top row, left) clears a space in the forest and lines it with a carpet
of leaves. Archbold's bowerbird does the same, but paves his palace with snail
shells. These two species may be said to build piazze—and human piazze, I
would note, are often similarly used for purposes of sexual selection.
Macgregor's bowerbird builds a circular berm around a central sapling, bor-
dered on the outside by arrangements of leaves: he creates an obelisk or tower
(top row, right). In the second row, beginning on the left, the striped gardener
bowerbird constructs a true shelter with an open doorway through which you
can see a supporting pillar—a trunk wrapped in twigs from which the roof
hangs. On the right of the middle row we see the pylons or gateposts erected
by the Australian regent bowerbird. The satin and great gray bowerbirds (bottom row, left and center) build similar structures, while Lauterbach's bowerbird
(bottom row, right) erects four pylons or piers on a square plan.

Not only do some bowers resemble eighteenth-century garden structures, but they may not be all that different from the first human huts. In Banister Fletcher's 1890s vision of a prehistoric hut, for example (fig. 5.11), a circular space is cleared in a stand of saplings. An outer ring of trees is left in place just as with some of the bowerbirds' structures—though in Fletcher's drawing the saplings are bent into a domical shape (and one could of course thence proceed to the ribbed convex cone of Brunelleschi's dome). The similarity to a recently photographed bower is striking (fig. 5.12).

As a final variant on birds' buildings we have the male wren. He too is a real estate developer. He partially builds several nests that he then shows off to interested house-hunting females. The female who selects him then indicates which of his unfinished nests she prefers, and he completes it. Thereupon, like her weaverbird sisters, she lends a hand with the interior decoration, lining the twig-built sphere with feathers. As von Frisch points out, over the millennia these competitions probably perfected wrens' building standards—which is more evidence in favor of Vitruvius's theories about nest-weaving or hut-weaving competitions as inspirations for human architecture.[17]

5.11.

A primitive hut. From Fletcher, *History of Architecture.*

5.12.

A male Lauterbach's bowerbird in his bower. From Gould and Gould, *The Animal Mind.*

## ORNAMENTED BODIES

Architectural ornament is often called a variation on bodily ornament—a development from jewelry, tattooing, and clothes. (The latest research indicates that the earliest smelting of metals was not to make tools but to fashion ornaments.) Few creatures are as rich in natural body ornament as certain birds. The male bird of paradise's rectrices, or tail feathers (fig. 5.13), are pale crimson in color and gorgeously soft and long. They are composed of delicate, exceedingly regular chevroned barbs wrapped in soft streamers that surround their owner with a rich halo. The bright yellow of the back of the bird's head combine with his contrasting black throat, fierce bluish beak, and wary yellow eye to mix fascination with menace. It is hard to think of anything more glamorous. But these beautiful appendages actually impede flight. A quick getaway is difficult.

And yet of course the retrices have the thoroughly practical purpose of attracting females. When engaged in sexual display, male birds of paradise radically change their appearance:

*the breast shield is fully expanded and thrust forward, the nasal tufts are erected, and the cape is not only flicked forward but is also spread laterally, forming a complete semicircle above the bird's head and extending down behind the breast shield, producing together with the dark wings and underparts a complete black circle that is broken by the iridescent blue breast shield. At the base of the cape (just above the bird's actual eyes) a pair of iridescent blue-green "eye spots" become visible. . . . In this posture, with his mouth remaining closed, the male proceed[s] to dance around the female in short, sharp steps.*[18]

Who could say no to this? The tendency in some bird species to let their attractors dominate their bodies clearly parallels certain human practices. Our clothes and our costumes, our armor and our uniforms, create carapaces inside which our everyday selves are strikingly, and often misleadingly, showcased.

Images of male birds decked out in seductive ornamentation have long been part of our architectural tradition. Next to the illustrated bird of paradise in figure 5.13 is a transenna panel from the Byzantine cathedral at Torcello near Venice (fig. 5.14). Not only does the sculptor present two beautiful long-tailed marble peacocks, but the scene also has other biological aspects. As we will

5.14.

Torcello, Cathedral, trensenna, c1008. From Fletcher, *History of Architecture.*

5.13.

Male raggiana bird of paradise. From Johnsgard, *Arena Birds.*

Photo Bruce M. Beehler.

see, in the wild animals most commonly face off when two rival males are establishing a territorial boundary.[19]

But here that normally confrontational act has softened. The two opposed birds drink from a common cup. They almost genuflect to each other, their legs arched neatly away from any suggestion of challenge. Separated by a column on the axis of their reflective symmetry, and with their pear-shaped bodies wound in foliage spirals, the two birds drink in the Gospel's cooling draught. (Just to enrich the metaphor, the basic meaning of *transenna* is "trap for birds.") So these peacocks are trapped—happily, of course—at the boundaries of the paradise symbolized by the church's chancel.

Or take one of the commonest pieces of ornament in medieval architecture. The word *corbel* means "raven." So when you see a row of corbels topping a wall, a common architectural sight (fig. 5.15), the association is with a row of birds—birds, in this case, with wings set in perfect interlocking curves as they perch or prepare to fly off. Indeed, not just ravens but any birds that perch in rows make the point (fig. 5.16).

5.15.

Row of corbels from Sant'Ambrogio, Milan, 1140. From Fletcher, *History of Architecture.*

5.16.

Mick Ellison. A roosting row of crows. From the *New York Times,* 27 May 1997, C1.

## FLIGHT AND FEEDING

Some human buildings derive more from the notion of birds' flight than from birds' ornaments. This is especially true of those built by the Greeks. They called their temples *ptera*, "plumed things, winged things." And so, by trope, even such a thing as a peripteral ("around the ptera") colonnade, which rings a building, has an association with flight. The *pteroma* is the space between the walls of a temple and its colonnade, so that space is winged as well. In modern English a "flight" of stairs, or several of them, similarly speaks of flying; the stairs zigzag skyward.

Gables, to the Greeks, were known as "eagles," ἀετοί One should probably think of a hovering eagle with its long wings spread slightly downward, his brilliant eye and beak at the apex of a broad, low triangle. At Korkyra (fig. 5.17) the Gorgon-goddess who commands the gable runs, as in one of Artemis's hunting dances, while on her outspread wings she flies up and out toward us. Accompanied by panthers, by Pegasus, and by Chrysaor, and with snakes at her belt, she is not exactly reassuring. Indeed she is probably intended to be apotropaic—to keep trouble at bay.

5.18.

Detail from the tympanum of a

tomb (Gaetano Argenti, d. 1730,

designed by Ferdinando

Sanfelice?). In San Giovanni a

Carbonara, Naples. Photo

Mimmo Jodice.

5.19.

Antoni Gaudí. Windows of the chapel at the Colonia Güell, Barcelona. Designed 1890, begun 1908. From de Solá-Morales, *Gaudí*.

5.20.

Tawny frogmouth. From Peterson, *The Birds*.

The Greeks passed on this concetto of the gable or tympanum as a flying creature.[20] It appears everywhere in later architecture. In an eighteenth-century tomb in San Giovanni a Carbonara, Naples, for example (fig. 5.18), the brilliant perversity of Ferdinando Sanfelice crowns a corpse's skull with lilies and gives it thick muscular wings. Thus does the idea of a bodiless seraph get mated with a toothless, glowering cranium. Sometimes heaven-bound souls are depicted in the guise of such angels—newborns leaving the dead body below. But Sanfelice's flying skull shows, ascending, everything that should have been left below: fleshless bones, broken teeth, mortal coil.

Still today our buildings have wings (the White House's and the National Gallery's East Wings); still today, buttresses fly. But let us return to that greatest of architectural biologizers, Gaudí. His buildings are not only molecular and insectile; they also can be birdlike. The stained-glass windows of the chapel for the unfinished Colonia Güell, near Barcelona, for example, are clearly modeled on the yapping beaks of infant birds (figs. 5.19, 5.20). The gape, as ornithologists call it, especially when the gullet is bright red, is not merely a signal to the parent or feeder; in some species it is an attractor—perhaps because with it a male can suggest to a female the welcome possibilities of their deciding to set up house.

Gaudí's gaping windows, with their sharply angular upper bills and rounded lower ones, beg to be fed. But their hunger is theological. It will be appeased by the sunlight of sanctifying grace, a light often filtered through stained-glass symbols and stories. This is a thoroughly Franciscan and Gaudíesque idea:

Francis brought birds, including nestlings, home to his cell, where they gaped and he fed them. On other occasions he interpreted birdsong as the singing of God's praises, and even heard in it the voice of God himself, preaching to a congregation.[21]

## NORTHWEST COAST BIRD-ARCHITECTURE

No peoples, perhaps, have been more committed to the incorporation of birds (though they revere other fauna too) into their life, art, and architecture than the indigenous communities of the upper Pacific coast of North America. The Tlingit, who settled along the fringe of coast and coastal islands on Alaska's southern leg; the Haida to the south, on the Queen Charlotte Islands; and the Kwakiutl, partly on Vancouver's northeast coast and partly inland, as well as many linked communities, have been prolific in making large wooden images, masks, chests, blankets, and other objects that portray sacred ravens, eagles, thunderbirds, and waterbirds. The chief Northwest Coast god, creator of all things, is Raven.[22] He has fathered all lesser totems, all people and animals; procured territories for them; and laid down ecological rules. Raven and other birds are also totems or guiding spirits. A human devotee reveres the totem in life, assumes it into his or her body at special feasts, and, on dying, expects to become one with it and to be transported by it to heaven.

The houses of the Northwest Coast peoples are given the shapes and colorings of the inhabitants' totems.[23] The dwellings are normally constructed as part of a shoreline village, often on a high bluff over a beach. Tall flights of wooden steps lead down to the water where the canoes—they, too, transformed by carving and color into totem creatures—are lined up. The houses are made of heavy upright cedar logs or posts to which wide planks are attached with withes. The planks can be dismounted and moved to other villages when the group follows the migrations of their prey.

A Kwakiutl legend throws light on the bird-oriented thinking behind this architecture. A man named

*Qawatliqala, when about to take his prospective son-in-law to his house, warned him, "Take care, brother, when we enter my house! Follow close on my heels! Qawatliqala [a god] told his brother that the door of the house was dangerous." They walked up to the door together. The door had the shape of a*

5.21.

Kwakiutl village at Alert Bay.

Chief's house with frontal pole.

From Jonaitis, *Totem Poles*.

*raven. It opened and they jumped in, and the raven snapped at the son-in-*
*law. All the images in Qawatliqala's house were alive, the posts were alive,*
*and the Sisiul [cedar] beams.*[24]

The house, then, is a holy bird's extended phenotype, and also that of the bird's totem group. Raven guards his family and snaps at strangers. Like both the Gorgon at Korkyra and Sanfelice's skull, Raven is apotropaic. Similar mouths and beaks appear on house poles, which are shorter totem poles used as interior piers. All this is in addition to the painted animals that can be splayed across the house's facade, whose body parts are rendered in powerful curved geometric forms in brilliant blacks, reds, whites, and yellows.

Figure 5.21 presents such a house. The bird's open beak is the ceremonial entrance. With a powerful gesture his broad pentagonal wings defend the facade. A great magical bird's tail meanwhile spreads in an inverted triangle behind the pole, its feathers as stiff and erect as the pole itself. Note too that each of the raven's wing feathers is simultaneously the snout of a different animal—in Northwest Coast mythology, any given totem may thus be composed of other totems. In the photo the specific family and individual totems forming the raven's crest consist of an upper raven with spread wings, a killer whale, a beaver who is eating or regurgitating a bear, a waterbird, and a second bear who perches immediately on top of the raven at the base. Totem poles, in short, are both heraldry and mythic food chains.

Northwest Coast totemism includes intricate marriage laws and calendars of feasts.[25] The key to it all is the transformation of one animal into another—including humans. These transformations occur when a totemist moves, marries, comes of age, or ceremonially eats his or her totem's flesh. At the ceremonies, masked dancers embody the transformations. Take the raven mask. Its outer form (fig. 5.22) represents the god with his powerful black beak, red-rimmed and marked by dark grayish-red stripes, and his deep, angry eyes. When this outer beak is "opened," however, it hinges outward into four radiating pointed parts. Inside, carved across the gullet, is the round, hook-nosed face of a god known as Raven of the Sea (fig. 5.23). He is human in shape but covered with blue stripes. Along the inside of Raven-the-bird's beak, parts of other creatures are painted in red, blue, and black. Raven's sharp teeth are ready to chew the body parts of the other totems that he will devour at the feast. Remembering that this mask will be worn by a human, we can set still another being inside these concentrically enveloped beings. Thus do the creatures "consume" one another just as totem animals do. The transformation masks accord with the Northwest Coast belief that no organism in nature survives except by ingesting other organisms (which of course is perfectly true). All creatures, in short, are made of other creatures. And a house, with its inhabitants, is just one more such creature.

5.22.

Kwakiutl wooden transformation mask of Raven (outer face). From Drury Inlet, collected 1901. American Museum of Natural History, New York.

5.23.

Raven of the Sea (inner face). Both 5.22 and 5.23 from Jonaitis, *Totem Poles*.

5.24.

Bella Coola. A carved eagle
holds a lady's coffin, 1895.
Royal British Columbia
Museum, Victoria. Ethnology
Division, PN 4588.

Death is another occasion when totemic bird-architecture plays an important
role. When a chieftain or shaman dies, his body, or part of it, is put into a small
model of a house. There, after a certain number of days, Raven—or sometimes
another god, such as Eagle—descends from heaven, takes up the dead person's soul, and soars back there with it. Often on the model house the bird will
be carved and painted as it was about to fly off. Sometimes an opening for the
soul's escape will be made in one of the walls. One such model house in New
York's American Museum of Natural History, raised on stilts and with a carved
figure inside, is filled with the colossal form of a thunderbird about to sail up
to heaven with the occupant's soul.

Or instead of the model house there can be a sculpture of the great bird soar-
ing up with the departed person. We see this in figure 5.24. A giant eagle—
Eagle himself, perhaps—his hooked beak raised like an archer's arrow, perches
before a village. His crest is the coffin containing a woman's soul.

If birds are descended from dinosaurs, and if they then evolved into the smaller
creatures we now know, then there is a certain poetic justice in the Northwest
Coast peoples' building birds at dinosaur scale. In this their bird-buildings are
a bit like our dinosaur-bridges. Maybe both we and they are unconsciously
keeping evolutionary memories alive. With the birds, too, our narrative has
begun to fill up with more individualized characters. Molecules and cells, after
all, are pretty anonymous, as (though less so) are vegetation and insects. But
with weaverbirds, bowerbirds, and, in a different way, with Raven, we come
upon dramas of individual struggle, like the weaverbird's realization of his
insufficient handiwork or the great eagle flying aloft with a woman's soul.

# Mammals: Territory and Reproductive Rights

6

Our look at Northwest Coast peoples has shown how mammals may relate to architecture. (Besides birds, after all, the buildings represent bears, whales, goats, wolves, beavers, and humans.)[1] Yet mammals are not, on the whole, great builders—some of the few exceptions are dormice, beavers, badgers, and ourselves. But, as I noted in the introduction, our fellow primates' nests are fairly skimpy.[2]

Nevertheless, we mammals, all of us, can be highly territorial. We recognize articulated spaces and landmarks. Indeed, it is probable that our human monumental impulse mainly arises out of this. We are concerned about the ownership of space. And our territories are breeding zones often strongly associated with our bodies. The notion of extended phenotypes comes into play as much with us as with bees and bowerbirds. In this chapter I will be suggesting that along with the human drive to monumentality and competitive sexual selection, another beginning point for our architecture is precisely this territorial sense.[3]

## PRIMATE TERRITORIES

Among primates, some territorial systems are very strict—as "strict," in their way, as any human-built geometric territory marked out by walls, gates, watchtowers, and statues.[4] Other primate territories are only vaguely bounded, though their reality may be strongly proclaimed once an interloper comes on the scene. J. G. Fleagle has found a way of analyzing several different primate territories visually, hence spatially.

In figure 6.1, all six species' territories reflect their sociosexual systems. In each group there is an alpha male with title to the main tract of land. The bushbabies (upper left) demonstrate how a small group of two males (in black) controls two partly overlapping ranges within the circle that abstractly symbolizes that group's total territory. The upper male's personal territory completely encloses that of a single female (in white). The lower male in the diagram, however, the beta, has two females in his harem, each with a territory that is at least partially her own—territory that does not overlap that of the other female but is partly outside the beta male's area. Thus his females each enjoy a sliver of private turf. In contrast, the upper female's territory is entirely overlapped by the alpha's.

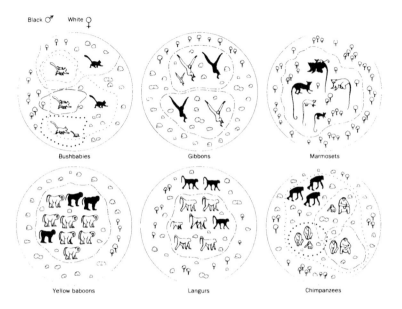

Black ♂ White ♀

Bushbabies    Gibbons    Marmosets

Yellow baboons    Langurs    Chimpanzees

6.1.

Six primate territories. From the *Cambridge Encyclopedia of Human Evolution,* after Fleagle, *Primate Adaptation.* Females are shown in white, males in black.

In the upper center are two gibbon groups. Their territory is adjacent but without overlaps. The upper male has one female and one daughter; the lower, the beta, a female only. Marmosets (upper right) have a single, large range containing several generations of males and females. Note that the large male on top cares for a daughter. The cohort consists of two major males and a young male, plus one major female and that female's daughter, along with the infant carried by the alpha male.

In the lower left diagram we see the arrangements favored by yellow baboons. Here, in another large single territory, three males live with seven females. Among the langurs in the center of the lower row, an alpha male, with a harem of six, patrols his territory while two outcast males, on the outside looking in, patrol the periphery. Finally, the female chimpanzees, lower right, have overlapping subterritories within a larger range patrolled by three males.

The upshot is that among these representative primates, territory maps breeding arrangements. A main territory is established primarily because an alpha male wishes to provide a haven (or prison, or both) for his female(s) and their offspring.[5] Within those main territories are subterritories that tend to be asso-

MAMMALS: TERRITORY AND REPRODUCTIVE RIGHTS

ciated with smaller groups in which couples are prominent. Larger unified territories, when there are no subdivisions, are linked both to large populations and to specific harem systems.

## Human Territories

What the corresponding territorial arrangements for prehumans and hominids were we do not know. But almost certainly there were territorial arrangements, probably in several varieties. And these prehuman territories, I am sure, went hand in hand with sexual institutions comparable to those that Fleagle portrays for nonhuman primates. Even though we know nothing about early hominid and human territoriality, there is reason to give weight to this long, precivilized era in our history. We humans have spent a much longer part of our past—longer by several millennia—inhabiting wild territories than we have in permanent dwellings. I assume that during this period we were hardwired with territorial adaptations, some of them still in force.

Territories are singled out and remembered by landmarks. Peter J. Wilson discusses the ways in which traditional societies identify their farmland, meadows, water holes, and ancestral monuments. In general, he writes, when a group has a sparse population and a large ranging area, territory seems less important than it does in more confined circumstances. Boundaries for big territories are not strongly marked and may not really exist at all. This is all the truer among migratory peoples. Yet, as he also observes, "all ethnographic accounts note a strong association between people and territory, especially landscape, among hunter-gatherers."[6] Tim Ingold has shown that today's hunter-gatherers (who of course may not be particularly representative of prehistoric ones) are especially concerned with specific objects and features: paths, tracks, sacred or burial sites, haunts, water holes, and the like.[7]

Indeed, one could make the case for a widespread if not universal human sense that territoriality and boundary recognition are deemed signs of superior culture. Undoubtedly when humans began to appreciate landmarks and hold territory permanently, especially with the advent of agriculture, boundaries gained importance. This in time led to artificial landmarks, such as divinized piles of stones or stone uprights,[8] and to such things as land measurement and boundary markers—to walls, columns, and apotropaic images like the magical bird painted on the Haida house in the previous chapter (see fig. 5.21).

In his 1975 book *The Experience of Landscape* Jay Appleton, a geographer, claims that we see and feel landscape—parks, gardens, paintings—in terms of a territorial sense inherited from the hunter-gatherers who came before us.[9] Thus, he says, in a "desirable" landscape, landscape that we admire as sublime, picturesque, or beautiful, we need somehow to sense that we ourselves are located where we can see without being seen. At base we like a terrain in which we can stalk prey. We must have bushes and hillocks to hide behind. This arrangement Appleton calls a "prospect." His other landscape categories involve horizons, refuges, vistas, magnets, offsets (which are like stage wings), and what he calls the "sky dado"—an arching form, like a tree branch, just above the horizon. And, he adds, all these features, however aestheticized in our conscious brains, are unconsciously linked to our cortical need to find prey and avoid predators. To borrow W. D. Hamilton's term, landscapes—even those of Claude Lorrain or Capability Brown—are domains of danger.[10]

Appleton's vision, then, is about promptings that are still felt when the need for them has long vanished. Or has it? One of the most brilliant analyses ever made of English landscape painting was done by David Solkin in something like Appleton's terms. Solkin proposes British landscape and garden design as what a biologist would call an alpha male's territory. He states this in Marxist terms: landscape, especially cultivated landscape, is a form of capital accumulation, while gardens represent surplus value, the exploitation of commodified labor, and so on. But terminology aside, what Solkin actually, or also, describes in these paintings meshes with Appleton's insights.[11] And it meshes with those I am presenting here, for I too in my non-Marxist way wish to emphasize the qualities in territory and its landmarks that denote ownership, proprietary rights, sovereignty, and the ways in which those claims can be architecturally and sculpturally made.

Let us look with Appletonian eyes at Leonardo's famous 1475 pen drawing, thought to be the first Western image purely of landscape (i.e., without figures; fig. 6.2). We will assume that the most primitive parts of our cerebral cortices continue to be those of a preliterate hunter-gatherer. The fierce precipice before us, the trees that might catch us as we fall, the placid distant river in its desirably open valley, the *castellum* on the far left with its watchtowers and battlements protecting its inner huddle of houses and its cultivated fields, and the town itself resolutely planted on the edge of another unscalable cliff: this,

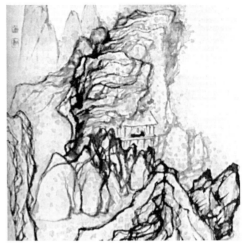

6.2.

Leonardo. Arno landscape,

1475. Uffizi, Florence.

6.3.

Tao Chi (1641–c1717).

Landscape. Album leaf. Private

collection, New York.

Appleton would say (I think), is the true language of Leonardo's drawing, addressing our deepest instincts—our combined need to be protected and to gain opportunities for predation.

In Tao Chi's monumental landscape (fig. 6.3), which I choose because it is culturally unrelated to Leonardo's (though it is not visually so dissimilar), we can find kindred associations. There are the powerful lineaments of the great rocks and cliffs among which the hut and its inhabitant are so inconspicuous—a "prospect." The hut itself, tucked beneath a beetling outcrop, is surely a "refuge." And in this scene, which ominously lacks a horizon and a "sky dado," so overwhelming is the torrential fall of mountain rock, so ferocious the foreground peaks, that the small, central refuge-house surely functions as a powerful "magnet" for the climber whose surroundings are full of hiding places—for prey, yes, but also for predators.

6.4.

Giovanni Battista Piranesi.

San Lorenzo fuori le Mura,

Rome. Etching, 1760–1761.

From Piranesi, *Piranesi:*

*Rome Recorded.*

6.5.

Detail of Piranesi plate.

6.6.

Persepolis, palace, *apadana*
(audience) hall. Double bull
capital. Louvre, Paris.

6.7.

Two male topi settle territorial

boundaries in a ritualized duel.

From Gould and Gould, *Sexual*

*Selection*. Photo Jonathan

Scott/Planet Earth Pictures.

## TERRITORIAL SYMBOLISM IN ARCHITECTURE

Such features need not be limited to the wilderness or to wild territories. Our cities, too, are jungles, deserts, or wildernesses that afford prospects, provide refuges, and protect us from hazards—or else present them.[12] I here go beyond Appleton's book. Think of Piranesi and such etchings as the *veduta* of the Roman church of San Lorenzo fuori le Mura (fig. 6.4). First of all, of course, churches are traditional "refuges." And that, by extension, can make the surrounding urban exterior a labyrinth of hazards, of predators' lairs. Indeed, this is just what we sense, it seems to me, in Piranesi's scene. Note the central foreground beggar or scavenger in his tatters (fig. 6.5), and his starveling dog burrowing in the gutter. If they aren't hunter-gatherers, who is? We might well feel threatened, I suppose, by these wretches; they are clearly capable of predation. Or perhaps we might be moved, if we were among the gentlemen in front of the church, to chase them out of the picture, thus turning the piazza from a hazard into a refuge. The act would reaffirm the territory, the boundary, marked by the bollards.

Territorial symbolism borrowed from the wild is endemic in high civilizations. Thus the creators of the kneeling bulls at Persepolis, which formed the capitals for the columns in a royal hypostyle hall (fig. 6.6), were probably thinking of the territorial encounters of male mammals (other capitals in the palace depict confronted bulls, unicorns, and griffins). I illustrate a pair of sub-Saharan antelopes called topi (*Damaliscis lunatus*; fig. 6.7). This particular animal may not have been known in ancient Persia, but there were and are plenty of similar species in the region—for example, Smith's gazelle, whose males duel just this way.[13] Thus does the architectural centerpiece of the human king's palace make the analogy between his lands and those of two territory-establishing antelope alphas. It is more than possible that the depiction of such agonistic beasts and birds in other art—the motif is common in practically every period— retains something that has survived the transition to settled communities; a bit of the property-declaring, family-protecting significance, concentrating on repro- ductive rights, that it has had throughout the millennia of prehistory, and that primates and other mammals still express.

François de Polignac, writing on early territorial symbolism in ancient Greece, shows that frequently the holiest sanctuaries were located not at the city cen- ters but precisely at their boundaries.[14] He claims that it was the border, the outer shape, not the urban heart of a territory that was its most empowering aspect. In particular, he says, the polis's outer boundary guaranteed its hopes for future reproduction, both agricultural and sexual. Disputed boundaries were traditionally marked by admonitory temples, tombs, altars, herms, and the like. The ruling council would often hold its meetings at these border shrines. Thus did the Megarians build their council chamber at the frontier. It was here, too, that the graves of the polis's founding heroes were located. In this way the archons could profit from the advice of the dead whose bodies and tombs physically marked out the geometric integrity of the state.[15] In a similar sense, it seems to me, the obelisk, bollards, Chigi mountains and starbursts, foun- tains, plumes, globe, and cross in Piranesi's etching (see fig. 6.4) are territorial markers. They are the warnings and admonitions of the papal rulers, who built the city's squares, walls, obelisks, and churches as ways of "marking" their land.

## Territorial Colossi

We have examined, several times, the notion of buildings as huge organisms. A creature-shaped building would be an extended phenotype. Building-sized, and indeed city-sized, nation-sized, and even, we will see, continent-sized and cosmos-sized shapes, of humans and other organisms, exist throughout many cultures. "Among the Para-Pierana of Colombia," we read, "the longhouse is . . . a creature, known here as the Roofing Father, who is both a human per- son and an enormous bird." The palm leaves composing the roof are likened to the bird's feathers. (We think of Raven and the Northwest Coast houses.) The head is at what is called the house's male end and the anus at its female end. Within the house, the line dividing men from women is the creature's digestive tract. The men's door is the bird's vagina. When a man enters the longhouse, he is a metaphor for ejaculated sperm, as the house turns into a womb. And when he exits he becomes metaphorically a newborn, and leaves via the house's vagina. The women, in contrast, enter through a women's door. They do so as metaphors for manioc, or nourishment, so their door is the building's mouth.[16]

European modernism can also conceptualize buildings this way. The German architect Frei Otto is as biological as Gaudí, or more so. The core of his flexible tower or monumental column project (fig. 6.8) is formed from vertebra-like disks in compression, held in place by muscles and tendons that consist of guy-lines. By lengthening or shortening these cables (via winches at the base) the structure can be curved and swiveled just like a human, or any mammalian, spine (fig. 6.9).[17] We recall that the cables on a suspension bridge (chapter 5) similarly bind the structure together, counteracting the compressive weight of its bones. I will add that in bridges, these cables allow for a certain amount of movement as a form of controlled wind-bracing. Otto may also have been thinking of the way skyscrapers are built so as to sway (but only a little) during windstorms. But the archings and rearings of this particular tower would probably be unsettlingly animalistic.

6.8.

Frei Otto. Flexible column. Project, 1963. From Glaeser, *Work of Frei Otto.*

6.9.

Frank H. Netter. The bones and ligaments of the vertebral column. From Netter, *Atlas of Human Anatomy.*

6.10.

Johann Bernhard Fischer von
Erlach. *The Colossus of Rhodes.*
From Fischer von Erlach,
*Entwurff einer historischen
Architektur* (1721).

Frei Otto gives us only a part of a mammal's body. In ancient times the most famous colossi had complete human physiques. And, more than is the case with Otto's tower, they were territorial—boundary markers, admonitions, and devices with which to subdivide and order a community. The Colossus of Rhodes—long since destroyed but often reimagined—portrayed the god Helios (Strabo 14.2.5). As the divinity who marked the sites of sunrise and sunset, with his ray-crowned face shining out to the east (Eos) and away from the darkness of the west (Zophos), Helios had any number of territorial meanings.[18] Like many landmarks he both welcomed and warned. The colossus lighted the mariner's way with his torch but, with his ready weapons, signaled protection.

The most famous reconstruction of the Rhodes Helios is probably that by the Austrian baroque architect Johann Fischer von Erlach (fig. 6.10). The nude god bestrides a narrow harbor entrance, each foot on a high seawall where microscopic humans walk. In the god's left hand is an arrow and in his right a great

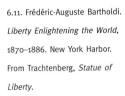

6.11. Frédéric-Auguste Bartholdi.
*Liberty Enlightening the World*,
1870–1886. New York Harbor.
From Trachtenberg, *Statue of
Liberty*.

smoking beacon. Solar beams shine from his head. And a ship sails through his spread legs into the inner harbor.[19]

Helios's torch and rayed crown reappear in many later colossal images, most famously in the Statue of Liberty (fig. 6.11).[20] Like Helios, Liberty is liminal and apotropaic. Once again the crown signifies east and west, sunrise and sunset. And once again the torch is a lamp of welcome—lifted beside the golden door, as Emma Lazarus's inscription puts it. Yet like Helios at Rhodes, Liberty on Bedloe's Island is also apotropaic.

In fact, she is not all that welcoming. Aren't her stern heavy face, baleful brow, imperial lips, huge thick arms, and crown of spikes more than a bit admonitory? In any event, those she welcomed, who went through Ellis Island, felt like personae non gratae often enough.[21] No wonder Kafka, in a strong misreading of Bartholdi's statue in the first sentence of his novel *Amerika*, has Liberty raising her sword rather than her lamp beside the Golden Door.[22]

MAMMALS: TERRITORY AND REPRODUCTIVE RIGHTS

## Territories of Human Shape

Colossi are legion. There is, for example, Vitruvius's description of a man-shaped city carved from a mountain (*De architectura* 2, preface). Its designer was Deinocrates—well named, since the word means "dreadful power." Here the colossus is not simply an entrance guardian but is the city itself, carved out of living rock on the peak of Mount Athos in Greece. Like the communal buildings of the Para-Pierana, Deinocrates' colossus grants human access to its body through its orifices.

Later in the story, Deinocrates presented plans for a quite different new city, to be built by Alexander and named after him. As an item in his résumé Deinocrates tells Alexander about the Greek mountain he had carved into the shape of a man-shaped city.[23] In order to make memorable his presentation to the emperor, Deinocrates oiled his body, dressed himself in a lion skin and olive crown, and carried a club—Hercules, obviously. And Hercules was appropriate, since that hero's labors were mostly territorial: clearing land, eliminating pests, cleaning stables, and otherwise civilizing various settlement areas.

Down the ages draughtsmen have often sketched this vision. Francesco di Giorgio Martini produced two designs. In the earlier (fig. 6.12) the figure is recumbent. Its physique consists of the town's walls, towers, and main buildings. The man's feet are round bastions, his stomach a circular piazza; the cathedral grows from his heart and lungs. Another set of circular bastions marks his elbows. His head is crowned with a high, fortified tower. Between his legs is the triangular drill field. Thus did the army march and countermarch under a cock and balls half as big as the cathedral! Here again breeding and protective functions go hand in hand.[24]

In the eyes of seventeenth-century allegorists the plan of St. Peter's at Rome, with its colonnades, was also a recumbent colossus (fig. 6.13). Note that the prostrate Peter wears Michelangelo's dome as his papal crown (much as Francesco's figure wears its town's main fort). The saint's embracing arms turn into the oval sweeps of Bernini's colonnades.

Rudolf Wittkower discusses this drawing as an anonymous "counterproject" intended to criticize Bernini's plans.[25] Maybe so. But Bernini himself twice likened his colonnades to outstretched human arms. On one occasion he wrote: "since the Church of St. Peter [is] as it were the mother of all other [churches],

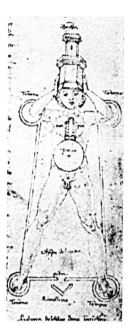

it should have a portico that actually shows itself receiving Catholics maternally into her open arms, to confirm them in their beliefs, [and receiving] heretics to reunite them with the Church, and infidels to illuminate them in the true faith."[26] (To be consistent, of course, Bernini's own sketch of such a figure would have shown the female, Ecclesia, and not St. Peter. But never mind: the analogy strengthens our theme.) Bernini makes his colonnades and the great basilica a human phenotype—a reproductive one, we note.

Bernini made the same analogy, buildings = bodies, on another occasion. When he was in France in 1665,

*he said that galleries were like arms with regard to the head . . . and he took the pencil and demonstrated this on paper. He said that he was actually thinking of the church of St. Peter in Rome, whose portal appeared low in everyone's judgment; he found a remedy and suggested to the pope to have two wings of colonnades built, which would make the portal look taller than it was; and he showed this with his pencil, demonstrating that it was like two arms and a head.*[27]

Could the drawing in figure 6.13 have anything to do with this?

6.14.

Cologne, 1587. Map of Europe
as queen, with Spain as head.
Yale University Map Collection.

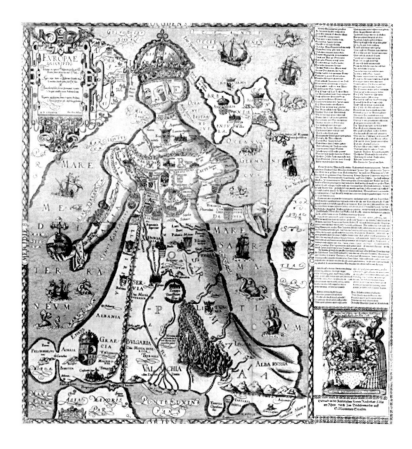

Deinocrates' city of Mount Athos extends the human phenotype to mountain size. An allegorical map printed in Cologne in 1587 proposes the whole of Europe as a colossus—as a peace goddess's extended phenotype. Europa appears as a crowned lady dressed in a long gown. (To create this likeness the landmass has been revolved so that Spain is on top; see figure 6.14.) Though fully dressed, moreover, the lady's anatomy is analyzed in accompanying verses: her head is Spain, with her right cheek Aragon and her left Navarre. The upper part of her bosom is France. The Rhine flows around her breasts and the Danube descends down her body to her skirt's hem at Wallachia. Italy is her right arm, Denmark her left. In her belly, we read, lies the strong stomach of Germany. Bohemia marks her umbilicus. Her right thigh is Hungary, Poland her left, and her feet are Greece and Muscovy. Thus is the beautiful Europa, Zeus's prize (Ovid, *Metamorphoses* 2.858ff.; illustrated in one of the map's vignettes), literally fleshed out at continental scale.

## PROCREATING COLOSSI

Often these territorial colossi have procreative roles—as one would expect, since they are often breeding territories. For example, a sandpainting by an Australian aborigine (fig. 6.15) represents a colossal mother whose living body, still directing them, is fused into a hill and lake. The mother is horned and carries two long bobbins of possum-fur string. The numbers on the painting refer to landscape features linked to different parts of her body—trees, clouds, and ceremonial zones. The picture shows how a progenitor of the current population, a mother who lives on as a specific set of landscape features, guides and preserves her descendants.[28]

Similar ideas reappear in our own culture. In figure 6.16 is a project for a Dalmatian resort village by an architect named R. Porro. He exploits the shape of an Adriatic beach whose natural features had already suggested a huge torso tanning itself. Within the upper torso are rental housing, a central square, administration offices, civil services, a restaurant, and so on, as well as such delights as a labyrinth. A men's meeting place and family housing are also located here. Porro's settlement is a synthetic cubist beachboy with massive hair, streamlined dark glasses, and washboard abdomen. His arms and hands make a symmetrical gesture of offering, circling a pelvis enlivened with a blossom at the figure's genital center.[29]

6.15.

Bokarra (Manggalili clan, Australia). A Yolngu landscape colossus. From Tilley, *Phenomenology of Landscape.*

6.16.

R. Porro. Project for a seaside resort village at Vela Luca, Korkula Island, former Yugoslavia, 1970. From *L'Architecture d'Aujourd'hui,* 1970.

6.17.

The Cosmic Man, Mahapurusha,
imposed on a temple mandala.
From a Hindu architectural
manual. From Michell,
*Hindu Temple.*

Other colossi, similarly procreative, are found in the East. In India the Hindu temples we see today were built beginning about 2,000 years ago. Normally they are massive, squarish masonry structures on high platforms. Their outer shape consists of a heavy stone or brick tower rising from a lower ring of walls. Steps, porches, corridors, and chambers are embedded in this ring.

The temples contain invisible colossi. These are represented by the mandalas (*mandala* is Sanskrit for "circle") or meditation diagrams that Hindus and Buddhists fashion. Mandalas relate temple plans to the cosmos. A mandala usually involves a square as well as a circle, and is symmetrical and concentric. I reproduce one that represents both a temple sanctuary, or womb chamber, and a male divinity in the lotus position (fig. 6.17). The notion is not too different from the image of Europa we just looked at, especially if we imagine the goddess crisscrossed by lines of latitude and longitude. The mandala's subsquares or *padas* are dedicated to different parts of the heavens, to different gods, to different parts of the human physique, and also the plan elements of the temple's tower. The central nine *padas*, the shrine's lotus heart, are sacred to Brahma. The peripheral squares—the arms and legs of the main divinity—belong to protective planetary gods.

According to Peter J. Wilson, mandala, as a plural, are also the auras of charisma surrounding certain Hindu and Buddhist rulers.[30] The kings often express

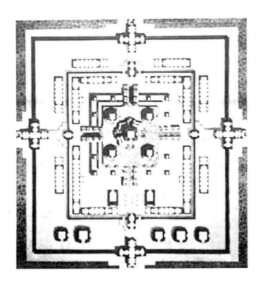

6.18.

Angkor (Cambodia). Temple
Mountain of Pre Rup, 961.
Plan. From Delaporte,
*Voyage au Cambodge.*

and intensify this special attractive power by building not just temples but whole architectural complexes based on mandala designs. One such group, at the ancient Cambodian city of Angkor, is Pre Rup, dating from 961 CE (fig. 6.18). Like other architectural mandalas, this one maps the unseen body, legs spread and arms akimbo, vitals filling the central square, of its royal builder, the god-king Rajendra Varman II. A central quincunx of small temples lies on processional cross-axes leading through similar concentric, symmetrical, L-shaped architectural ranges to Greek-cross gateways at the complex's cardinal points. These are all set exactly north, east, south, and west.[31] The quincunx is centered on the god-king's imagined heart, viscera, and genitals.[32]

Here I would like to point out something that I think may not yet have been sufficiently noted: as far as I know, these Cambodian complexes, the earliest of which belong to the ninth century CE, are the first large-scale, rigorously symmetrical building groups in all of architectural history. At any rate there is nothing known to me that is comparably regular, and with the same kinds of multiple reflective symmetry, from the ancient Near East, Egypt, Greece, or Rome.[33] The ultimate source of the idea could well be Chang'an, the Chinese city that already in the third century BCE had a regular bilaterally symmetrical grid (though we don't know whether the buildings themselves matched up left and right, top and bottom, tower for tower, loggia for loggia, window for window, door for door, as they do in Cambodia).[34]

MAMMALS: TERRITORY AND REPRODUCTIVE RIGHTS

The most famous such Cambodian complex is Angkor Wat. This, like the others, portrays several different things. It chiefly represents a celestial palace that the son of Indra, god of storms, built on the sacred Hindu mountain, five-peaked Meru in the Himalayas. Indra decided that his son should inhabit the mortals' world, so the celestial architect Viswakarman built Angkor Wat as a replica of the palace on Meru. Indra's later issue ruled the kingdom. The present complex at Angkor Wat was mostly built by another child of Indra, Jayavarman VII, who reigned from 1181 to 1220.

The mandalic plans of these complexes, then, map out the bodies of cosmic deities and of divine kings—universal procreators. But the plans can be procreative in another way, one that is more pointed. They can express the notion of the allegorical father's body superimposed on that of an allegorical female. Thus an inscription at Angkor Tom by its builder (again Jayavarman VII) reads: "[This city is] a beautiful young girl of honorable family, worthy of her fiancé and ardently in love with him, whom the king married so that the happiness of the inhabitants would be born of the union."[35] Here in Southeast Asia, then, a breeding territory with its landmarks and protective structures is once more fused into images of colossal human bodies.

I believe that it was because we humans insisted on defining our territories with ever-increasing precision that our prehuman instinct for building was evoked. That so many monuments—defense towers, the Apadana Hall at Persepolis, the Colossus of Rhodes, the Statue of Liberty, the Piazza San Pietro, Pre Rup, Angkor Wat—are not dwellings, not nests, but proclamations of territory is key. Other primates have territories but do not sculpture them with walls, gates, towers, and the like. We—borrowing ideas from other territorial and building species—do. And so our drama continues: a sudden shift in mammalian evolution makes human cities gleam on the horizon.

# PENIS PARADIGMS

7

## THE PENIS AS AN ARCHITECTURAL ATTRACTOR

For the next three chapters we turn from landmarks and territories themselves to one of their chief raisons d'être—reproduction. In this and the next chapter I discuss, respectively, the architectural use of male and female reproductive organs. The final chapter will deal with reproduction itself—the fertilization, growth, and adaptation of new architectural "organisms."

Evolutionally the penis and its mate, the vulva/vagina, are among nature's oldest creations. They date from long before the origin of mammals. Both organs are already present, for example, among certain exceedingly ancient gastropods, including the cerithiids—a genus of snails with long, dark spiral shells suitably known as horns.[1]

In his book *Sexual Selection and Animal Genitalia*, William G. Eberhard has shown that throughout the animal kingdom penises exist not only as practical devices for implanting sperm but in various theatrical and extravagant forms as well. They can show up, for example, as enlarged self-replicas, and sometimes in arrays of dummies, looking a bit like the rows of cannon on an eighteenth-century man-o'-war.[2] The purpose of the arrays is to give females added visual and tactile stimulation—stimulation that the females of course select for. As a result, many penises have evolved well beyond the necessities of their basic function. Like the peacock's tail or the orchid's flamboyant flower, or even the geometric magnetism of marrying molecules, the penis is not just a reproductive organ. It is an attractor.[3]

Before going on to its architectural appearances let us look first at the penis per se (see fig. 7.16). The organ consists of a tube of concentric tissues in multiple layers. The basic tube is known as the shaft or stalk. Down its middle is a conduit, the urethra, which discharges urine and is also part of the ejaculatory duct through which sperm passes during climax. The slotted opening at the top that discharges the sperm is called the meatus. The soft, lobed cone of flesh surrounding the meatus is the glans (in Latin, "acorn" or "fountain"). The glans in turn has a thick necking of skin, called the prepuce (another word for fountain). This is removed in circumcision.

Inside the penis shaft are thick, concentric cylinders surrounding the urethra. These are the three corpora, or bodies of specialized tissue; the corpus spongiosum and the larger, two-part corpus cavernosum. During erection these cor-

7.1.

Phallus on the Maitreya temple, Thiksey Cloister, Ladalch, Tibet, 1983. From Gassner, *Phallos.*

pora engorge with blood, which provides the necessary rigidity. The corpora are separated from each other by other tissue layers called fascias and "tunics" (tunicae).

The human race has long had a powerful penchant for using the penis as an architectural paradigm (the latter word's primary meaning in Greek, by the way, is "architect's model"). We are always reading that obelisks, columns, spires, skyscrapers, towers, and the like are phallic. In 1786 Richard Payne Knight roundly claimed that the obelisk, the cross, and "the spires and pinnacles with which our churches are . . . decorated" are expressions of "the male organs of generation."[4] (Knight indeed traced all religion to phallic cults.)[5] Two hundred years later, post-Freud, Dolores Hayden prints a picture of the Chrysler Building ejaculating (i.e., with a spray of searchlight beams at its tip). And Donald Trump proudly points to his skyscraper on Central Park West, the Trump International Hotel and Tower, as "the stiffest building in the city."[6]

Many other cultures, past and present, have revered the penis architecturally. Jutta Gassner describes a host of phallic buildings in her book *Phallos: Fruchtbarkeitssymbol oder Abwehrzauber?* She shows how phallic bosses and beam ends protect walls in Pompeii and Pakistan, and how phallic joists hold up roofs and invigilate entrances in Tibetan monasteries (fig. 7.1).[7]

The Egyptians and Greeks had penis-gods. For the Greeks, the most important was Priapus. We saw him in Virgil, armed with a sickle, guarding flowerbeds. Whole cities were sacred to him. At Delos, just outside the gate to the Heraion, an avenue of choragic monuments (honoring competition winners) was erected to him (fig. 7.2).[8] Their tall, limestone pedestals support the partially castrated shafts of colossal marble penises resting like field mortars on paired testicles. One wonders what sort of competitions these prizes were given for. Priapus's name, in Greek, is related to προιέσθαι, ποιήσας and so on, which tropes a number of appropriate associations—ejaculation, creation, building construction, poetry.[9]

Phallused architecture was endemic in ancient America, and in Africa it still is. Gassner prints examples from Ethiopia (fig. 7.3) of conical roofs with finials. These strongly recall the fibrillated organs in Eberhard's book (fig. 7.4).[10] In Ethiopia similar objects decorate the conical shields of the warriors, emphasizing the penis's apotropaic role.[11]

## SPERM COMPETITION

Note that these African phalloi have been endowed with hyperlarge glanses and that some stalks have more than one glans. In this, and in their general form of bulb-headed stems, the African penises resemble individual human spermatozoa. The African craftsmen, to be sure, probably had not seen actual human sperm, which are visible only through a microscope; but here perhaps I can once again assert the power of homology. Nor is it strange, given the self-similar scaling throughout nature that we have looked at, that individual sperm should resemble penises—real ones or, alternatively, the larger penises portrayed in art.

But among themselves, sperm can have considerable variation in appearance. The most important kind, known as the macro, is the only one that actually fertilizes an egg. "His" head wears a cap filled with fluids that are important for

7.2.

Avenue of Priapus, Delos,

Greece, third century BCE.

From Johns, *Sex or Symbol?*

7.3.

Phallic finials for conical roofs. Upper two from Konso; lower examples from Darassa and Guraghe, Ethiopia. From Gassner, *Phallos.*

his journey through the female labyrinth and his attempt to reach her egg (fig. 7.5, top of left-hand column). This cap, indeed, contains his DNA. Macros can course like champion swimmers through a woman's body fluids, their tails powerfully whipping them along. Other sperm, helpers to these champions, are less glamorous. Some are microcephalic—their heads contain no DNA at all. Still others have heads shaped like cigars, lollipops, dumbbells, or pears. Some have what might be called chaotic heads. And there are sperm with two, three, and even four heads. Some have long tails, some short; and some have tails like Goldilocks's curls, or else multiple tails.[12] To me, at least, most of these sperms also resemble weapons. It is fitting, then, that Robin Baker and Mark Bellis, the great experts on this subject, describe the battlements, traps, and hostile rivals that sperm encounter. The oft-drawn parallel between penises and guns seems appropriate also to the penis's ammunition.

But let's look at sperm competition a little differently; we return here to the notion of the colossal. Human sperm is microscopic. But much further back in evolution there were creatures whose sperm, and their equipment for discharging it, were huge. Very large sperm are no oddity even today. For example, *Drosophila bifurca*, a fruit fly species, has male sex cells that, uncoiled, reach 2.3 inches in length-many times the fly's own length and thousands of times longer than any human sperm. And there are other species with jumbo sperm. To make a trans-species comparison that no biologist would approve of, a six-foot man with sperm at *bifurca* scale would unleash gametes 120 feet

7.4.

Genitalia of slugs, genus *Milax*. From Eberhard, *Sexual Selection and Animal Genitalia*.

7.5.

Human sperm shapes. From Baker and Bellis, *Human Sperm Competition*.

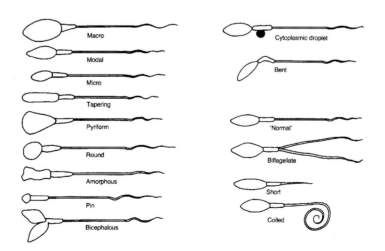

long. Combined with proper amounts of seminal fluid, human ejaculation at *bifurca* scale would be monumental, a matter of geysers and fountains.[13] And we recall that in Latin glans, meatus, and prepuce (from *prae-putium*, fore-fountain) all mean just that—fountain. Furthermore the *bifurca*, in order to contain its giant sperm, has testes totaling about 11 percent of its body weight.[14] By that standard our six-foot human, weighing, say, 185 pounds, would have 20-pound testicles and a penis to match.

Though not so astonishing as this, human penises are larger, in proportion, than those of other primates—the single exception being the well-hung bonobo. So while early evolution may have eventually diminished the size of the human penis with respect to some possibly larger ancestral scale, we can be more certain of recent pressure favoring enlargement. A. F. Dixson has shown that female sexual selection, in primates generally, has continually favored larger and larger testes, a longer baculum (a penis bone—we don't have them), and prolongation of the hard-on after ejaculation. This has happened in all species where females mate with a number of males.[15] Here, perhaps, is further evidence, for humans, of a cortical desire to regain, from a distantly pre-human state, lost, gargantuan penises that can emit floods of sperm. This would explain the enormous male appendages we see or read about all down the ages in ribald art, literature, and theater. Not to mention the even huger ones we build in architecture.

## Homunculi

There is one further aspect of sperm we should discuss. This too ties in with sperm competition. For centuries it was thought that individual sperm consisted not of the limp lollipops we see today in biology textbooks but of microscopic, perfectly formed adult human beings.[16] Probably the idea can be traced back to a statement by Aristotle (*De generatione animalium* 33b25ff.). He writes of blooded animals in general: "the male emits semen into the female, and upon entry of the semen the young animals are 'set' and constituted, and assume their proper shape." Over the centuries this developed into a doctrine called preformation or, sometimes, preexistence. To some it meant that an embryo, though its substance came from the mother, was given its shape by the father's homunculus (or, for nonhumans, by animalculi that had their own species' proper shape).[17] Homunculi were much in mind during the Renaissance and baroque; Paracelsus wrote a whole book on them.

7.6.

Nicolas Hartsoeker. Drawing of
human sperm cell containing a
homunculus. From Hartsoeker,
*Essai de dioptrique* (1694).

7.7.

Vincenzo Re. Fireworks apparatus in front of the Castel
Nuovo, Naples, 1749. From Re,
*Narrazione delle solenni reali
feste fatte* (1749).

Homunculi had their supernatural side. They could grow up into fairies and other magic beings. Alchemists thought they could make artificial homunculi. Thus did sperm possess a prestige that was magico-religious as well as biological. Curiously, belief in these ideas was strengthened around 1600 by the invention of the microscope, which for the first time made human sperm cells actually visible. When Antoni van Leeuwenhoek was showing off his new invention to his fellow scientist Jan Swammerdam, Swammerdam convinced himself that he could see homunculi when he put human sperm under the lens.[18] Another convert was Nicolas Hartsoeker, who examined his homunculus enclosed within a real sperm cell (fig. 7.6).

Does all this change now that we know that homunculi don't exist?[19] To the historian the salient fact is that they were believed in for centuries. This is why I will describe the statues on phallic fountains and other constructed erections as ejaculated homunculi. The human beings who interacted with these building-sized phalluses can be seen similarly. It is an ancient vision: the Greeks carried colossal phalloi in Dionysos processions.[20] Made of wood, fabric, and other temporary materials, these structures towered up on their bearers' shoulders. The third-century BCE historian Callixinus describes one that was 120 ells high (about 180 feet, the equivalent of a six-story tower), painted with golden stripes, and with a golden star topping its glans.[21] Thus did the people in the parade make homunculi of themselves. These Greek parade penises have had several kinds of descendants. Among them, I believe, are the *guglie* (finials) still carried upright in festivals today in southern Italy. Similar phalloi, elaborated and transformed into permanent sculptural monuments, decorate Naples. The monuments often embody, albeit baroquely, the anatomical makeup of the human penis. In Vincenzo Re's mid-eighteenth-century *guglia* for a fireworks show in the Piazza Castello, Naples (fig. 7.7), note the crowned meatus, the double-torused glans, the banded ornament on the shaft, and the heavy vulvar base through which the shaft rises.[22]

And Re's creation teems with homunculus-like statues. The main dedicatee, Pallas Athene, has been ejaculated directly from the meatus. Other homunculi (and feminculae) stand at strategic spots along the shaft. We noted that this particular structure was a fireworks machine. So, at the crucial moment, its summit and flanks would have burst into further ejaculations. Colorful arrays of "seed" would soar heavenward, like Dolores Hayden's vision of the Chrysler Building. The iconography, by the way, is appropriately genetic and territorial,

7.8.

Isernia (Abruzzi). Festival of
the Guglia. Detail of photo by
Mimmo Jodice.

dealing as it does with the rivers of the realm; the birth, lands, and lineage of
the kings' new son, Filippo; and the House of Bourbon's breeding future.

I mentioned contemporary processions with *guglie*. In figure 7.8 we see 1980s
devotees dancing around a sacred phallus in Isernia, a town in the Abruzzi. It
was in this very town, in the eighteenth century, that Payne Knight had seen
the phallic celebrations for St. Cosmas. In these, during a three-day annual fair,
people carried images of the saint's gonads in procession. The monks sold
replicas of them to women as foretastes of the miraculously boosted sexual
powers their menfolk would possess as a result of St. Cosmas's interventions.[23]

While most phallic architecture involves towers, steeples, finials, and the like,
there is at least one architectural penis that forms a building's plan. It is often
discussed: Claude-Nicolas Ledoux's Oikéma, or House of Pleasure (fig. 7.9).[24]
But it has not been noted, I think, that it may be taken as a sagittal section of
testes, shaft, urethra, and glans. Further, as a bordello, the Oikéma's functions
would involve sperm competition and sexual selection. Its male users—its
homunculi—would indeed even follow a spermatic course through its rooms

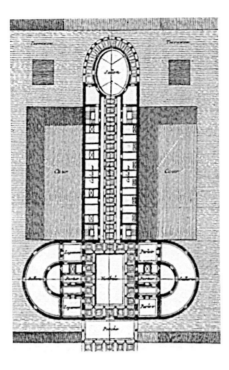

7.9.

Claude-Nicolas Ledoux. House of Pleasure for Montmartre, 1790. From Ledoux, *L'Architecture* (1804).

and corridors. The porch, centralized between the testicles, is the prostate gland with its prostatic ducts. The testes are the paired symmetrical semicircular galleries flanking a courtyard and twin parlors. These latter take up the space that in a real penis would be occupied by the urethra and the ejaculatory ducts at the shaft's base. After issuing from the testicles, the homunculi-clients would then proceed along the building's urethra, which is a corridor with flanking bedrooms or cellules (i.e., the corpora). There, male and female gametes pair up, perhaps to become zygotes. The glans, finally, is an oval salon with exterior colonnade.[25]

## OBELISKS

The ancient Egyptian obelisk, I will propose, is another form of architectural penis.[26] The obelisk began as, or at least came to be, a stone transformation—a "statue"—of Osiris's member. Here, paraphrased from Diodorus Siculus's (admittedly postpharaonic) account (1.21–22.6), is one version of how this happened:

*Osiris was slain by the giant Typhon, who carved his body into twenty-six pieces. These Typhon scattered up and down the Nile. Isis, Osiris's queen, sailed along the river to locate them. Wherever she found a body part she built a tomb for it. But when it came to Osiris's penis (αἰδοῖον) she was apparently not satisfied with just one monument. She commanded that statues (εἴδολα) of it be set up and worshiped in a number of temples. Inspired by Isis's devotion, the Greeks, too, honor the male member, giving it the name of Phallos.*

In short, images of Osiris's αἰδοῖον (which means both "gonad" and "thing to be honored")[27] were to be set up in the temples and given (and now I quote Diodorus directly) "the highest regard and reverence in the rites and sacrifices accorded to the god." Older Egyptian prayers frequently pay just such special honors to the penis, with phrases such as "[Neferhotep], who takes his place near his sister when she treasures the phallus (⟨hieroglyphs⟩) of her father, so that his phallus is kept safe."[28]

But what did these myths and honors have to do with obelisks? For one thing, obelisks were reproductive: they symbolized the sun's generative powers. As with statues and stelae, the texts say that obelisks gestate in the quarry and are born when erected. The obelisks' inscriptions detail the procreations, births, and mingled divine bloodlines of the dedicator's genome. Hatshepsut's 97-foot obelisk at Karnak is typical. The queen asserts that she was begotten by the god Amun, there she is also the holy egg begotten by Ra, and that she will give birth to a glorious posterity. To reinforce the point, the shaft is inscribed with the ithyphallic image of Amun Kamutef, "bull of his mother."[29]

The pyramidal tip of an obelisk was known as its *ben-ben*. That word is linked to *ben* and *benen*, which mean male reproductive virility. Indeed, the *benben* was revered as Atum's ejaculated sperm as well as representing the procreative sun "swelling up" on the horizon.[30]

Henri Frankfort brings together more evidence about obelisks' role as hyper-begetters. Originally, we learn, Amun was the very first piece of living tissue. He begat the first two complete human-shaped bodies, those of the gods Shu and Tefnut, who in turn begat humanity.[31] Amun's act was explained as a sort of metaphorical masturbation—the scattering of seed. At each daily dawn, in this story, and also at the beginning of each pharoah's reign, the original pro-creation had to be repeated.[32] Like the Tantric Hindus and Buddhists of more

7.10.

1658 medal showing the
obelisk in the Piazza San
Pietro. From Krautheimer,
*The Rome of Alexander VII.*
This medal shows a proposed
but unbuilt extension of
Bernini's colonnades, filling
their eastern central opening.

recent times, the Egyptians thought of the continuity of cosmos and nation as being dependent on continual sacred coitus—coitus, you might say, non-interruptus.

In later times obelisks could have a meaning that was almost exclusively sexual. Ptolemy Philadelphus erected one to his wife, Arsinoë, as a tribute to their conjugal relationship (Pliny, *Historia naturalis* 26.14). Hadrian similarly raised an obelisk on the Pincian Hill to his lover Antinoos. Part of the inscription reads: "He [Hadrian] has penetrated everywhere, he has traveled the earth in its four directions, and the bulls and their cows responded in joy" (Dio Cassius 69). This, by the way, approximates to what Victorian biologists would call *panspermia* (universe-wide trans-species insemination; or even the transport of living seed to Earth from the cosmos).[33]

But of course penises, like the sperm they carry, are linked to male-male rivalry, to war as well as reproduction. On conquering his foe, a New Kingdom victor would display the piled-up penises of the defeated army,[34] proclaiming in effect that the vanquished lord had lost his and his people's reproductive future. Obelisks make similar statements. They frequently record the military triumphs of their erectors, and they are territorial. They establish entrances and boundaries, carrying out the admonitory and apotropaic functions that go with the other markers used for breeding territories.[35]

The Roman conquerors of Egypt brought obelisks to their own cities, and especially to Rome, where the monuments continued to symbolize ownership, procreation, and territory (note the obelisk on the far left in the Piranesi etching of San Lorenzo fuori le Mura, fig. 6.4). In figure 7.10 I illustrate a 1658 medallion showing the obelisk in Piazza San Pietro. Caligula, we are told, had captured the St. Peter's obelisk and taken it to Rome. In 1586 it was moved to its present location from a nearby site in Nero's Circus. Later on, at St. Peter's, it symbolized Christ's triumph over paganism, just as its earlier location, or locations, had proclaimed Rome's triumph over Egypt—and had proclaimed, in the obelisk's first setting, the triumph of its dedicating pharaoh over some predecessor or enemy (the shaft now lacks its original inscriptions).

Sixtus V was especially keen on obelisks.[36] He reestablished five, situating all of them in broad vulval piazze. Besides those of San Pietro and Santa Maria del Popolo, he erected the obelisks of Santa Maria Maggiore, the Lateran, and

126

7.11.

Ippolito Caffi (1809–1866).

Obelisk in the Piazza del

Popolo (1232–1200 BCE), with

Santa Maria di Montesanto

(1676) and Santa Maria dei

Miracoli (1678). Detail.

Courtesy Art and Architecture

Library, Yale University. Slides

and Photographs Collection.

the Esquiline. Michele Mercati, whose 1589 book *Gli obelischi di Roma* might be called a handbook of papal obelistics, pays full attention to their role as markers for breeding territories. Just as they themselves symbolize the all-fertilizing sun, he says, so their erectors are the sun's all-conquering offspring. Think of the obelisk of the Piazza del Popolo in Rome (fig. 7.11).[37] Here one can add the reproductive cults of the two testicular churches that flank it, both dedicated as they are to the Immaculate Conception, that is, to various cults of sacred seed.[38]

And the Christianizing process to which the monument was subjected, far from erasing or denying the obelisk's original reproductive nature, has enhanced it. The slender pharaonic member has been considerably lengthened by its high pedestal and a lofty added glans; that is, the orb and cross. (Here we recall the star-topped glans of Callixenus's processional phallus.) These glans forms are repeated in the lanterns of the churches' domes, much as subsidiary phalloi accumulate in Roman phallic sculptures—or for that matter in the penis arrays we see in nonhuman species such as nematodes. Known as the Falminian obelisk, the Popolo monument comes from Heliopolis. Sixtus's inscription speaks as usual of solar begetting, generative joy, new birth, reborn glory, and

7.12.

Gianlorenzo Bernini. Study for
the *Fountain of the Four Rivers*,
Piazza Navona, Rome, 1650.
Biblioteca Apostolica Vaticana,
Vatican City.

resulting majesty and honor. The piazza's neoclassical sculptural program, with
its statues of the seasons and its river-fountains, also focuses on territory, status, fecundity, and reproductive power.[39]

One other Roman and papal obelisk should be mentioned: that in the Piazza
Navona (fig. 7.12).[40] This forms the upper two-thirds of Bernini's *Fountain of
the Four Rivers* (1648-1651), which was intended by Sixtus's successor, Innocent
X, as a continuation of Sixtus's obelisk program.[41] Once more the new alpha's
succession and territory are inscribed: the obelisk maps the church's worldwide,
ocean-borne sway. The figures, by Bernini's shop, represent the main rivers of
the four continents: the Nile, the Ganges, the Rio de la Plata, and the Danube.
The gods of these rivers—muscular, shaggy old men borrowed from classical
sculpture—have abandoned their usual recumbent attitudes. They clamber
around their common cave as if marveling at its towering source of new peoples. The concetto, I suspect, is that the four great rivers of the world have
their spiritual source, their birth, in a single place—Rome.

As a final note, there are Egyptian images in which pharaohs honor what
appear to be model obelisks.[42] Such a miniature, especially when held in the
hands, suggests a sort of codpiece. The idea is particularly explicit in Domenico

7.14. Greek black figure vase, fifth century BCE. Detail of masturbating satyr. Berlin, Staatliche Museen. F1761.

7.13.

Frontispiece from

Domenico Fontana,

*Della trasportazione*

*dell'obelisco vaticano*

(1590).

Fontana's frontispiece for his 1590 book on the Vatican monument (fig. 7.13).[43] Embedded in a High Renaissance niche and framed by telamons, putti, and aristo-architectural paraphernalia, Fontana stolidly gazes forth as he fondles his miniature obelisk. Here, if ever, is a penis paradigm, a παράδειγμα—an architect's model. As to possible sources for the portrait, curiously comparable images appear on Greek pots—for example, a black figure vase now in Berlin on which a grinning, goggle-eyed satyr (not without a certain resemblance to Domenico Fontana) similarly shows off his personal obelisk (fig. 7.14).

## THE PENIS AS A TOWER

It is a commonplace that whole buildings—towers and skyscrapers—can resemble penises. Are there correspondences of function as well as shape? I return to what I said at the beginning of this chapter. Like any tower, the penis is made up of concentric layers of sheathing and other materials that reinforce it, stiffen it, and translate matter and fluids from one part of it to another (see fig. 7.16)—that protect it and control its temperature. The layers of cladding in a modern office tower, the insulation, the waterproofing, the brick or block, the columns, the studs, and the interior plasterboard, as well as all the different coatings these elements receive, are the architectural equivalents to the layers of tissues and the biochemical transporters, suppressors, enhancers, lubricants, and so on that compose the penis and allow it to function.

In addition to the glans and shaft, which are essentially vessels for sperm delivery, the domical prostate gland stores the fluid that will transport the sperm, arrayed for their struggles, past the urogenital diaphragm and through the urethra. With its urethral crest, ducts, sinuses, and utricle, the prostate is thus a kind of entrance rotunda or *salle des pas perdus* (or maybe a parking garage), buried in the pelvis and leading up to the tower-shaft. Or: think of a skyscraper rising up from an underground network of steam, water, sewer, electricity, and telephone lines, all of them cognate to the meshes of veins and arteries, of ducts, bladders, bulbs, elbow joints (crures), and canals (fossae) that rise from inside the pelvis and weave into and service the penis (fig. 7.16).[44]

A whole book could be written about the penis paradigm vis-à-vis skyscrapers. Let's look at just one building—the Nebraska State Capitol in Lincoln, designed in 1916 by Bertram G. Goodhue (fig. 7.15).[45] (On the Internet it has been billed as "the penis of the plains.") From a broad-spreading base of massed symmetrical low-rise offices, corridors, and halls, soars an office tower. Everything is penile in shape, proportion, and location. The tower's base is its urogenital diaphragm. The shaft is a four-sided lattice or corpus spongiosum of windows, the glans a slender octagon whose meatus is a gilded dome.

7.15. Bertram G. Goodhue, Nebraska State Capitol, Lincoln (1916; 1920–1932). From Watkin, *History of Western Architecture.*

7.16.
Sagittal section of human penis. Adapted from Netter, *Atlas of Human Anatomy.*

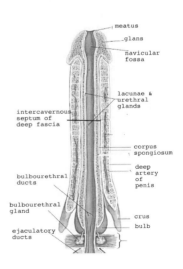

At the building's summit there is even an ejaculated homunculus. This is Lee Lawrie's statue, *The Sower*. What could possibly be more appropriate? *The Sower* casts his seed immediately above an octagonal memorial chamber in the glans's center. (He staggers, this exceedingly unfortunate figure, knock-kneed and unhappy, perhaps from fatigue.) The memorial chamber honors Nebraska's war dead. To a biologist like Robin Baker such a juxtaposition—dead heroes below, active seed-spreader above—would suggest the process of "shedding sperm." The war dead would be the "aged blockers and killers," now set aside, while *The Sower* would represent the fresh sperm ready for a fertile spot.[46] The rest of the decorative program at Lincoln appropriately expresses "the energies of life" (floor of the central rotunda), the advent of the pioneers and home-steaders into their newly seized territories, and their reproductive victories over the native flora and fauna (including nonpioneer humans).

The penis paradigm also prevails in Hindu architecture, as I began to show in the previous chapter. The central feature of the temple is a sculpture of Shiva's penis, called a *linga*, which is subject to constant bathing and ornamentation,[47] and which stands beneath the tower's core. Ancient drawings of the towers make plain their penile essence. Note (fig. 7.17) the vertical duct going up the tower's center—its urethra—and the swollen layers flanking it, shaped and sit-uated respectively as shaft, fascias, glans, and meatus. But it is more than a matter of just the towers, or even of the "womb chambers" or *garbagrihas* from which the towers rise. The interior space of this chamber is thought to consist of inchoate matter called *vastu purusha*, *purusha* being not only a man but also a kind of matter with "unknown" form that is occupied by the gods and that then receives "mandala" or form.[48] Every Hindu structure, from a hermit's retreat to a city plan, follows a *vastu purusha* mandala.[49] The concentric square shapes within the mandala's perimeter, at the tower's base, emanate from or are generated by the linga. The linga, in essence, is a stone portrait of Shiva's penis standing at the mandala's center. The linga contains the god himself when he is properly invoked, and he is sometimes portrayed emerging from it (see fig. 7.18).[50]

7.17.

Seventeenth-century Orissan section through a Hindu temple tower. Below, the mandala governing the plan. From Michell, *Hindu Temple*.

The mandala's circles, which also centered on the linga, are extensions of the yoni, a perforated disk that normally represents Parvati's vulva—Parvati being Shiva's wife. Her yoni is the linga's base, so that the latter seems to have been inserted into it and to rise upward from it. The room containing the linga and yoni, the womb chamber, is thus by extension a monumental female reproductive tract.[51] (In the next chapter, we examine this question further.) By the same token the temple's exterior tower, rising over the womb chamber, is an architectural linga set into the yoni formed by the temple's ground plan. Like the human penis, that of Shiva, and the linga, these towers partake of the key Hindu theological process of emission and reabsorption.[52] And then, continuing with our vision of self-similar upward scaling, the cosmos itself turns into a female genital tract.

Wendy Doniger O'Flaherty explains that the insertion of the linga into the yoni expresses a state of equilibrium in Shiva's life, one that was achieved after a period of blocked lust and accompanying destruction. For example, in one origin myth, Shiva's linga fell off; disembodied, it raged through earth, hell, and heaven like a towering inferno, burning everything in its path. Then Brahma said: "as long as the linga is not still, there will be nothing auspicious in the universe." He meant that only when the unleashed linga was set into a yoni would it quiet down. This was done, and linga worship, with Shiva as the god both of creation and destruction, was established.[53]

Some of these ideas are readable in the celebrated Shiva linga from the Parasuramesvar temple, Gudimallam (c50 BCE-50 CE?), in figure 7.18 (no yoni is shown).[54] This is very probably the oldest known example of a stone cult linga dedicated to Shiva. The god stands before the shaft of a five-foot penis, which has the hooded ferocity of a storm trooper. The god's destructive powers, however, seem present but not active. That quiescence may also be indicated by the crushed creature on whose shoulders Shiva stands, which could be Kama, the lust god. He, we hear, becomes bodiless when Shiva's desires are satisfied.[55] In any event, Shiva himself, armed, smiling, and at rest, here forsakes his role as a destroyer and stands calmly, ready to govern human affairs.

7.18.

A five-foot linga,

Parasuramesvara temple,

Gudimallam, Andhra Pradesh,

India, c50 BCE–50 CE? From

O'Flaherty, *Asceticism and*

*Eroticism.*

The linga behind Shiva is enormous, but others are bigger. Some, in their temple wombs, are so tall that a gallery is erected at the glans level so worshipers can anoint it with milk and other semenlike substances.[56] These latter are known as *bodhichitta*, the god's ejaculated sperm.[57] An oft-mentioned visionary linga stretches so far up into heaven and down into Earth that its bottom and top are lost to view. This imagined linga is worshiped with special fervor.[58] Thus is it the greatest of towers, an ur-skyscraper.

7.19.

Nagara temple, India.

Elevation of tower, with names

of its parts. From Desai,

*Erotic Sculpture of India.*

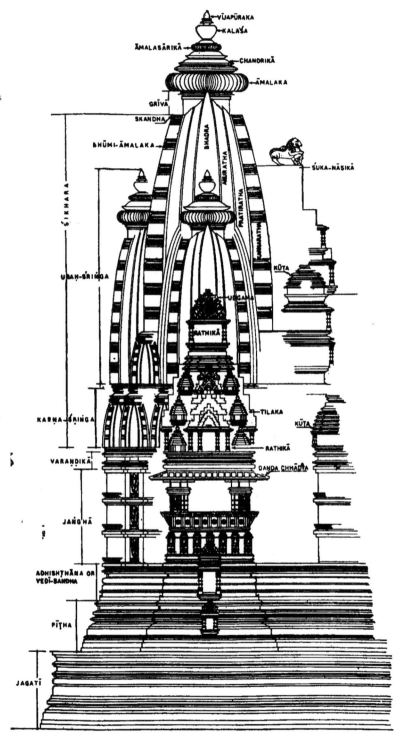

In my view, the Hindu temple monumentalizes this concept of the yoni as a controlling vessel, a governor, for the linga's great but otherwise ruinous energies.[59] Devangana Desai, who has written brilliantly about these subjects, prints an elevation of a typical Indian Hindu tower (fig. 7.19). In her drawing we sense the tower's role as a gigantic invaginated penis, its sheathed power still patent in the glanslike crest with its swollen moldings (identified respectively as *amalaka*, *chandrika*, *amalasarika*, *kalasa*, and *vijapuraka*). The shaft supporting this crowning complex is equally composed of silhouettes suggesting muscular exertion, this time vertical, and respectively labeled *badhra*, *anuratha*, and *pratiratha*. These would be the architectural equivalents of the anatomical penis's corpora and fascias. The other elements in the design are self-similar miniatures of the central linga, grouped into an impressive array of one main and four subsidiary towers that recalls the five peaks of Mount Meru, home of the gods.

However, it is in Hindu Cambodia, rather than in India itself, that the most impressive monuments of this tradition stand. Beginning in the ninth century CE, immense temple complexes—gloriously symmetrical towered stone cities—began to rise. As noted earlier, the most famous of them is Angkor Wat, sometimes described as the largest religious building ever erected.[60] But there is also the Khmer temple known as Bayon, also at Angkor, built by the god-king

7.20.

Bayon. Erected during the reign of Jayavarman VII (1181–1220). From Vassiliou, *Angkor*. Drawing by Jacques Dumarçay.

7.21.

The Shiva face on one of the

linga towers at Bayon. From

Vassiliou, *Angkor.*

Jayavarman VII (1181–1220). At least as originally intended (figs. 7.20, 21), Bayon was to be as grand or grander than Angkor Wat.[61] These complexes make use of quincunx plans and five-tower groups and subgroups. The different heights of the towers also reflect the statuses of the inner and outer gods of the mandala's *padas.* But at Bayon the glanslike moldings, which ornament only the tops of the towers in Desai's drawing, are developed all the way down the shaft while still preserving its entasis or curve of exertion. To my mind these glanslike moldings are multiplied yonis. They surround the shaft along its length like the "many bracelets" with which, in one legend, the wives of the Pine Forest sages decorated Shiva's erection. And then there are the omnipresent colossal faces of Shiva himself, eyes blissfully closed, lips in a heavy, dreaming smile. Thus does the god-king (for this is undoubtedly also Jayavarman) emerge not once but dozens of times from his towers. Lingas with such faces are known as *mukha-lingas* (figs. 7.21, 7.22).[62] In the Nepali example, red pigment ornaments Shiva's polos-like hairdo, known as the *jatamukata,* and his forehead, lips, and ears. It also appears on the linga's crest and in the tray formed by the yoni.[63]

Back to the West. I have said that whole towns were dedicated to Priapus. In a certain sense, this practice was not limited to Greece but can be observed in many parts of the world. Until its towers were destroyed, Florence and nearby

7.22.

A mukha-linga and yoni in

Pashupatinath, Nepal. From

Gessner, *Phallos.*

San Gimignano (where some of the towers are still visible) were transformed by medieval ruling families into towering groves of male members (fig. 7.23).[64] The same may be said of the Northwest Coast villages forested with totem poles (fig. 7.24).

This is not simply a question of tall towers being "phallic" in general shape. Both the Italian and the North American erections express specific facts about territory, genetic inheritance, and status. The Northwest Coast poles display the totem animals of the different families inhabiting the adjacent houses, and the flat brick or limestone sides of the Tuscan towers were originally ornamented with flags and sculptured or painted coats of arms. These latter also recorded, by means of their bundled weapons and beasts, each family's matrimonial and military conquests and alliances—the histories, in short, of their breeding territories.[65] Both kinds of building, then, represent monumental stacks of sperm —spermathecas (repositories for male sex cells) of seed that has been selected, become fertile, and passed on the elder generations' genes. And, once again, the human makers and users of these great phalloi turn into homunculi. The poles and the towers are "penis paradigms" in the literal sense of the Greek παραδείγματα, models, but now at larger rather than smaller scale.

There are any number of other monumental phalloi. When it was first built, a cartoonist known as Jacobo saw Gaudí's Casa Milá as a jumble of giant, habitable penises—shafts with their own windows and domed and balconied glanses (fig. 7.25). A later example, also in Barcelona, is a concrete column by Miró

7.23.

The towers of San Gimignano, Tuscany. From Barni, *Il Tempo delle torri.*

7.24.

The Haida village of Masset, late nineteenth century. From Jonaitis, *Totem Poles.*

7.25.

Jacobo. Caricature of Gaudí's
Casa Milá, Barcelona, in
*El Papitu*, 1911. From Torii,
*Gaudí.*

7.26.

Joan Miró (with Joan Gardy-
Artigas). *Woman and Bird,*
1981–1982. Barcelona.

7.27.

A Roman enameled bronze stud
shaped like a phallus with what
is identified as an eye in its
glans and a vulva in its shaft,
second–third century CE.
London, British Museum. From
Johns, *Sex or Symbol?*

dominating an urban square (fig. 7.26). This is a single 24-foot uncircumcized penis with powerful glandular entasis. It is made of concrete with appliqués of colorful Gaudí-like pottery shards. The glans, furnished with a round black eye, is topped by a hollow cylinder and pair of horns. The shaft is breached by a huge vulval slit lined with blackish tiles. While the title of the piece is *Woman and Bird*, and while it does resemble other birds by Miró, the penile resemblance is also hard to deny. An eyed penis pierced by (rather than piercing) a vulva? Why not? There are, after all, plenty of penis-shaped female statues; Miró himself made them.[66] Ancient phalloi with comparable eyes and vulvas are also common (fig. 7.27).

We have looked at more than a few architectural penises fitting Eberhard's definition: flamboyant, theatrical, hyperbolic, stimulating to females. Maybe Richard Payne Knight was correct. We have also advanced our tale into the very vitals of the human body—the center of its forces of selection and reproduction, and hence survival. Now, too, for the first time in the drama, we seen the actions and effects not of whole bodies but of body parts. We look at the architectural role of organs freed from their physiological and anatomical contexts, to act out scenarios on the wider architectural stage.

# THE FEMALE GENITAL PALACE

## The Reproductive Tract

Architectural expressions of the human female reproductive tract are exceedingly ancient. They are often religious. Indeed, some forms of Buddhism consider that Buddha-hood itself lies in female sexuality—which, after all, and in ways more complex than male sexuality, is responsible for reproduction, hence species survival, hence "eternal life."[1]

Probably the earliest of all architectural interiors are the natural caverns that Paleolithic humans filled with art.[2] These groupings of defiles, canals, tunnels, pools, and biomorphic chambers, with their shifting levels and contrasting spaces, strikingly evoke the complexities of female interior anatomy—as do their darkness, their fluids, their oozing walls, and their redolences. When one contemplates the adventures of human sperm seeking out the prized egg within the female labyrinth, and then enlarges this picture to architectural scale, one might well think of such caverns.

But, of course, the human female interior is not ornamented with paintings and sculptures. In the caves, in contrast, thirty thousand years and more ago, artists covered some of these surfaces with images of plants, panthers, giant elk, bear, lions, horses, and the like. These made the caverns even more anatomical, furnishing them with portrayals of prey and forage. Otherwise, or in addition, the painted and engraved organisms could conceivably represent the earth mother's future offspring lodged in her belly, waiting to be born.

8.1.

La Grotte Chauvet at Vallon-Pont-d'Arc, in the Ardèche, near Avignon. By the author, after Chauvet, Deschamps, and Hillaire, *La Grotte Chauvet.*

8.2.

A sagittal section of the reproductive parts of the female pelvis. After Vannini and Pogliani, *Color Atlas of Human Anatomy.*

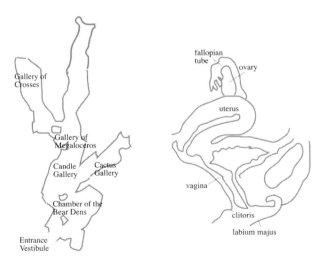

8.3.

Vallon-Pont-d'Arc, France.

Grotte Chauvet, stalagtite

formation. From Chauvet,

Deschamps, and Hillaire,

*La Grotte Chauvet.*

8.4.

Frank H. Netter. Left half of

the perineum and uterus of a

human female. From Netter,

*Atlas of Human Anatomy.*

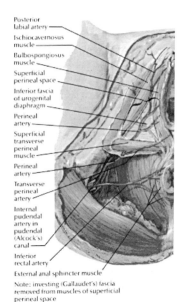

Posterior
labial artery
Ischiocavernosus
muscle
Bulbospongiosus
muscle
Superficial
perineal space
Inferior fascia
of urogenital
diaphragm
Perineal
artery
Superficial
transverse
perineal
muscle
Perineal
artery
Transverse
perineal
artery
Internal
pudendal
artery in
pudendal
(Alcock's)
canal
Inferior
rectal artery
External anal sphincter muscle
Note: investing (Gallaudet's) fascia
removed from muscles of superficial
perineal space

Sometimes there are more specific analogies. In the plan of the Grotte Chauvet at Vallon-Pont-d'Arc, in the Ardèche region of France, the cave's Gallery of the Megaloceros (large horn) is more or less a fallopian tube, the open chamber below it an ovary, and the Chamber of Bear Dens a uterus.[3] The entrance passage can represent-at least at the Cro-Magnon level of knowledge-the complex's vagina, clitoris, labia majora, and so on (figs. 8.1, 8.2).

Other anatomical aspects of such caves are the pink and white fistulous stalagtites and stalagmites that weave through the walls like linear organs, and the veins and arteries of dark red that lace the smooth white crystallized rock surfaces. All these things are extraordinarily reminiscent of the interior reproductive areas of the human body (figs. 8.3, 8.4).

Built structures that derive from or reflect the female interior often mirror, and amplify, its reproductive character. Normally, for example, birds' nests serve solely as shelters for the young. (The parents do not sleep in them but roost nearby.) Such nests are therefore really extended phenotypes of the womb— containers designed to continue, in a new, larger enclosure, the protection begun within the mother's body and then later still provided by the form of the egg. The nest is an "egg" for the egg, as the egg is a "womb" for the womb.

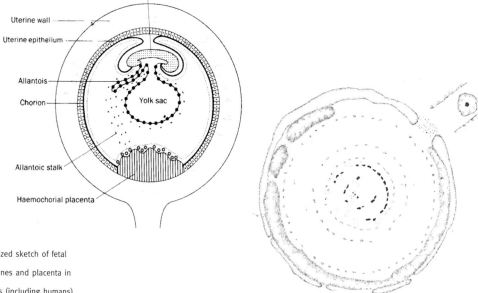

Uterine wall

Uterine epithelium

Allantois

Chorion

Yolk sac

Allantoic stalk

Haemochorial placenta

8.5.

Generalized sketch of fetal
membranes and placenta in
primates (including humans).
From the *Cambridge
Encyclopedia of Human
Evolution.*

8.6.

Stonehenge, plan. First
begun c2800 BCE. From Burl,
*Rings of Stone.*

Thus are birds' nests extended phenotypes. They belong to yet another of our
graduated isomorphic sequences. The egg-shaped nests of the African weaverbird are particularly appropriate examples (see fig. 5.7).[4]

One finds similar shapes and functions in human architecture. We recall the prehistoric village of Lemba, Cyprus, from chapter 1, whose houses are literally cellular (see fig. 1.26). But they are also placental (fig. 8.5),[5] and so are any
number of prehistoric structures. (Hunting societies would be familiar with
mammalian anatomy.) Stonehenge apparently combined fertility and death rituals with more practical needs for public meetings and markets. The other
stone circles—in Britain, in Ireland, and on the Continent—probably had similar purposes. But note, again, the placental qualities of Stonehenge's circular-
ity and enclosure, of its concentric layered wrappings, and of the distribution
of its inner encircling wall-like features (fig. 8.6). One can even make specific
comparisons, on the one hand, between the placenta's chorions (vein-carrying
outer membranes) and uterine epithelia (cellular envelopes), and, on the other,
Stonehenge's outer circle; also between the yolk sacs in the placentas and
Stonehenge's central upright sarsen. Even the embryo itself could be replaced,
in our analogy, by the human body that was buried at the opening of

Stonehenge's inner horseshoe-shaped colonnade. This person's rebirth in eternity would thus be marked by an enormous womb whose stone and earth "tissues" were those of a huge placenta.[6]

Let us turn to a civilization in part contemporary with Stonehenge's, but probably richer and more intricate. The ancient Egyptians' knowledge of human anatomy was achieved in large part through their embalming procedures, which separated and divinized individual organs.[7] We have seen, indeed, that one Egyptian concept of the world and the cosmos was as a huge reproductive system. But now it is appropriate to mention a further peculiarity in Egyptian life. Diodorus remarks on it: Egypt's woman-centeredness. He even admits, ruefully, that in Egypt the women dominate the men. In marriage ceremonies, for example, the groom vows to obey the bride rather than the other way around. And in many Egyptian households the wife rules, while the husband cares for the children (Diodorus 1.27.2ff.). Such an arrangement is un-Greek and un-Roman, and the comments of Diodorus (d. 21 BCE) may reflect a situation that only came into existence after pharaonic times; but they do throw some light on why, in that earlier period, the Egyptians designed major structures in the form of female body parts.

Thus James P. Allen has shown that Egyptian royal tombs may reflect and emulate the spaces and labyrinthine interconnections of a woman's reproductive system.[8] This could explain why so much Egyptian interior architecture consists of passages, rooms, and shafts that, at least in Old and Middle Kingdom pyramids, had hidden exterior entrances. The Pyramid Texts tell us that a pyramid's entrance corridor was, to its builders, a "birth canal."[9] Such architecture also evokes the intricate orifices, hollows, and channels inside Mother Earth that the Cro-Magnons filled with pictured prey, progeny, or both.

Nut, the sky goddess—and here I again depend on Allen—is also an expanse of territory with openings, *akhets*, at either end through which the departed pharaoh enters and leaves. The pharaoh makes a daily sojourn within the goddess's womb, a sojourn identical to the sun's course through the skies. The redness of dawn and sunset is the blood of the king's daily birth and death. As a New Kingdom cosmological text puts it, the pharaoh "floats in [Nut's] redness."[10] The entrances to the goddess's interior were seen, also, as sea gates, like locks in a river or canal. In his afterlife the king travels through the system by boat. Thus the soul-boats found in Egyptian tombs may be thought of

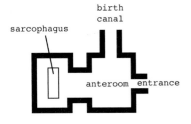

birth
canal
sarcophagus

anteroom   entrance

8.7.

Scheme of an Egyptian

tomb with birth canal. After

Allen, "Cosmology of the

Pyramid Texts."

8.8.

Female urogenital diaphragm.

From Netter, *Atlas of Human

Anatomy.*

8.9.

Cross-section through the

Great Pyramid at Giza,

2750–2500 BCE. From Fletcher,

*History of Architecture.*

as organic entities—corpuscles, perhaps embryos, maybe even homunculi—traveling through the fluid-filled veins and vessels of Nut's colossal body.

The plans of some Egyptian royal tombs map out equivalent reproductive tracts. Thus in figure 8.7 the sarcophagus stands in the funeral chamber, which is entered through a doorway. This anteroom, however, has not only a major entrance but also an upper birth canal. Normally the latter leads out to the tomb's exterior wall. The birth canal is as narrow, and its exterior apertures are as invisible, as are human birth canals and their uterine gates and locks, their fossae and venae cavae.

The cross-section of the human female reproductive system illustrated alongside a vertical section of the Great Pyramid at Giza (figs. 8.8, 8.9) extends these ideas. Both systems involve chambers or volumes interconnected by narrow approach corridors, some at steep angles. In the pyramid, the larger volumes—the king's and queen's chambers—reflect the placement and scale of a vagina and a female urethra. Note also the pyramidal silhouette of the urogenital diaphragm's fascia, and observe that, as a fascia, it even gets an architectural name. The same goes for the female's vestibular bulb and greater vestibular gland. Also, just as the whole of the reproductive system is encased in a thick mass of muscles (those of the sphincter urethrae and the deep transverse perineal), so the pyramid's chambers and corridors are encased in the mass of its masonry. Finally, both systems have (or had) outer claddings; the pyramid its electrum and limestone or granite, and the genital system its ischio-pubic ramus—together with the outer tissues and skin that also protect and stiffen

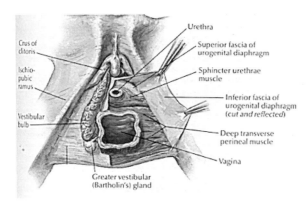

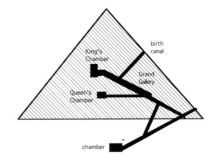

it. In all these ways I would read the pyramid as a colossal compaction of reproductive organs, fit to reproduce a god-king and send him off on his cosmic journey.

## MORE SPERM COMPETITION

We have seen that different types of sperm cells form cohorts around their designated chief, the macro, and swim in a group into the female's labyrinthine world.[11] The goal is her egg. But the egg is not stationary: "she" too has a journey to make. Here is the scene as described by Robin Baker:

*A short distance away from the end of each oviduct, suspended like a relatively huge planet next to a black hole, is an ovary. Tiny hairs on the inside of the oviduct create a current in the body fluid so that when an egg is released by an ovary, it is slowly wafted toward the black hole of the oviduct. Like a waiting hand, the fingerlike projections funnel the egg into the tube. From here, the egg begins its five-day journey down toward the womb.*[12]

Baker calls the egg a fortress, one that can be breached across three lines of defense—her cumulus, her zona, and her vitelline membrane. The successful sperm hacks his way through these defenses at a special entry spot called the *infundabulum*. Here he glues himself to the egg wall and cuts it open with a spike mounted on his head much like the horn on a Prussian helmet. Once he conquers all the difficulties, the egg embraces him and sends a message all over her surface that makes her impenetrable to any other sperm.

But there is more to sperm competition. Females of many species store sperm they have collected from several sources. Insects can park it temporarily in organs called *spermathecae*. (Note the analogy with *bibliotheca* and *oenotheca*—repositories from which books and wine can be selected.) The female will collect gametes from a partner, but at the same time she may well suspect that someone better might come along. If that happens, she is able to ignore the old sperms and latch on to the new. The better stocked her spermatheca, the wider her choice of future fathers for her offspring—hence the better her chances (and her progeny's) for survival. And even though human females don't have spermathecas, they do have what are called crypts in the uterus wall where sperm can be stored, sometimes for several days, and then used to fertilize an egg.[13] All this happens without the female's active or conscious intervention. It is purely a matter of biochemistry.

THE FEMALE GENITAL PALACE

## Anatomies and Their Names

Similar ideas about interior anatomy and the cosmos reappear in Greece and Rome. The Latin *occidens*, which gives us our word for the Occident, the West, is the place where the sun disappears. As a verb it also means "setting," "dying." And *oriens*, the Orient, the East, means "rising," "originating," "being born." Roman towns, camps, and (often) buildings were laid out along axes geared to these directions. Thus did the eastern part of a building, camp, or town have associations with birth, and the western part with death. Even today, when we speak of "Western" culture the word has a tinge of doom. To "go west" is to die. And when in 1918 Oswald Spengler called his book *Der Untergang des Abendlandes* he was playing on the German language's equation of West ("evening lands"), sunset (*Untergang*), and death. (These associations are absent from the book's English title, *The Decline of the West*.) But we saw that any such death, like the sun's or the pharaoh's, is followed by a new act of reproduction.

Thus, as before in this book, questions of terminology arise. Human organs do not greatly differ from individual to individual, culture to culture, and age to age. But the names for these organs, and their supposed functions, do differ—and strikingly so. When we look at modern diagrams of female anatomy we are told about bladders, uteruses, ovaries, fallopian tubes, ureters, kidneys, peritonea, recta, and so on. In modern languages, most of these terms refer only to these organs. But in the languages from which the terms were taken, usually ancient Greek or Latin, much broader meanings are involved. Thus a *meatus* (the opening in a penis glans) is in Latin any sort of passageway, channel, or course: a star's course is its meatus. Urethra, οὐρήθρα, can mean the physiological urethra but also a tank—which once again helps us think of it at architectural scale.

A penis, by the way, refers primarily not to what we call a penis but to any tail. And penis has appropriate links, or tropes, with other *pene-* words such as penetralia, penetrate, penes (within, under the control of), and Penates, the Roman gods of the household. This cluster emphasizes one of my central notions—that the penis is often to be seen not as an ithyphallic exterior male organ but, instead, as being inside the female tract. One of the obvious examples is the Hindu belief that Shiva's linga is calmed into a state of peaceful power when it resides in Parvati's yoni, but there are many others. In Latin a *vagina* can be any sort of sheath. When Caesar puts his sword into its scabbard he says he's putting it into its vagina. Gourds were grown in wooden vaginas or sheaths that gave them the desired phallic shape.

A rectum (from the Greek ῥεκτήρ) is a worker, a doer, one who is active and busy. In Latin a *uterus* is both an anatomical uterus and also any sort of bulging cavity; for example, a bird's nest or ship's hull. In *Aeneid* 2.20 the Trojan horse is described as a cavern filled with armed men; Virgil also calls that a uterus. (Thus, when I envisaged the Grotte Chauvet filled with animal fetuses I might have cited Virgil.) The word "ovaries" derives from the Latin *ovarium*, the structure that held the *ova*, or egg-shaped objects, used for recording the laps of chariot races. All these broader meanings for reproductive organs firm up our sense that when the latter were first studied and named, they were seen as buildinglike artifacts subject to human functions.

## Vaginal Fountains and Fetal Skyscrapers

Perhaps the greatest age of female genital imagery in architecture, at least in the West, was that of the rococo.[14] Then, the shapes of shells and flowers were manipulated into large hilly configurations—wall elements, fountains, and basins. The likenesses of these objects, and other rococo designs, to female genitalia are often startling (figs. 8.10, 8.11). The "hills," by the way, often served as backdrops for couples engaged in precopulative play. Even when an

8.10.
Detail of illustration from Jean Modon, *Le galand Chasseur*, 1730. Metropolitan Museum of Art, New York. Harry Brisbane Dick Fund, 1930.

8.11. Parous vulva. From Netter, *Atlas of Human Anatomy*.

artist dresses his giant vulva in shells and foliage, making it a grotto or bower, there is no mistaking that it is also a vaginal opening—complete with clitoris and labia, a froth of pubic hair, and the usual soft flaps and indentations. In many rococo designs, even details like the vestibular fossa and the hymeneal caruncle can be identified. When these constructs operate as fountain orifices—well, that's just one more way of animating the analogy.

At this point I'll revisit the skyscraper, now to note its metaphorical role in female rather than male reproduction. In his book *Delirious New York*, Rem Koolhaas (unknowingly, I think) provides a Shiva-esque interpretation of Manhattan skyscrapers. He sees them, under the night sky, as being in "a cosmic container, the murky [Hugh] Ferrissian Void: a pitch-black architectural womb that gives birth to the consecutive stages of the skyscraper in a sequence of sometimes overlapping pregnancies, and that promises to generate ever-new ones."[15] This sentence—itself pretty murky—means, one gathers, that at night Manhattan's massed skyscrapers are penises or embryos inside a cosmic womb. The vision is illustrated by a drawing in which an awed homunculus, silhouetted on a suburban hill (and ejaculating?) gazes at a glowing, jagged mass of buildings towering up into blackness (fig. 8.12).

A painting by Madelon Vriesendorp, *Après l'amour*, also reproduced in Koolhaas's book (fig. 8.13), brings out skyscrapers' femaleness in a different way. The Empire State Building and the Chrysler Building have just had sex (their condom was the Goodyear Blimp). I read the Empire State Building, on

8.12. Unidentified drawing in Koolhaas, *Delirious New York.*

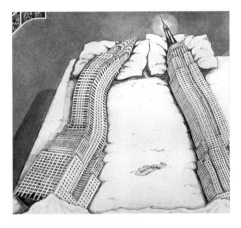

8.13. Madelon Vriesendorp,
*Après l'amour,* detail. From
Koolhaas, *Delirious New York.*

the right, as the male. (His dirigible tower is engorged with red and his searchlight is turned on.) The curvaceous Chrysler Building, with her phallic headpiece
composed of coaxial vaginae dentatae, is obviously the female. In this latter
detail Vriesendorp's concetto reverses Koolhaas's. We have not multiple penises
in a cosmic vagina but multiple vaginas in a cosmic penis. (As to the question
of whether two penises, one male, one female, can make love, the answer,
based on antique precedents, is "of course!")[16]

## Samarasa

So far the most intensely reproductive architecture we have looked at is that
of the Hindu temple.[17] We have seen that mandalas embody lingas and yonis,
and that this imagery reappears, scaled up, in the temple's womb-chamber and
tower. Let us now look at the Tantric Hindu concept of *samarasa.* This is a mystical sexual union between gods and worshipers that exists to some extent
throughout Hinduism and in some forms of Buddhism.[18] In Hinduism's Tantric
branch, this union is the great mystical event. Its theater is the temple.

In addition to their linga-and-yoni shape, temple exteriors are often carved with
layered horizontal friezes of exuberantly intertwined figures. Much of the sculpture is erotic—both in the participants' nubile physiques and scanty dress and,
much more, in their actions. In Tantric temples to Shiva these figures are the
god's attendant deities. They may be said to compose the temple's walls like
atlantes or termini.[19] By anointing the linga with *bodhichitta,* or sacred sperm,
Tantric and other worshipers also emphasize that the room at the tower's base

8.14.

Ten-rupee stamp from Trombay,
India, depicting an atomic reactor. From O'Flaherty, *Asceticism
and Eroticism*.

8.15.

Mushroom cloud over Bikini
Atoll, Marshall Islands, 25 July
1946. From the *New York
Times*, 5 March 1997, A4. Photo
Associated Press.

is the goddess's reproductive tract.[20] We saw something similar, though in a purely male context, in Egyptian beliefs about obelisks impregnating the cosmos with their *ben-bens* gilded with sacred sperm and in our interpretation of the homunculus-statues standing atop, or around, *guglie* and other penis-towers. All such imagery, let us note, turns the spaces surrounding these phalluses into implied vaginas.

Sanskrit architectural terms echo these notions. There are the ritual terms for the parts of the tower, such as *jangha*, shank; *gandi*, torso; and *bhanga*, a curve. Terms that are more explicitly erotic—such as *bhoga*, sexual enjoyment; *maithuna*, a couple; and m*ukha-linga*, the linga carved with a divine face—describe the sculptures cladding the temple.[21] In some forms of Tantrism the sexual acrobatics are intended to arrest the flow of semen and prevent ejaculation (in Hindu theology, emission). This, it is claimed, sends the semen back into the body and up into the head, where its reproductive nature produces a form of bliss, which turns erotic force into the mental force of yoga.[22] All this is the other half of the Hindu theological concept of emission: reabsorption.

In Tantric ritual the participants in the *maithuna* bathe, perfume, and decorate each other with flowers.[23] The couples bask in crimson robes and enjoy wine, drugs, and incense. These liturgies have their geometrical and architectural aspects. The male draws out mandalas consisting of concentric circles, hexagons, triangles, and other shapes. Different parts of the diagram match different parts of the worshipers' bodies. Filled with the presence of Shiva, the male touches his partner, or *shakti*, on her forehead, eyes, nostrils, mouth, earlobes, at the hollow of her throat, and on her breasts, arms, hands, navel, thighs, vulva, knees, and feet. The vertices of the mandala's lines, its *marmas*, stand for each place where the worshipers' bodies touch. Then, says the ritual, the couple "twine together like vines." As in the sculpture they contemplate, and as in the temple surrounding them, linga and yoni unite in an act of controlled and peaceful power.[24]

We saw that without its yoni, Shiva's linga terrorized his people. Thus, it was known as "the golden seed of fire."[25] To the modern Hindu eye, an atomic bomb has something of that linga's destructive rage. So it is not surprising to see, on an Indian stamp, an atomic reactor that is shaped both like the mushroom cloud and also like a yoni-embedded linga (figs. 8.14, 8.15). When the atomic linga is set into the yoni provided by the power plant, the result is peace and constructive energy.

## EGGS, FRUIT, NUTS, BREASTS, AND DOMES

Many lingas—for example, the one just illustrated—resemble breasts as much as they do penises. And, of course, breasts are equally important as attractors. They also have the crucial practical function of nurture. They are therefore like eggs, fruit, and nuts: they store and dispense food for the newborn. Indeed the purpose of all this analogical procreation, all along, has been to fertilize analogical eggs.

The egg has inspired an abundance of architectural ornament; almost no image has been more fertile. "Oval" is a common name for a type of street. Baroque, rococo, and neoclassical architects, especially, relished oval rooms. The most famous such room in this country, the Oval Office in the East Wing of the White House, is where plans are laid, policies hatched, and sometimes, apparently, chicks chased.

8.16.

Ovolo moldings. From Fletcher, *History of Architecture.*

At the same time, architecture has often enshrined the egg as the model for those commonest of moldings, variously called the egg-and-dart, egg-and-claw, ovolo, or egg-and-tongue (fig. 8.16). Eggs were even more important in antiq-

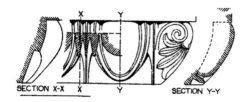
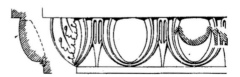

uity than they are today. Not only did they symbolize reproduction and the continuation of the race, but they were also sacrificed to the gods. A goddess might manifest herself before her worshipers in the form of a consecrated egg.[26] The Madonna of the Immaculate Conception often appears inside a mandorla—an egg-shaped frame (*mandorla* = almond, a tree's egg); no wonder egg-shaped ornamentation has been common.

Eggs and domes make me think again of Santa Maria del Fiore (see fig. 4.17). In chapter 4 I analyzed it as a beehive; but now I am reminded of Vasari's tale of Brunelleschi and the egg (known in another, less appropriate, version with Columbus as the hero). In Vasari, Brunelleschi is asked by rival experts to divulge his method for building the dome. Instead of doing so he passes an egg around among them and asks each to stand it on end. When they all fail he solves the problem by slightly crushing the egg on one end. The experts exclaim: "why, any of us could have done that!" To which Brunelleschi replies: "yes; and once you had seen my designs you could any of you build my dome."[27]

That much is well known. But so far as I know, Vasari and his commentators do not sufficiently remark that Brunelleschi's egg had his dome's shape.[28] Nor is the similarity merely a formal one. Like a real egg, the dome has a thin, hard outer shell and an inner lattice, equivalent to the molecular lattice of an eggshell's membrane; the dome also has air spaces and lined-up oculi that pipe light and air down through its inner space.[29] The oculi can therefore be likened to the albuminous corridors, known as *chalazae*, that in a bird's egg create communication links between the inside of the shell and the yolk (figs. 8.17, 8.18).

8.17.

Filippo Brunelleschi.

Conjectural scheme for the frame of the dome of the Florence Cathedral, 1420–1436. From Kostof, *History of Architecture.*

8.18.

Sagittal section of an egg interior. Author.

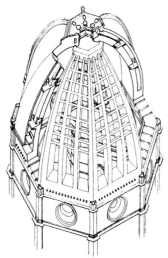
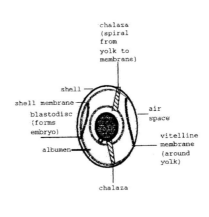

8.19.

Ernst Haeckel. The human egg.
From Haeckel, *Anthropogenie
oder Entwicklungsgeschichte
des Menschen* (1874).

8.20.

Michelangelo. Interior of
dome of St. Peter's with
decorations by Giuseppe
Cesari, Cavaliere d'Arpino,
1590. Art and Architecture
Library, Yale University. Slides
and Photographs Collection.

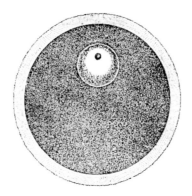

8.21.

Hannes Meyer and Hans
Wittwer, competition drawing
for the League of Nations
Building, Geneva, 1926–1927.
Detail. From Blau and Kaufman,
*Architecture and Its Image.*

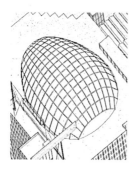

Indeed not just Brunelleschi's but any dome has a fundamental eggishness. Conversely, we can call an egg a double dome—a three-dimensional continuous curve with round or oval ends. Or we can put it biologically: a dome is half an egg. And once again, this is true not just in shape: for the iconography of dome interiors, like that of egg interiors, is often filled with reproductive potential and future sustenance. Eggs are filled with physical nourishment, domes with spiritual: both promise survival. In Ernst Haeckel's illustration of a human egg (fig. 8.19), the celebrated biologist almost calls it a dome—a "kugelrunde Zelle" (spherical cell; but *Kugel* is also dome, and a *Kugelgewölbe* is a cupola like Michelangelo's). The "eye" of Haeckel's egg-dome is its seed vesicle, nucleus, and nucleolus. Michelangelo's dome (fig. 8.20), has comparable elements in comparable places. The nucleus is the circular opening or eye, the nucleolus would be the Cavaliere d'Arpino's figure of the blessing God, and the seed vesicle would be the gold-backed dedicatory inscription to St. Peter and Sixtus V framing the nucleus.

Even modernists play riffs on the theme. In figure 8.21 is a project by Hannes Meyer and Hans Wittwer for the League of Nations Building, Geneva (1926–1927).[30] Despite their antibiological, antiornamental functionalism, these International Style architects have made the domed roof of the auditorium an unequivocal egg. It is not round or symmetrically oval, as in most architectural ova, but a true hen's egg with wide and narrow ends—its specific shape underlined, topographically, by the glass lattice (recall an egg's vitelline membrane) of the roof. Flying overhead, one could look down at the politicians nourishing their embryonic organization.

Domes like these frequently represent the heavens, which in many religions are known as the cosmic egg. E. Baldwin Smith observes that cosmic eggs were particularly significant for the Egyptians, Romans, Persians, Byzantine Greeks, and the inhabitants of the Indian subcontinent.[31] Words for *dome* in different languages are instructive in this respect. Almost all of them tie the dome to the sustaining activities of life, to eggs or egglike forms of reproductive nurture. Thus there will be onion domes, melon domes, bulb domes, pinecone domes, and the like. The builders of the Taj Mahal called its cupolas "guava domes" (see fig. 8.25).[32]

Any number of other building types are shaped like giant eggs, at least in that they are oval in plan or elevation. One thinks of everything from amphitheaters like the Colosseum to Buckminster Fuller in his more ooid modes (see fig. 1.4). Or there is Ascanio Vittozzi's Santuario di Vicoforte at Mondovì, south of Turin (figs. 8.22, 8.23). Writing in 1602, Federico Zuccaro links the church's shape to the Madonna's body. He explains that the oval excels other forms in beauty by as much as a woman's body is more beautiful than a man's. And, he goes on, "how much more beautiful than any other woman's body is that of the Glorious Virgin . . . such that I believe that this egg-shaped form, as the most gracious of all, has been chosen as the most proper and authentic [of those forms] derived in proportion from the human body."[33]

8.22.

Ascanio Vittozzi and others. Mondovì (Piedmont), Santuario di Vicoforte, begun 1596. Interior. From Lotz, "Die ovalen Kirchenraüme des Cinquecento."

8.23.

Mondovì. Plan. From *Piemonte*.

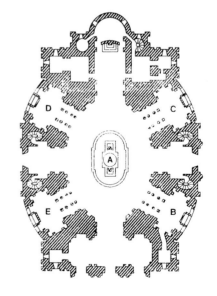

The egg motif appears, first and foremost, in the church's enormous ellipsoidal dome. We see it again in the oval windows and the floor plans of the chapels. Note, too, that in scale the church's nave is about the right size and shape for a yolk, while the central oval tomb (A) would be the yolk's nucleolus. Moreover, the extreme thickness of the surrounding walls, which contain the four egg-shaped chapels, gives them just the proper scale and distribution for a supply of albumin (compare fig. 8.18).

The interior of Vittozzi's church develops the eggish essence of its shell. The dome's oval perimeter and its concave volume dominate the interior. The roundels puncturing that perimeter are also oval. The dome frescoes (1745–1748, by Mattia Bortoloni, Giuseppe Galli da Bibiena, and Felice Biella) depict the Virgin's life and Assumption as witnessed by the church. At the base are scenes from her earthly life. Above, she arrives before the Trinity, witnessed by doctors of the church, saints, apostles, prophets, sibyls, and angels. So the contents of the great egg depict the coming lifespan of its divine contents and the Virgin's postmortem new birth into eternity. They depict, in short, her ontogeny. As with so much architectural imagery, egg-derived and otherwise, the theme is immortality—continuity through reproduction.

When Zuccaro says that the Madonna's body is shaped like an egg, he is clearly referring to the traditional painted imagery of the Immaculate Conception—the Virgin standing inside an oval. Often the oval is formed by clouds and the chorusing infant heads called thrones. Accordingly, what we sense in Vittozzi's building is, first, the egg from which the Virgin was born and then a second egg that is the one inside her body—the vessel of Christ's embryo and fetus, immaculately fertilized.[34] And then there had been the Virgin's own Immaculate Conception. When this is depicted in art, as noted, she appears as a perfectly formed adult human standing inside an egg-shaped nimbus. In short, the Immaculata appears as a homunculus. Perhaps these thoughts will do something to elucidate not only Mondovì but the crowd of oval *Frauenkirchen* built throughout Germany and Austria in the seventeenth and eighteenth centuries.

But there is another potent association with eggs and ovals in the age of the baroque. By about 1600 it had become clear to astronomers that the planets do not revolve in circular orbits, as hitherto supposed, but in ellipses.[35] Curiously, the newly proven fact of elliptical orbits, I believe, strengthened the myth that the heavens are "oval" in the sense of being maternal—or even that

8.24.

Allison. From *D-Cup Superstars*,
February 1992.

8.25.

Agra, India. Ustad Ahmad, the
Taj Mahal dome, completed
1643. From Begley and Desai,
*Taj Mahal*.

they are "cosmic eggs," perhaps nested. Kepler's proof of elliptical orbits would thus paradoxically have reinforced older magical notions much as, in these same years, the sperm in Hartsoeker's microscope reinforced the idea, for some, that sperm were homunculi.

Let us turn finally to breasts. Eggs, nuts, and fruits are often attractors—for instance, in still-life painting (and in life). In figure painting (and in life), the same is true of breasts (fig. 8.24). Evolutionary biologists tell us that women's breasts have been selected for size well beyond the needs of nurture.[36] And, indeed, compared with those of other primates, human breasts are gigantic. A great deal of attention is also paid to their shape, texture, and sartorial showcasing.[37]

Human breasts, furthermore, often have just the subtle conical crests and soft cylindrical bases that we see in domes. Domes are in fact even huger breasts—breasts at the scale of recumbent colossi. Like breasts, they shelter and express the building's holiest interior zones. A dome will rise up over the temple's shrine, altar, or tomb just as breasts rise over a woman's heart.

These ideas are beautifully embodied in the Taj Mahal (fig. 8.25). Shah Jehan, the Mughal emperor who ruled a vast empire in the middle 1600s, built this tomb for his queen, Mumtaz, after her premature death in 1631. She had died in childbirth, and in the funeral odes written at the time her presence, as a royal mother and vessel of the dynasty's survival, is everywhere. She is "the shadow of the divine nourisher," "who most . . . years became pregnant with some unique pearl worthy of the crown of sovereignty."[38] Thereby (and paradoxically) she is "the queen of the domes of chastity," who "abides in the cupolas of divine foregivennness." "Her cupola is the sky"; "she is the sky's tenth roof," and her tomb is "the eighth layer of the world and its dome."[39] The exquisite domes of the Taj are an architectural threnody to the queen's breasts. Indeed more than almost any other building, this great tomb is a sacred model, παράδειγμα, of queenly reproduction and nurture.

We noted at the beginning of the chapter that architectural expressions of the human female reproductive system are ancient. And we have learned that these expressions are pervasive and often beautiful. Not just Buddhism and Hinduism but many religions and cultures have considered that part of their essence lies in the physical setting of female reproduction. And who can deny it? Most religions teach that salvation and immortality lie in rebirth. And rebirth, like birth, requires a female context. Thus do the organs of reproduction, as inscribed in our monumental architecture, fulfill their destiny. So it is to reproduction itself that we turn next.

# THE BIOLOGY OF ARCHITECTURAL REPRODUCTION

9

I will propose several varieties of architectural reproduction. Three of them are based respectively on Mendelian genetics, on DNA transcription, and on fractals. I will then look at reproduction in two further senses: first, cladistics, or the genealogies of what I will call architectural clades; and, second, Darwinian adaptation in architecture. But these are only a very few of the ways in which architecture and reproductive biology can intertwine.

In the first chapter we saw that non- or prebiotic forms—for example, molecules and crystals—can "marry" and reproduce. More generally, and indeed all through human history, the application of words and phrases like "engender," "generate," "give birth to," and so on to nonorganic things shows how deeply ingrained the analogy of biological reproduction is. Architectural historians, in particular, often see buildings genetically, as parents and offspring, cousins and siblings—as mapping out inheritances. It is commonplace to read such statements as "this design unites the Pantheon dome with the portico of the Theseum." Such propositions are directly comparable to descriptions of inherited traits in a biological organism—the mother's eyes and the father's nose. They even evoke the genetic engineering of fruit flies, which can produce abnormal eye or body color, or grow antennae with eyes on the ends of them, or put a leg where a wing should be.[1] Such "monstrosities" also occur in architectural inheritance.

## Mendelian Genetics

Science writers are always calling the genome a blueprint; now I will call a blueprint a genome. In fact, architectural genomes may be even simpler than blueprints—and more ancient. Thus from Vitruvius, *De architectura* 3.2ff., one can assemble each of his categories for designing a temple—Ionic, tetrastyle, eustyle, and so on—which prescribe the order, specify that it has four columns in front and none down the sides and across the back, indicate that the spacing of the columns follows a given formula, and so forth, right on down to the measurements or proportions of step risers, door size, tympanum, column bases, moldings, and all else. Every aspect of the design has a name and numerical algorithm. Once all the names have been put together and a module dictated (say, one column diameter = three feet), if you give these directions to two different architects not in communication with each other, they will then theoretically produce two identical, or almost identical, designs ("almost," because Vitruvius usually provides parameters rather than unique measures and proportions). Vitruvius's algorithms are nothing more nor less than genome-like codes: when expressed in full-scale stone monuments, they "reproduce" the temple that has been condensed and coded.

A more recent attempt, more incisive than most, to achieve a Mendel-like reproduction in architecture was that of J.-N.-L. Durand, the early-nineteenth-century French theorist and teacher (fig. 9.1).[2] Note how, in the three facades on the left, a basic armature, (a), shown throughout in black, is preserved and transformed. The armature consists of a tall pilastered frontispiece, a pediment, and a central door. Also, two tall parapets flank steps leading up to that door. This basic building can be furnished with sets of Mendelian options (shown in gray). Two derived designs or offspring (b, c) preserve the armature's essence, but the inheritance can be varied: (b) makes the frontispiece two-story, with an entrance above a pair of lateral stairs, wings with half-pediments, windows, and an upper central window above a main entablature. In (c), in contrast, an upper flat-headed window turns into a thermal window (i.e., with a wide arch), and the pair of lateral wings lose their windows and get niches instead. The trim on the door also changes, and the steps return but as a shorter flight.

Nor would it require much effort to reshuffle these eminently shuffleable elements—two possible aisle facades, two possible doors, two possible tympana—into still other variations, as in (d). In the new variant, which is my own creation, I have combined the high basement of (a), the wings of (b), and the frontispiece of (c).

Durand's (and my own) shuffling of traits resembles Gregor Mendel's mid-nineteenth-century manipulation of pea plants. That, we recall, had involved "particulate" inheritance as opposed to the "blending" kind. In other words, a trait

9.1.
J.-N.-L. Durand. Facade variations (a, b, c) from the *Précis des leçons* (1802–1805). Far right (d): a further variation (author).

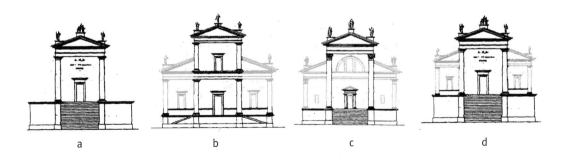

a          b          c          d

either reappears intact in the individual offspring or it doesn't reappear at all. But in Mendel as in Durand, the combinations of these traits are independent of the combinations found in the parent or parents.

We move to the 1930s, by which time Mendel's unjustly ignored experiments were receiving attention.[3] By then it was recognized that "particulate inheritance" depended on genes and chromosomes. Chromosomes are the rodlike elements in every organism that carry its molecules of DNA. Normally chromosomes are arranged in pairs. In a strange, incomplete, but fascinating way, the Austrian scholar Hans Sedlmayr applied insights derived from this chromosome biology to Borromini.[4]

First, Sedlmayr compares four versions of the developing plan of San Carlo alle Quattro Fontane with three of its presumed architectural models or forebears (fig. 9.2, top row). He reproduces the plans as shown, in what he refers to as a "genetic" format. I will accept his implications; namely, that Vignola's plan, of an oval church crossed symmetrically by four embrasures, is reflected in the Borromini plan below it; that the compound-curved Greek cross from Hadrian's Villa is similarly "reproduced" in the Borromini plan below it; and that the Borromini plan labeled as the fifth scheme for San Carlo (fig. 9.2, bottom row, extreme right) can be seen as an oval version of San Lorenzo's inner colonnade.

9.2.

Top row, from left to right: Vignola, Sant'Anna dei Palafrenieri; Hadrian's Villa, domed hall; San Lorenzo, Milan. Bottom row, left to right: Borromini: second, third, fourth, and fifth plans for San Carlo alle Quattro Fontane. All from Sedlmayr, *Die Architektur Borrominis.*

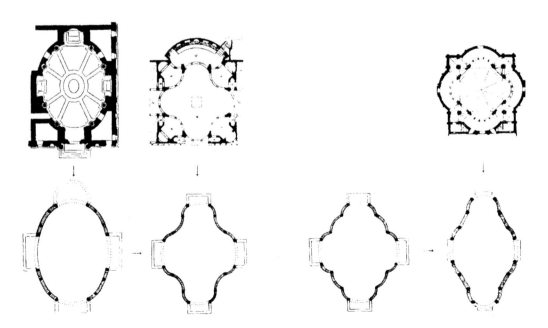

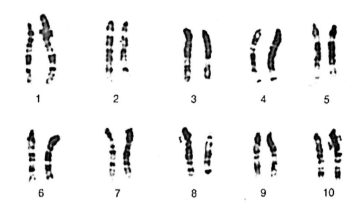

9.3.

The first ten pairs of chromo-
somes from a female mouse
arranged in their proper pairs.
From Anthony Griffiths et al.,
*Introduction to Genetic
Analysis.*

I give in figure 9.3 an example of how, in the neo-Mendelian analysis that was current in Sedlmayr's Vienna, chromosomes were arrayed for study—and still are. Note that the pairs are similar to, but more irregular than, the vermicular wall-sections of buildings that Sedlmayr prints.

Sedlmayr is Mendelian, or genetic, in another way. In crossing his plants, Mendel had discovered that there was a total of seven pairs of characteristics—two possible colors, two possible textures, and so on—that could reappear in the offspring.[5] Similarly, for Sedlmayr, Borromini's wall systems were composed from a pool or genotype of five different particulates or genes, as we see in the top row in figure 9.4. These could be combined as, for example, in the bottom row, where gene 1, the concave wall-section, is expressed twice; gene 2, the convex wall-section, once; gene 4, the large column, four times; and gene 5, the small column, six times. Gene 3, the triangular section of corona molding, is absent in the offspring or phenotype illustrated. Using modern terminology one could say that gene 1 was transmitted along with its allele or copy,

9.4.

The five "genetic elements"
of Borromini's architecture
according to Sedlmayr.
Redrawn by the author from
Sedlmayr, *Borromini.*

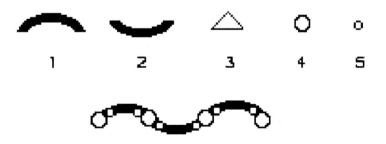

gene 2 was transmitted alone, gene 4 was transmitted with three alleles, and gene 5 with five. This makes 1, 4, and 5 dominant (they are expressed in the phenotype or resulting organism), while the absent 3 is recessive (it is not expressed but can be passed on to a later generation—that is, it can appear in some subsequent building that was "bred" by this lineage). When a recessive feature appears, Sedlmayr uses more genetics terminology: he refers to *latente Umformungen*, "latent mutations." For him, in short, one Borromini design flows from others in the same way that Mendel's pea plants beget varied offspring via expressed and unexpressed "genetic elements" (Sedlmayr's term).[6]

Figure 9.4 in fact maps out the facade plan of the lower floor of San Carlo. The upper floor uses the same three traits but with a slightly varied "phenotype." The historians' task, says Sedlmayr, is to explain how these genic elements fit into chromosome-plans, which in turn dictate the phenotype or finished physical body of the architectural organism. These same terms and principles could also serve for Durand's facades in figure 9.1.

## Architectural DNA and the Chaos Game

We turn now from Mendelian ideas to those of Benoit Mandelbrot and his many followers—to fractals.[7] Let's begin with something that anticipates the latter: the Sierpinski gasket (fig. 9.5). Note that the "gasket," or outer triangle, is composed of rational groupings, or sets, of isomorphic triangles at different scales. The creation of a Sierpinski gasket usually involves one or more rules that are applied over and over, in a process known as an iterated function system (IFS). The IFS is found throughout nature; gene transcription and editing, for example, are done this way. The gasket reproduced here consists of set numbers of isomorphic triangles that create ever-larger triangles. These increase at rational levels—for example, each immediately larger triangle is always twice as big as its smaller neighbor (only this specific increase can form a proper Sierpinski gasket). Such constancy is called *recursion*. At every point in the process, an outer triangle is formed by the inner ones. But a Sierpinski gasket, simply by continuing with its IFS, theoretically could go on growing forever.

Let us return to DNA. A set of commands somewhat similar to the IFS that produces the Sierpinski gasket can be applied to DNA.[8] This procedure turns what seems chaotic and linear into clear, graphic geometric order. As an example

9.5.

A Sierpinski gasket.

From Peak and Frame,

*Chaos under Control.*

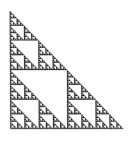

9.6.

Computer mapping of the
DNA sequence of the protein
amylase: (a) raw form;
(b) massaged form.
From Peak and Frame,
*Chaos under Control.*

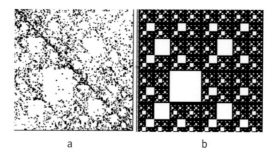

a                                   b

(which I gratefully take from David Peak and Michael Frame, who got it from its originator, H. Noel Jeffrey): among the most random or chaotic-seeming structures in biology are the sequences of base pairs of DNA spirals. In chapter 1, we saw that each bond or step unites two chemical base pairs formed from the proteins adenine, thymine, cytosine, or guanine (indicated as A, T, C, and G). Take the enzyme amylase (associated with hydrolysis: splitting a chemical bond and adding elements of water); one of its two DNA spirals starts off GAATTCAAGTTGGTGCAAAACT, proceeds onward for thousands more pairs. The order of these letters looks random, but as Peak and Frame show, the entire string can be rationally mapped. First, locate the four nucleotides—A, T, C, and G, respectively—at the four corners of a square drawn by a computer. Then set in motion an iterated function system: that is, ask the computer to make dots according to a set of rules that are repeated over and over in a pattern determined by the DNA sequence. Each new dot must be halfway between one of the square's corners and the last dot the computer has made. The corner toward which the computer should move is determined by the DNA code itself—in other words, for amylase, the first corner will be G, the second A, the third A, the fourth T, and so on, as in the list just given.

Figure 9.6 illustrates what the computer produces when the entire thousand-fold sequence of one of amylase's two DNA strands is mapped out. In (a) are the raw results obtained with one complete strand of amylase's double helix. Looking at that square, we must keep in mind that it preserves the exact order of the entire string. One could ask the computer to reconvert it back into letters and have, once more, half the genome of amylase in the form of its "random" list of letters.[9]

Figure 9.6(b) reproduces one of the smaller square-groups. The detail emphasizes that the total pattern is always repeated at recursively shrunken scale and

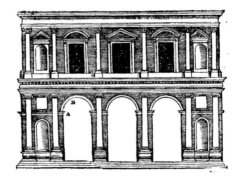

that still smaller, still similar groups form its background—on down to the unseeable or unprintable.

This rational restatement of what had seemed chaotic can be made even more rational (fig. 9.6[b]). The pattern can be enhanced, with only the most innocent degree of falsification, to produce the clear, sharp set of squares pictured. Note, also, that for each group of smaller squares plus a larger one, the prevailing pattern is always the same. (However, the outer square perimeter of the whole is not recursive with the inner squares.)

## THE POGGIOREALE PRINCIPLE

The geometrical pattern formed by a DNA code brings to mind the plan of a square building with variously sized courtyards. I myself think of a specific Renaissance experiment in this genre. This villa, now destroyed, was Alfonso II of Aragon's retreat at Poggioreale outside Naples; it dated from the mid-1480s.[10] A rationalized version of the actual building—one of the earliest Western projects I know of with four identical facades based on a square plan with double bilateral mirror symmetry—was published by Sebastiano Serlio (fig. 9.7).

The roughness of Serlio's woodcut forces us to use approximate values. But we do note that as with the Sierpinski gasket and the DNA square, isomorphic shapes—squares—are here repeated as common fractions of each other. To put it differently, the whole plan is made out of whole-number clusterings of the small, square rooms in the villa's four corners. Approximately seven of these rooms make each side; three of them make the outer colonnades, five the courtyard colonnade, and three the inner sides of the stepped pool in the center. In a sense, therefore, the plan is simply a graphic rearrangement of the DNA pattern for amylase! Or, at least, it could be mapped out by the same sort of iterated function system that maps out DNA.

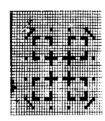

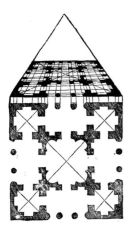

This Poggioreale principle, as I call it, has a multitude of progeny, with ramifications forward and back (i.e., siblings, cousins, and ancestors), and well beyond the West.[11] Gülru Necipoglu illustrates a Turkish Poggio-type plan (with added exterior peripteral piers) from the collection of the Qajar architect Mirza Akbar, dating from the late eighteenth or early nineteenth century (fig. 9.8).[12] And Serlio himself made a simpler version of his Poggioreale layout (fig. 9.9) to show students how to convert a plan into a perspective view.

Many Western architects have used such lattices to make plans and elevations. The grids themselves may be uniform or regular (i.e., like a plaid, with changing but repeated widths).[13] The gamut runs at least from the High Renaissance Italian architect Antonio da Sangallo up through Louis Kahn. Thomas Jefferson embraced the idea. Most famously, Durand also made a specialty of it—using it as yet another reproductive principle. In Durand's circle, the technique was called *quadrillage* and could produce everything from small villas to palaces and prisons (fig. 9.10).

I point out the plan's recursions: if we call the prison's corner blocks $x$ (and again the plan is rough, so we must settle for approximate values), then each side of the main square is $5x$. The sides of the corner blocks also determine the widths of the three interior courtyards, while their lengths are $4x$. The chaos game could easily plot out such a plan, and probably suitable elevations as well. Durand's pool of further possible plans (fig. 9.11) suggests many more plays with the Poggioreale principle—plays not only with a basic square rationally subdivided into quarter squares and half squares (the plans on the left)

9.8.

Islamic lattice design for a building. London, Victoria and Albert Museum. From Necipoglu, *Topkapi Scroll.*

9.9.

Sebastiano Serlio. Lattice-generated building plan. From Serlio, *Tutte l'opere d'architettura.*

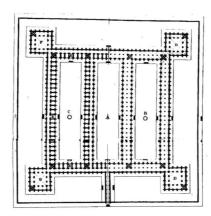

9.10. J.-N.-L. Durand and J. T. Thibault. Plan of a prison. From Durand, *Précis de leçons.*

THE BIOLOGY OF ARCHITECTURAL REPRODUCTION

9.11.

J.-N.-L. Durand. "Ensemble
d'édifices résultants des
divisions du carré, du
parallélograme, et de leurs
combinaisons avec le cercle."
From Durand, *Précis des
leçons.*

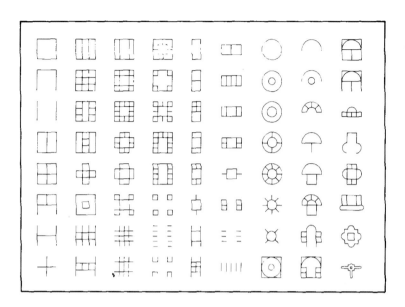

but also with circles, semicircles, and circle-and-square compounds derived from the same initial matrix.

The similarity of these images to mandalas might also intrigue us. They further remind me of the shape grammars for architectural plans and designs that have been developed more recently by William J. Mitchell, G. Stiny, and others.[14] But, mainly, the Poggioreale principle reflects an episode in the history of reproductive architecture that has yet to find its chronicler.

When that happens, I hope that she or he will consider yet another version of Poggioreale's plan—one that was unconsciously re-created by Hans Lauwerier, a mathematician and computer scientist, as a true fractal (fig. 9.12).[15] Here the basic formula consists of asking the computer to combine line segments of several different lengths. Each new segment must be rotated by a set value, 45° or 90°, with respect to its predecessor. At the same time, the computer must also duplicate its action in mirror symmetry across its vertical and horizontal axes. A fantasy of squares, mixed with the perimeters of Greek crosses, at several different sizes, quickly builds up.

The result is a complex variation on the Poggio plan. In this version the main square, or "court," is rotated 45°; and each of its corners gets a miniature square, with the corner pavilions moved to the center of each side. But the main corner pavilions are exactly as in Poggio, and each of these pavilions even has mini-pavilions at its own corners. As a practical architectural plan, this would be complex but certainly buildable; what it might be used for is another matter.[16]

## FRACTAL REPRODUCTION

All these things—Sierpinski gaskets, the Poggioreale principle, Lauwerier meanders—have to do with fractals. So then what is a fractal? It is a geometrical motif that repeats itself over and over at ever-smaller scale. The scale shifts are not necessarily recursive. Nonetheless, fractals are strongly tied in with our interest in the scaling (up or down) of self-similar shapes. For earlier fractal-like phenomena, we can go back to chapter 1 and Buckminster Fuller's tensegrity, or to the successive stages in the growth of a homunculus, or to the successive upward scalings of the linga and the yoni from human to colossal to architectural to cosmic. Indeed any architect who builds something shaped like a chrysanthemum capitulum, a rib cage, or a mollusk shell is in a general way playing with the idea of fractals.

There is another geometrical construct that turns out to be fractal, the Koch curve. It was originally discovered by Helge Koch in 1904.[17] Take a triangle

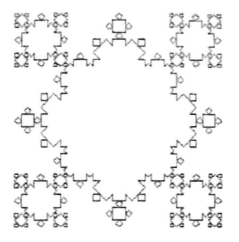

9.12.

Hans Lauwerier. A fractal meander program for the computer. From Lauwerier, *Fractals*.

(fig. 9.13, top). Impose on it a similar triangle upside down, in such a way that the points of the new triangle penetrate the middle third of each side of the original triangle (center). The result is a star of David. Next, consider each of the six points of that star as a triangle on its own, and repeat the process with suitably smaller triangles (bottom). Do this over and over again, each time adding and overlapping recursively diminished triangles. (Yes, it's another IFS.) Note that the component forms are all isomorphic—all 60° triangles or parts thereof.

But here comes something different: the final outcome of the process (fig. 9.14), with its twinkling baroque edge, would be about the same size as the original star of David formed from only twelve lines. And it would enclose approximately the same area. But, at least theoretically, the boundary of the new curve could be infinitely long—after all, one could go on subdividing forever. This is what makes the Koch curve fractal. Because of these notions, especially as they have been developed by Mandelbrot, all our concepts of dimension and extent have been changed. We have had to alter our idea of what a line or a curve might actually be.[18]

9.13.

The first three steps in making

a Koch curve. Author.

9.14.

A Koch curve. Extended version

of top side of star of David.

Author.

9.15.

A fractal formed from a series of Koch islands. Adapted from Lauwerier, *Fractals.*

9.16.

Michelangelo's St. Peter's transformed into a Greek cross. Author.

A single Koch curve can be joined by other, identical Koch curves to form what is called a *Koch island* (fig. 9.15).[19] This, we note, greatly resembles a central-plan building. Indeed, by repeating the island at different scales, and then superimposing the self-similar repeats at those different scales, we achieve something very close to the thick, writhing, anfractuous forms of a Renaissance plan (fig. 9.16). Both the Renaissance plan and the Koch island are essentially complex rotational spirals.

In the illustration I have doctored Michelangelo's plan to make it more Koch-like. But Michelangelo's desire for a central plan like this, rather than the Latin-cross plan of St. Peter's that was actually built, is well known.[20] Or are you disturbed that the Koch island is a hexagon and Michelangelo's plan a square? The Renaissance scheme can easily turn into a hexagon, or an octagon, thereby replacing $C_4$ rotation respectively with $C_6$ and $C_8$ (figs. 9.17, 9.18). It could in fact be just about any sort of polygon.

9.17.

Michelangelo's St. Peter's, as earlier, turned into a hexagon. Author.

9.18.

Michelangelo's St. Peter's, as earlier, turned into an octagon. Author.

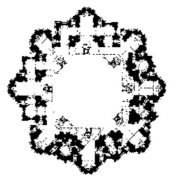

THE BIOLOGY OF ARCHITECTURAL REPRODUCTION

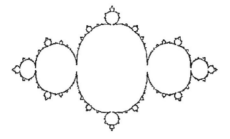

9.19.

A Julia fractal: the "San Marco."

From Lauwerier, *Fractals.*

There are other architectural and reproductive aspects to fractals. Figure 9.19 displays what is called a *Julia set* (a set of numbers in the plane), named after another of Mandelbrot's inspirers, Gaston Julia. Mandelbrot has dubbed this set the "San Marco" because the numbers produce a form reminding him of the lower facade of that Venetian church, as reflected in water when the piazza is flooded. In figure 9.20, thanks to Adobe Photoshop, I have contrived something of this effect. Not only do we see a basic architectural form repeated in the set, fringe-wise, at different scales around each arch, but, as with Poggioreale and the various versions of St. Peter's, the Julia set is laid out in mirror symmetry across central horizontal and central vertical axes. The same, of course, is true of San Marco and its reflection. Also, the diminutions in the sizes of San Marco's arches as they progress outward from the center approximate those in the Julia set.[21] Neither arrangement, however, is recursive.

9.20.

Lower facade of San Marco, Venice (begun 1063), with added effect of mirror reflection in the flooded piazza. Adapted from Watkin, *History of Western Architecture.*

But there is more to the St. Peter's part of the story. Before Michelangelo came on the scene as architect in 1546, the new church had been under construction for almost half a century. The first of the immediately preceding architects had been Bramante. In 1506 he created several schemes for the projected new building. One of these (fig. 9.21) is intricately fractal in what I will call a Renaissance way. How? I will begin by briefly paraphrasing (and annotating) myself: "Symmetrically clustered within the inside corners formed by the cross's arms [domes 1 and 2 on the plan] are four miniature Greek crosses [domes 3 and 4]. These together make up the basic cube of the church's body. The arms of these smaller crosses consist of further miniatures [not numbered]. And their corners, in turn, are filled in with smaller chapels or niches."[22] In other words, like a Koch island, Bramante's plan repeats self-similar units placed fringe-wise around a central, larger version—the matrix, the mother—of that unit.[23] So far, Bramante's plan is fractal.

But here we come to what I meant by "fractal in a Renaissance way." The "arches" of the San Marco Julia set (and those of San Marco itself) do not recurse; similarly, the diameters of Michelangelo's two differently sized domes in figures 9.16 to 9.18 are not rationally related, nor are other major dimensions of his plan—either as built or as doctored by me.

Yet the spaces in Bramante's plan are recursive, and just in the way that the squares and their clusterings in Serlio's Poggioreale are recursive—and, for that matter, like those in the chaos-game version of the amylase chain. In Bramante,

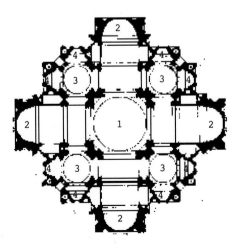

9.21.

Reconstruction of one of Bramante's 1506 projects for St. Peter's. From Wolff Metternich, *Die frühen St.-Peter-Entwürfe.* Corner octagonal chapels omitted.

THE BIOLOGY OF ARCHITECTURAL REPRODUCTION

dome 1 = 1, dome 2 = $\frac{2}{3}$ of 1, dome 3 = $\frac{1}{2}$ of 1, dome 4 = $\frac{1}{4}$ of 1, and dome 5 = $\frac{1}{8}$ of 1. Dome 1, in the center, is the largest and is unique. Dome 2 I will consider as appearing twice, but split, making the four semidomes for the arms of the main Greek cross. Dome 3 appears in four places, capping the four chapels set in squares around dome 1. Dome 4 appears four times, split into 8 semidomes. Dome 5, half the diameter of Dome 4, covers the niches or small apses that exist all throughout the plan. In all, this smallest of the church's "body parts" appears 96 times. Note also that dome 4, split into semidomes, supplies the apses around the compartment crowned by dome 3, and that the same happens with dome 5 vis-à-vis dome 4.[24]

## CLADISTICS: THOUGHTS ON ARCHITECTURAL HERITABILITY

Let us look further at what happens to buildings as they "breed" and cluster into populations. I will propose that one can study these events by using cladistics. I borrow the term from evolutionary biologists, who study genetically related groups such as species, orders, phyla, and the like. Any such group is called a *clade* (from the Greek *klados*—sprout, arm, branch, blood vessel). The implication is that the group is organized like a tree. So cladistics takes up a theme from the introduction, where I illustrated Ernst Haeckel's tree showing the descent of man and Banister Fletcher's tree of architectural history.

As explanatory devices, however, those nineteenth-century trees had shortcomings. For one thing, the consecutive order in which each "sprout" or clade appears is unclear—or else is clearly wrong. In Haeckel's tree (see fig. 0.4, bottom part) did the Infusoria (protozoa in decaying organic matter) precede or come after the ovularia (Haeckel's term for organisms that reproduce via eggs)? They seem coeval. And then in Fletcher's tree (fig. 0.3) Chinese architecture comes into being at the same time as "Peruvian" (Incan), which obviously wasn't so, since Chinese architecture came into existence a good 5,000 years earlier.

Another flaw is that both trees have built-in hierarchies favoring a main central line of descent, with lesser offspring quite literally marginalized. Thus in Haeckel the early phyla lead up to a final one, that which contains humans and which, as "MAN," is supreme over all its predecessors. In Fletcher's tree this central line leads to what he calls the Modern Style. Such inappropriate messianism (in large part due to the two trees' being bilaterally symmetrical with main vertical axes) is averted in cladistic analysis. No clade is more important

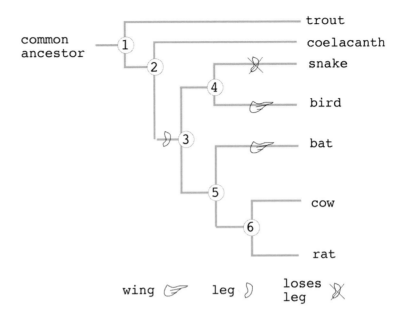

9.22.

A cladogram of tetrapod

(four-legged-animal) lineage.

Adapted from Siebert,

"Tree Statistics."

than any other. The Haeckel-Fletcher system may be good for tracing royal bloodlines, primogeniture, and so on, but it does not reflect the way actual genetic descent works.[25] The cladogram is a more accurate, less value-ridden way of diagramming inheritance—and hence history.

Figure 9.22 presents a cladogram taken from evolutionary biology. On the far left is an as-yet unidentified common ancestral species. This branches (1) directly into a new species, the trout, and (2) into a bifurcation—first the coelacanth (a living fish virtually unchanged since the Paleozoic) and then into a further branching, (3). At (3) each branch splits once again, at (4), and then again at (5). The branching at (4) generates snakes and birds; that at (5), bats. A final branching (6) produces cows and rats.[26] In other words, the cladogram teaches us, in a stepwise fashion, how cows/rats relate to fish.

What is important to note in this cladogram is that when the key new trait, legs, appears, just before (3), it reappears in all subsequent branchings. This happens because biological heredity is conservative; like goes to like. And the rule holds true even though one such appearance may be followed by a loss: the snakes who emerged from branch (4) eventually lost their legs.[27] There were other transformations. The birds who emerged from (4) and the bats who

174

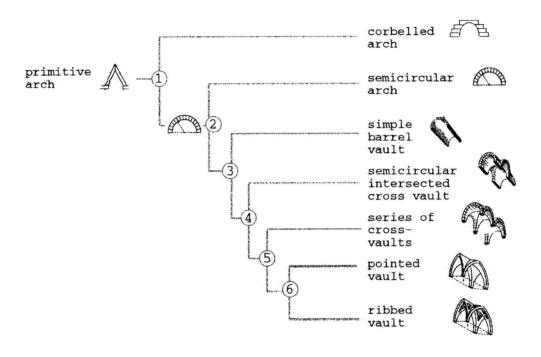

corbelled arch

primitive arch

1

semicircular arch

2

simple barrel vault

3

semicircular intersected cross vault

4

series of cross-vaults

5

pointed vault

6

ribbed vault

9.23.

Simplified cladogram of types
of arch and vault. Author.

emerged from (5) turned their forelegs into two (evolutionarily unrelated) kinds of wings. Nevertheless, cows and rats have this in common: they are (a) mammals and (b) use all four of their legs as legs.

Here is how we might do a cladogram for an architectural lineage, one that leads from the earliest simplest form of masonry arch to an elaborated Gothic vault. Figure 9.23 assumes that the oldest type of stone arch (which survived into Anglo-Saxon architecture) consists of two longish blocks laid against one another in the form of a triangle (far left). This is the group's common ancestor. Like all its progeny it creates a window, door, or other opening while at the same time supporting superincumbent masonry. At (1) this "primitive" arch splits into two types. One is the corbeled arch; more elaborate than the triangular one, it makes use of smaller blocks horizontally laid. The curvature of a corbeled arch is adjustable. It can therefore span a greater variety of openings than can the triangular arch, which is limited by the size and breakableness of single blocks. However, in the corbeled arch, since each block projects slightly beyond the one beneath it, there is a tendency for the upper blocks to be

unstable and to tip forward into the opening. The problem is solved by lock-
ing the arch blocks in place with the "surcharged" masonry on their inner ends.
But this of course means heavier and costlier construction. Later on, cheaper
methods of achieving the same effect would be possible.

The invention of the semicircular arch solved several of these problems. In this
arch all the constituent stones, or voussoirs, are cut so that their joints radiate
from the arch's center, as shown in the cladogram. Such arches are more stable than corbeled arches and yet can be built of lighter materials. They provide
an even greater variety of openings than had been possible earlier.

Above all, semicircular arches had a strong effect on a building technique that
came to be dominant in several parts of the world: vaulting. A vault is simply
a very deep arch—one that continues along its axis to cover an interior space.
Corbeled vaults can be built, as can corbeled domes (see the Treasury of
Atreus; fig. 4.16). And masonry vaults, corbeled or not, are an improvement on
wooden roofs. (Paradoxically, masonry vaults usually have to be protected by
wooden roofs; but these latter, unlike the wooden roof that is a building's only
cover, can be renewed and replaced without interfering with the spaces below.)

In any case, it was the semicircular rather than the corbeled vault that blos-
somed and separated into many new groups or clades. As noted, a simple
semicircular arch, continued along an axis, results in a barrel vault (3). But the
barrel vault has the disadvantage of being able to cover only a space as wide
as the vault itself. This means that most barrel-vaulted spaces are narrow. The
problem is solved at (4) when one barrel vault is crossed by another of the
same height and width, resulting in an intersection—most familiar nowadays in
vaulted churches with nave, transepts, and crossing. But suppose you want a
really wide space, square or rectangular—for a mosque, say, or a railway station. That space can be covered by an assemblage of cross-vaults, which can
extend themselves both north and south, and also east and west: that is, along
multiple parallel axes (5). In other words, massed cross-vaults provide something like a hypostyle, but with the many structural improvements (e.g., fewer
supports) that vaulting offers.

There is one further evolution in our cladogram, from the bifurcation at (5) into
(6). This produces a planar pointed vault and a ribbed vault (the latter may be
semicircular or pointed). There is a distinct disadvantage to semicircular vaults:

if a vault of smaller width meets one of larger width, the tops of the two will not meet (the height of a semicircle has to be half its width), or else the narrower vault will have to be stilted so that its crest is at the level of that of the wide vault. Either way, the result is both ugly and unstable. The problem is solved if the two vaults have pointed rather than a semicircular profiles. The graphic profile of the narrow vault can be steeper than that of the wide one, so that the tops do meet, are stable, and are also visually satisfying, since the two vaults spring from the same level. Then, too, pointed vaults have less diagonal thrust than do semicircular ones, so they need less buttressing.[28] Most important, the builder can now for the first time vault rectangular as well as square bays or compartments.

Finally, a note on construction. Much of the way a building looks is a function of the process, the order of events, with which it was erected. All of these vaults and arches (except the corbeled type) must be constructed with temporary wooden forms called *centering*. Centering fills the space to be vaulted and supports the blocks as they are being laid. (Masonry vaults and arches become self-supporting only when every single block is in place.) The amount of centering needed for a good-sized vault can be considerable. As an alternative, that same vault can be constructed in skeleton form, which makes possible more economical centering. Then, when the stone skeleton can stand alone, its openings can be filled in, without centering, by simple panels called *webbing*, shown in gray in figure 9.23.[29]

All this adds up to an evolutionary process not unlike the development pictured in figure 9.22. The leg in animal evolution is like the radiating joint in the evolution of vaults. Legs made the development of land creatures possible. Radiating joints made possible the many varieties of vault, and hence the great efflorescence of masonry architecture, that we now have. The difference between the two clade trees is, of course, that Nature, with her unconscious processes of natural selection, created the different groups of animals. And one clade of animals is not better than another. The arch/vault clade tree was consciously evolved, by people—people who were anxious to improve on earlier forms. And the "clades" of arches and vaults get better and better at doing what was needed.

A word of warning: I have been drastically simplifying. Moreover, my sequence is in large part the product of my common sense plus my imagination. I do know that corbeled arches are probably more ancient than semicircular ones, but I do not know that barrel vaults preceded intersecting vaults, or that multiple cross-vaults came after single ones. It is pretty certain that pointed vaults succeeded semicircular (pointed-arch Gothic came after round-arched Romanesque, and the events can be dated); and I know that ribbed vaults came after the planar kind. But even so, my cladogram raises many questions— such as: just when did all these branchings occur? (Though biologists will tell you that cladograms show sequences, not dates.)

In other words I have diminished but not eliminated the problematic chronologies in Fletcher's tree. But never mind. The "fossil record" of the paleontologists, and for that matter the sequences of evolutionary biology in general, also has holes. In both cases we can only hope that future research will fill them up.

This chapter on heritability—on the elaboration of clades—completes my tale. Note that that tale, as traced throughout this book, has expanded in a scalar chain from molecular and cellular size upward through sequences of different organisms grouped into self-similar chains. On the way we have buzzed with insects as we built skyscrapers and geometric grids, soared with the birds, risen to the level of the cosmos, wreathed our artifacts with flowers, gone head-to-head with mammals at boundaries, and ornamented our territories with walls and gates, factories and dwellings, and symbols of sexual reproduction. Now it is time, briefly, to look back as a way of suggesting other ways forward.

# WHERE TO NOW?

We have looked at quite a few ways of digging out architecture's biological roots. But there are plenty of others—ways that I've either barely mentioned or completely omitted. For example, while we looked at the immense architectures of certain ant and termite species, and at cognate human pyramids, cathedrals, and skyscrapers, many other animal builders—beavers, bumblebees, and various unmentioned insects and birds—could well have been discussed.

For another example, our look at DNA and similar nature-derived spirals in architecture yielded many instances—spiral capitals, spiral staircases, spiral columns, spiral towers, spiral jetties, and spirals left- and right-handed, Archimedean, and equiangular. Yet all this, much as it is, only begins to tap the possibilities for studying the spiral and radial symmetries that human architecture has derived from nature. The same goes for ornamented animal bodies. Apart from those discussed, any number of creatures can be sources for human design, from butterflies to snakes to leopards to zebras. The world of botany harbors many more.

Or take the "gephirosaur," my made-up two-headed bridge dinosaur that looks (and functions) like a suspension bridge (see fig. 5.3). My technique, of fabricating an animal-like construct in order to make comparisons with human architecture, has, I believe, an extremely fruitful road ahead of it in architectural writing. Indeed, many "botanical" and "zoological" buildings quite simply are such madeup biological organisms. Gaudí could furnish material for a whole book all by himself.

A highly relevant subject that I left entirely aside was morphology. This is the zoological or botanical bauplan: the practical limits of size, shape, and design among organisms. A study of architecture in terms of biological morphology could have all sorts of new outcomes. The physics of animal and plant morphology would play out powerfully in such studies.[1]

I did, however, elaborate on the ways that flora, both as they grow and as humans rearrange or even reimagine them, serve architectural analysis. We looked at phyllotaxis in terms of Fibonacci sequences, at spiral arrangements in stems, leaves, and tendrils, and at the cyclical symmetries of blossoms, domes, and pavements. To the old idea that the origins of human architecture lie in weaving we added the new one that human weaving is related to, and possibly derived from, that of birds.

But here, too, there could have been so much more. Even my longer discussions have gross gaps. Take vegetable ornament. I devoted some 8,000 words to it, but I could have done better with 80,000. We saw how Ruskin, Riegl, Baltrušaitis, and Elizabeth Mendell worked with the subject. But it would have been useful to consider it at greater length, and with other writers (as well as with the craftsmen who carved what the writers wrote about). One omission I particularly regret is Louis Sullivan's botanical fantasies, which brought unprecedented delicacy and beauty, as well as gorgeously tricky symmetries, to his terra-cotta ornament. And of course Sullivan himself wrote memorably about his own work.[2]

Following Sedlmayr, we also looked at how one can invoke, for architecture, Mendelian genetics and particulate inheritance. Here the possibilities for further explorations are legion. The whole library of Victorian villa books, for example, lies open before us. Then, again under the rubric of reproduction, I looked at the tradition of the Tree of Architecture and Tree of Life in terms of cladistics.[3] Here a further new departure would be to look at fractal trees—for example, those published by Mandelbrot in *The Fractal Geometry of Nature*—to see how they might apply.[4] We took some time, using Sierpinski gaskets, Julia sets, Koch curves, and the like as our playground, to concoct several architectural games. But this whole subject of architectural *quadrillage* needs further study.

And, speaking of reproduction, we saw the immense role in architecture of reproductive organs. Architectural penises, testicles, vulvas, and uteruses—as well as eggs and breasts and their botanical counterparts, nuts and fruits—appear in many cultures that were not discussed. These reproductive shapes take the form of everything from domes to ornamental friezes.

There were many roads not taken. We could have looked at architecture through the lenses of natural and sexual selection. We did see how the latter affects birds' nests, and often birds' colors and markings as well. And of course all the structures whose striking sexual imagery we examined—pyramids and towers, caves and skyscrapers—are ipso facto sexually selective: they magnify, enhance, intensify, and exaggerate sexual attractors. Their underlying purpose is to stimulate.

We might have examined architecture in the light of Darwinian adaptation. Here one would take off from Stephen Jay Gould and Richard Lewontin's classic article "The Spandrels of San Marco."[5] This essay (which is about pendentives, not spandrels), makes a direct analogy between biology and building. To be sure, the authors misunderstand what it is that pendentives do structurally. Nevertheless, the article insinuates a fascinating thought: if pendentives are adaptations (Gould and Lewontin say they're not), then one might imagine architectural adaptations more generally, adaptations that act within a Darwinian scenario for the history of architecture. One could therefore proceed to define, as rigorously as possible, what such an architectural adaptation might be. One could then move on, still in the architectural context, to the pseudo-adaptations that biologists also study—the "sports" created by plant and animal breeders and the temporary genetic fluctuations found in certain hybrids.

One could even propose (and here Peter J. Wilson, in *The Domestication of the Human Species*, has already spoken) that the monumental impulse, in and of itself, is an adaptation. In other words, just as land animals adapted by creating legs, and vaults adapted by creating ribs, so we humans have ensured our survival by elaborating our territories into towns and cities, creating the adaptation that is architecture.

Consider another path, untrodden but promising: in biology, a parasite is any organism that lives on or in another organism, and eats either its host's food or—a frequent alternative—its host.[6] But parasites are not all bad; indeed, they have been one of nature's essential strategies. Nor are they all microscopic. Cowbirds lay their eggs in other species' nests, knowing or at least hoping that the rightful occupants will feed and rear the foreign chicks.[7] Bees like the mason bee, *Osmia bicolor*, occupy abandoned snail shells and refit them with walling made from pebbles. They too are parasites of a sort. They don't eat their hosts but they do exploit the hosts' abandoned body parts.[8]

But for centuries, for most of its existence, the word *parasite* has in fact referred to human beings, which makes it all the easier to apply it to architecture. A building's users are also its users-up—its parasites. Think of what happens, say, to a historic cathedral, castle, or palace. The visitors wear out carpets and floors, mark the walls, and bore, annoy, insult, manipulate, or otherwise wear down the staff (we will consider the staff to be the monument's auto-immune system). Yet at the same time, the very presence of these tourist-parasites is flattering. They are there to admire. They want to take something of the building's beauty with them. (Sometimes they do this quite literally.) The whole history of *Ruinenlust*, of ruin worship, could be rewritten as a study in parasitism. (By the same token we might call the mason bees "ruin fanciers.")

And then there is a fundamental question that I have sometimes raised but have always shrugged off: what about the distinction between our conscious human impulse to build and that same impulse in other species, where, presumably, it is unconscious? This brings up the whole question of human consciousness, with which philosophers and "cognitive scientists" so often bore us. But boring or not, the concept of human consciousness does have the more interesting subset of animal, vegetable, even mineral consciousness.[9] As we saw in chapter 1, lower organisms, and even inanimate matter, seem to judge and select. Molecules of a given shape prefer to unite with their similars or complements. It is clear, also, that the youthful slapdash weaverbird whose handiwork appears in figure 5.7 became conscious that the nest he'd built was inadequate. So he decided to build a better one. Can one speak here only of instinct and not of intention? The further study of building instincts, impulses, or whatever they are, would be one way to answer such questions.

But the most important theme I have introduced in this book has been that of self-similar forms that are scaled upward and downward in size. I posed it first in discussing Fuller's tensegrity, where self-similar shapes rise from the scale of atoms to the scale of geodesic domes. The concept is also fractal. Bramante designed a chapel (the central vaults and dome of his 1506 St. Peter's plan) that was reproduced, and multiplied, as its own fractal fringe, at $\frac{2}{3}$, $\frac{1}{2}$, $\frac{1}{4}$, and $\frac{1}{8}$ scale. At the lower and upper ends of another such scale there could be cells as cities and cities as cells, or molecules as finials and finials as molecules. Between the largest and the smallest forms in each chain, there can be imagined or invisible clones at appropriate scales. We recall that Fuller's tensegrity sequence from atom to truss had intermediate self-similar forms, invisibly created by gases.

This led to a new look at colossi—to the notion, dream, wish, or actuality that we build and inhabit giant plants, animals, or body parts. It pleases us to linger under a dome spiraled according to the symmetries in a sunflower or a rose; Domenikus Zimmermann constructed a church-sized seashell for the worshipers at the Wies. We saw the figure sculpture on phallic buildings as homunculi. A colossus was created that shrank its human users and relocated them a considerable distance down the stream of scaled self-similar images. We humans have put unparalleled energies into elaborating this concept, mainly through architecture. It makes us see all creation as extending far beyond ourselves toward infinite smallness and infinite largeness. Why? Only energetic inquiry will give this simple question the profound answer it deserves.

So I end my look at architecture's biological roots. The discussion has illuminated a long and, I hope, fascinating drama of encounters, enactments, fusions, and correspondences between biology and architecture. It is as if our subject were a huge unvisited museum, its exhibits all set up but unlighted. I have shone a flashlight here and there in some of the galleries, indicating the vastness of the collections. But for now, just knowing that they all exist, waiting to be studied, has to be enough. As Alberti would say (or perhaps he would have said it sooner), "De his hactenus"—enough of these things.

# NOTES

INTRODUCTION

1

Nikolaus Pevsner, *Outline of European Architecture* (1942; reprint, Harmondsworth; Penguin, 1944), xvi. On this passage, see now Joseph Rykwert, *The Dancing Column: On Order in Architecture* (Cambridge, Mass.: MIT Press, 1996), 374ff.

2

Thomas Munro, *Evolution and the Arts* (Cleveland: Cleveland Museum of Art, 1957), surveys the earlier literature. For more recent writings, see Alexander Alland, *The Artistic Animal: An Inquiry into the Biological Roots of Art* (Garden City, N.Y.: Anchor Books, 1977); Ellen Dissanayake, *Homo Aestheticus: Where Art Comes from and Why* (New York: Free Press, 1992); John Frazer, *An Evolutionary Architecture* (London: Architectural Association, 1995); Johan Bettum, "An Evolutionary Architecture," *AA Files,* no. 30 (autumn 1995), 70ff.; Philip Steadman, *The Evolution of Designs: The Biological Analogy in Architecture and the Applied Arts* (Cambridge: Cambridge University Press, 1979); and John Frazer et al., in "The Interactivator" in *Architects in Cyberspace,* special issue of *Architectural Design* 65, nos. 11–12 (1995), 79ff. These writings discuss morphogenesis, self-constructing structure, genes, sexual reproduction, and environment, all in terms of human architecture. See also Stephen Toulmin and June Goodfield, *The Architecture of Matter* (New York: Harper and Row, 1962).

3

Karl von Frisch, *Aus dem Leben der Bienen* (Berlin: Springer, 1953), 159.

4

See Ennio Francia, *1506–1606: Storia della costruzione del nuovo San Pietro* (Rome: De Luca, 1989).

5

For more on our human debts and correspondences to our animal forebears and cousins, see Jared Diamond, *The Third Chimpanzee: The Evolution and Future of the Human Animal* (New York: HarperCollins, 1992). Animal art is discussed at 168ff.

6

On imitating the shelter of animals, see especially Joseph Rykwert, *On Adam's House in Paradise: The Idea of the Primitive Hut in Architectural History* (New York: Museum of Modern Art, 1972).

7

Cesare Cesariano, *Vitruvius, de Architectura* (Como: Gottardus de Ponte, 1521), on Vitruvius 2.fol. 32r. On Vitruvius's primitive hut, see also Elisa Romano, *La capanna e il tempio: Vitruvio o dell'architettura* (Palermo: Palumbo, 1987), 108ff.

8

Ernst Haeckel, *The Evolution of Man: A Popular Exposition of the Principal Points of Human Ontogeny and Phylogeny* (New York: Appleton, 1879), 2:pl. xv.

9

Mark Ridley, *Evolution* (Boston: Blackwell, 1993), 44ff., on homologies. See also S. V. Meyen, "Plant Morphology in Its Nomothetical Aspects," *Botanical Review* 39, no. 3 (1974), 205ff., which further distinguishes between convergence (distant species developing similarities) and parallelism (similar species doing so).

10

Stephen Jay Gould, "Common Pathways of Illumination," *Natural History,* December 1994, 14. He discusses the similarities between squids' and humans' eyes.

11

The main modern studies of animal architecture are David Hancocks, *Master Builders of the Animal World* (New York: Harper and Brothers, 1973); Karl von Frisch with the collaboration of Otto von Frisch, *Animal Architecture,* trans. Lisbeth Gombrich (New York: Harcourt Brace Jovanovich, 1974); and Michael H. Hansell, *Animal Architecture and Building Behaviour* (London: Longmans, 1984). See also [Juhani Pallasmaa], *Animal Architecture,* exhibition catalogue (Helsinki: Museum of Finnish Architecture, 1992), and the excellent chapter on animal architecture in James L. Gould and Carol Grant Gould, *The Animal Mind* (New York: Scientific American Library, 1994), 114ff.

12

Juan José Soler, Anders Pape Møller, and Manuel Soler, "Nest Building, Sexual Selection, and Parental Investment," *Evolutionary Ecology* (in press 1997), n. 21.

13

Monogamy may have something to do with this aptitude for building. Beavers and humans are monogamous; and badgers are so de facto, since they have clans in which there is only one breeding pair (Anders Pape Møller, personal communication).

14

Richard Dawkins, *The Extended Phenotype: The Gene as the Unit of Selection* (Oxford: Oxford University Press, 1982), 195ff.

15

Dawkins calls cultural extended phenotypes "memes" (*Extended Phenotype,* 109). The meme, a "unit of reproduction residing in the brain," "may be in the form of words, music, visual images, styles of clothes, facial or hand gestures, skills." I have not considered the term *meme* to be necessary to my argument.

16

Peter J. Wilson, *The Domestication of the Human Species* (New Haven: Yale University Press, 1988).

# 1

MOLECULES, VIRUSES, AND CELLS

1

Leslie E. Orgel, "The Origin of Life on Earth," *Scientific American,* October 1994, 76ff., with earlier bibliography. Also on evolution without selection, see Roger V. Jean, "On the Origins of Spiral Symmetry in Plants," in István Hargittai and Clifford A. Pickover, eds., *Spiral Symmetry* (Singapore: World Scientific, 1992), 323ff.

2

Kevin Kelly, *Out of Control: The Rise of Neo-Biological Civilization* (Reading, Mass.: Addison-Wesley, 1994); Claus Emmeche, *The Garden in the Machine: The Emerging Science of Artificial Life* (Princeton: Princeton University Press, 1994).

3

George M. Whitesides, "Self-Assembling Materials," *Scientific American,* September 1995, 146ff.; Manfred Eigen, *Steps Towards Life,* trans. Paul Woolley (Oxford: Oxford University Press, 1992), 12ff., and idem, "Self-

Replication and Molecular Evolution," in D. S. Bendall, ed., *Evolution from Molecules to Men* (Cambridge: Cambridge University Press, 1983), 105ff.

4

Julius Rebek, Jr., "Synthetic Self-Replicating Molecules," *Scientific American,* July 1994, 48ff., with earlier bibliography.

5

Manfred Eigen, "Wie entsteht Information? Prinzipien der Selbstorganisation in der Biologie," *Berichtete der Bunsengesellschaft für Physikalische Chemie* 80 (1976), 1059ff.; see also Rebek, "Self-Replicating Molecules."

6

A. Lima-de-Faria proposes in *Evolution without Selection: Form and Function by Autoevolution* (Amsterdam: Elzevier, 1988) to dispense entirely with the concept of selection. It is not, he says, that these shapes select each other, or that the environment selects for them—rather, they self-assemble. For the present, however, I will see self-assembly only as one more form of selection.

7

Arnold J. Levine, *Viruses* (New York: Scientific American Library, 1992), 195ff.

8

R. M. Fleming et al., "Crystalline Fullerenes," in George S. Hammond and Valerie J. Kuck, eds., *Fullerenes: Synthesis, Properties, and Chemistry of Large Carbon Clusters* (Washington, D.C.: American Chemical Society, 1992), and Sergiu M. Gorum et al., "Low Resolution Single-Crystal X-Ray Structure of Solvated Fullerenes," in ibid., 25ff.

9

Benoit B. Mandelbrot, *The Fractal Geometry of Nature,* new ed. (New York: Freeman, 1983).

10

*Standard proximity* packing is also known as *locally stable* packing. See L. Fejes Tóth, "Symmetry Induced by Economy," in István Hargittai, ed., *Symmetry: Unifying Human Understanding* (New York: Pergamon Press, 1983), 83ff.

11

See David Goodsell, *Our Molecular Nature: The Body's Motors, Machines, and Messages* (New York: Copernicus, 1996).

**12**
For instances of how Fuller's tensegrity principles can be seen at work in cell structure and molecular biology, see Donald E. Ingber, "The Architecture of Life," *Scientific American,* January 1998, 48ff. Ingber also shows how buckyballs may be considered tensegrity spheres.

**13**
Philip Ball, *Designing the Molecular World: Chemistry at the Frontier* (Princeton: Princeton University Press, 1994), 43ff., see also P. W. Fowler and D. E. Manopoulos, *An Atlas of Fullerenes* (Oxford: Clarendon Press, 1995), 165, which illustrates that there are 181 general fullerene isomers with $C_{60}$ rotations.

**14**
Ball, *Molecular World,* 44.

**15**
Anthony Alofsin, *Frank Lloyd Wright: The Lost Years, 1910–1922* (Chicago: University of Chicago Press, 1993), 301ff.; idem, "Frank Lloyd Wright and Modernism," in Terence Riley, ed., *Frank Lloyd Wright, Architect* (New York: Museum of Modern Art, 1994), 40; Neil Levine, *The Architecture of Frank Lloyd Wright* (Princeton: Princeton University Press, 1996).

**16**
Anthony J. F. Griffiths et al., *Introduction to Genetic Analysis,* 5th ed. (New York: Freeman, 1993); also Robert Olby, *The Path to the Double Helix* (Seattle: University of Washington Press, 1974), 321ff., and Goodsell, *Our Molecular Nature,* 26ff.

**17**
This is a chain of collagen-like sequences of 78 amino acids. See François Jacob, "Molecules: Tinkering in Evolution," in Bendall, *Evolution,* 131ff.

**18**
David Ruelle, *Chance and Chaos* (Princeton: Princeton University Press, 1991), 152ff. Cf. Eigen, "Wie entsteht Information?"

**19**
The drawing is in the Paris Bibliothèque Nationale and dates from 1487–1488, long before Leonardo went to France. The stair at Chambord was not built until 1544, twenty-five years after Leonardo's death. See Carlo Pedretti, *A Chronology of Leonardo da Vinci's Architectural Studies after 1500* (Geneva: Droz, 1962), 121ff.; idem, *Leonardo architetto* (New York: Rizzoli, 1978), 263; and also Jean Guillaume, "Léonard de Vinci et l'architecture française, 1. Le Problème de Chambord,"

*Revue de l'art,* no. 25 (1974), 71ff. For spiral staircases geenrally, see John Templer, *The Staircase: History and Theories* (Cambridge, Mass.: MIT Press, 1994), 53ff.

**20**
Robin Evans, *The Projective Cast: Architecture and Its Three Geometries* (Cambridge, Mass.: MIT Press, 1995), 214ff.

**21**
Joseph Rykwert, *The Dancing Column: On Order in Architecture* (Cambridge, Mass.: MIT Press, 1996), has a full bibliography.

**22**
For the Trajan column, particularly, as a vehicle of communication, see Renate Scheiper, *Bildpropaganda der römischen Kaiserszeit* (Bonn: R. Habell, 1982), esp. 152ff. See also Rykwert, *Dancing Column,* 514 n. 73.

**23**
Achim Arbeiter, *Alt-St. Peter in Geschichte und Wissenschaft* (Berlin: Gebr. Mann, 1988), 166ff.

**24**
Juan Antonio Ramírez, "Guarino Guarini, Fray Juan Ricci, and the Complete Solomonic Orders," *Art History* 4 (June 1981), 175ff., and idem, "Sinédoque: Columnas Salomonicas," in *Dios, Arquitecto: J. B. Villalpando y el templo de Salomón,* by Ramírez, René Taylor, André Corboz, Robert Jan van Pelt, and Antonio Martinez Ripold (Madrid: Siruela, 1991), 17ff. with bibliography. Also Enrico Mauceri, "Colonne tortili così dette del Tempio di Salomone," *L'Arte* 1 (1898), 377ff.

**25**
But Rykwert does not discuss the literal dancing of columns in his *Dancing Column.* For that, see Indra Kagis McEwen, *Socrates' Ancestor: An Essay on Architectural Beginnings* (Cambridge, Mass.: MIT Press), 1993. On Bernini, see William Chandler Kirwin, *Powers Matchless: The Pontificate of Urban VIII, the Baldachin, and Gian Lorenzo Bernini* (New York: P. Lang, 1997).

**26**
Ian Stewart and Martin Golubitsky, *Fearful Symmetry: Is God a Geometer?* (Oxford: Blackwell, 1992), 104ff.

**27**
David Peak and Michael Frame, *Chaos under Control: The Art and Science of Complexity* (New York: Freeman, 1994), 113ff.

188

28
Christina Lodder, *Russian Constructivism* (New Haven: Yale University Press, 1983), 55ff.

29
The connection is suggested by Ulrich Conrads and Hans Sperlich, *Architecture of Fantasy* (New York: Praeger, 1962), 177. On Tatlin, see John Milner, *Vladimir Tatlin and the Russian Avant-Garde* (New Haven: Yale University Press, 1983), 151ff., and *Vladimir Tatlin: Leben Werk Werkung: Ein internationale Symposium,* ed. Jürgen Harten (Cologne: Dumont, 1993), especially Aleksander Flaker's ingenious if eccentric "Die Spiral als optimate Projektion," 64ff.

30
Edith Balas, "The Unbuilt Architecture of the Early Modern Sculptors," *Gazette des Beaux-Arts,* ser. 6, 110, no. 1426 (1987), 181ff.

31
Stewart and Golubitsky, *Fearful Symmetry,* 73ff. For non-biotic reproduction, see Martin Gardner, *The Ambidextrous Universe* (New York: Basic Books, 1964), 91ff.; Paul J. Fagan and Michael D. Ward, "Building Molecular Crystals," *Scientific American,* July 1992, 48ff.

32
D'Arcy Wentworth Thompson, *On Growth and Form,* complete rev. ed. (1942; reprint, New York: Dover, 1992), 645ff.

33
A. G. Graham Cairns-Smith, *Seven Clues to the Origin of Life* (Cambridge: Cambridge University Press, 1990), 101ff., 110ff.; Jack Cohen and Ian Stewart, *The Collapse of Chaos: Discovering Simplicity in a Complex World* (New York: Penguin, 1994), 102.

34
Noel F. Kennon, *Patterns in Crystals* (New York: Wiley, 1978), 63. For more, see Donald E. Sands, *Introduction to Crystallography* (New York: Dover, 1975).

35
Marc-Antoine Gaudin, *L'Architecture du monde des atomes* (Paris: Gaulthier-Villars, 1873).

36
Vera Kowitz, *La Tour Eiffel* (Essen: Die blaue Eule, 1989); Caroline Mathieu and Françoise Cachin, *1889: La Tour Eiffel et l'Exposition Universelle,* exhibition catalogue (Paris: Musée d'Orsay, 1989); Bertrand Lemoine, *Gustave Eiffel* (Paris: Hazan, 1984).

37
Ronald E. Cohen and Lars Stixrude, "High Pressure Elasticity of Iron and Anistropy of Earth's Inner Core," *Science,* 31 March 1995, 1972ff.

38
Carter Wiseman, *I. M. Pei: A Profile in American Architecture* (New York: Abrams, 1990), 292ff.

39
Kennon, *Patterns in Crystals,* 107.

40
These criticisms are all quoted by Alan Riding, "An Ultramodern Design, Old-Fashioned Outrage," *New York Times,* 3 July 1996, C9. See also "Daniel Libeskind: Architect of the V & A's Proposed Extension," *Country Life,* no. 24, (13 June 1996), 154ff., and the squibs in *Architectural Review* 200, no. 1193 (July 1996), 11; *Architects' Journal* 203, no. 20 (23 May 1996), 8ff.

41
Kennon, *Patterns in Crystals,* 97ff.

42
Eigen, *Steps towards Life,* 101ff.; Arnold Levine, *Viruses.*

43
Antoni van Leeuwenhoek, *Anatomia seu interiora rerum . . .* (Leyden: Boutesteyn, 1687). See also Marian Fournier, *The Fabric of Life: Microscopy in the Seventeenth Century* (Baltimore: Johns Hopkins University Press, 1996).

44
Conrads and Sperlich, *Architecture of Fantasy,* 116, 180; also Konrad Wachsmann, *Wendepunkt im Bauen* (Wiesbaden: Krausskopf, 1959).

45
Richard Buckminster Fuller (in collaboration with E. J. Applewhite), *Synergetics: Explorations in Geometry and Thinking* (New York: Macmillan, 1975), 119, and R. Buckminster Fuller and Robert W. Marks, *The Dymaxion World of Buckminster Fuller* (New York: Anchor Books, 1973), esp. 61ff.

46
Juan Bassegoda Nonell, *El gran Gaudí* (Barcelona: Ausa, 1989), 17. For illustrations of similar molecular configurations available to Gaudí, see Gaudin, *L'Architecture du monde des atomes.*

47
Goodsell, *Our Molecular Nature,* 81.

48
Vassos Karageorghis, *Cyprus from the Stone Age to the Romans* (London: Thames and Hudson, 1982), 33ff.

49
Hermann Finsterlin, undated letter to Iain Boyd Whyte, ed., *The Crystal Chain Letters: Architectural Fantasies by Bruno Taut and His Circle* (Cambridge, Mass.: MIT Press, 1985), 91.

50
James E. Rothman and Lelio Orci, "Budding Vesicles in Living Cells," *Scientific American,* March 1996, 70ff.

51
See O. Roger Anderson, *Radiolaria* (New York: Springer, 1983), though his micrographs are less glamorous than the drawings in Ernst Haeckel's classic *Die Radiolarien,* 3 vols. (Berlin: G. Reimer, 1862–1888).

52
The honeycomb in seventeenth-century Rome was associated with the Barberini, since their symbol was the honeybee (see chapter 4). However, Ariccia was Chigi territory, so Bernini's motif probably wasn't intended to suggest honeybees.

53
Ernst Haeckel, *Art Forms in Nature* (New York: Dover, 1974).

54
Erika Krause, "L'Influence de Ernst Haeckel sur l'art nouveau," in Jean Clair, ed., *L'Ame au corps: Arts et sciences 1793–1993,* exhibition catalogue (Paris: Grand Palais, 1993), 342ff.

55
Krause, "Ernst Haeckel," 342ff., with earlier bibliography.

## 2

### Leaves and Flowers

1
Dawn Friedman, "Determination of Spiral Symmetry in Plants and Polymers," in István Hargittai and Clifford A. Pickover, eds., *Spiral Symmetry* (Singapore: World Scientific, 1992, 253; R. V. Jean, *Phyllotaxis: A Systematic Study of Plant Morphogenesis* (Cambridge: Cambridge University Press, 1994), with earlier bibliography; and idem, "On the Origins of Spiral Symmetry in Plants," in Hargittai and Pickover, *Spiral Symmetry,* 323f.

2
Gottfried Gruben, *Die Tempel der Griechen* (Munich: Hirmer, 1986), 140.

3
Hellmut Baumann, *Die griechische Pflanzenwelt in Mythos, Kunst, und Literatur* (Munich: Hirmer, 1982), 188.

4
John Ruskin, *The Seven Lamps of Architecture* (1849; reprint, London: Everyman's Library, 1956), 114.

5
See Enrica Neri Lusanna, "L'atelier del 'Maestro dei mesi' nella scultura medievale della Cattedrale di Ferrara," in *La Cattedrale di Ferrara* (Ferrara: Belriguardo, 1982), 199ff.

6
Alois Riegl's *Stilfragen* is translated by Evelyn Kain as *Problems of Style: Foundations for a History of Ornament* (Princeton: Princeton University Press, 1992); see 267, 302ff., 308, 311ff., 326.

7
Riegl, *Problems of Style,* 229, 234ff.

8
Riegl, *Problems of Style,* 237.

9
Riegl, *Problems of Style,* 238.

10
Jurgis Baltrušaitis, *Le Stylistique ornementale dans la sculpture romane* (Paris: E. Leroux, 1931), 52ff.

11
Elizabeth Lawrence Mendell, *Romanesque Sculpture in Santonge* (New Haven: Yale University Press, 1940), 100ff. See also David Castriota, *The Ara Pacis Augustae and the Imagery of Abundance in Later Greek and Early Roman Imperial Art* (Princeton: Princeton University Press, 1996).

12
Jean, "Spiral Symmetry," 327. See also Stephen A. Wainwright, *Axis and Circumference: The Cylindrical Shape of Plants and Animals* (Cambridge, Mass.: Harvard University Press, 1988).

13
Leonardo da Vinci, *The Literary Works of Leonardo da Vinci,* 2nd ed., enl. and rev. Jean Paul Richter and Irma A. Richter (1939; reprint, New York: Dover, 1970), 1:269.

14
For the Leda, see *Leonardo da Vinci,* exhibition catalogue ([New Haven]: Yale University Press in association
with the South Bank Centre, 1989), nos. 14, 58, 74, 75.

15
For these drawings, see Martin Kemp, "The Vortex," in
*Leonardo da Vinci,* 118ff.

16
Leonardo Fibonacci, *The Book of Squares* (1225), trans.
and ed. L. E. Sigler (Boston: Academic Press, 1987);
Alfred Renyi, *Tagebuch über die Informationstheorie*
(Basel: Birkhaüser, 1982).

17
*The Fibonacci Quarterly,* official journal of the Fibonacci
Association. See also Peter S. Stevens, *Patterns in
Nature* (Boston: Little, Brown, 1974), 159ff.

18
Some of these are explored in Le Corbusier, *Le Modulor:
A Harmonious Measure to the Human Scale Universally
Applicable to Architecture and Mechanics,* 2nd ed.,
trans. Peter de Francia and Anna Bostock (Cambridge,
Mass.: Harvard University Press, 1954).

19
B. Zagorska-Marek, "Phyllotaxis Diversity in Magnolia
Flowers," *Acta Societatis Botanicorum Poloniae* 63, no.
2 (1994), 117ff. Roger V. Jean, studying the arrangement of plant sprouts as they first appear (primordia),
establishes what he calls a phyllotactic fraction. When
such a fraction is $5/13$, for example, it means that 13
sprouts have emerged in a 5-whorled spiral sequence
(*Phyllotaxis,* 118, 155ff.).

20
Jean, *Phyllotaxis,* 265.

21
But see P. I. Wilson, "The Geometry of Golden Section
Phyllotaxis," *Journal of Theoretical Biology* 177, no. 4
(1995), 315ff., and S. Douady and Y. Couder, "Phyllotaxis
as a Dynamical Self-Organization Process," *Journal of
Theoretical Biology* 178, no. 3 (1996), 255ff., 275ff.,
295ff.

22
A. Lima-de-Faria, *Evolution without Selection: Form and
Function by Auto-Evolution* (Amsterdam: Elsevier, 1988),
100. See also A. Remane, *Die Grundlagen des natürlichen Systems der vergleichenden Anatomie und
der Phylogenetik,* 2nd ed. (Leipzig: Akademische

Verlagsgesellschaft Geest und Portig, 1956); Rupert
Riedl, *Order in Living Organisms: A Systems Analysis*
(Chichester: Wiley, 1978), with earlier bibliography.

23
Lima-de-Faria, *Evolution without Selection,* 305ff.

24
Allan Temko, *Eero Saarinen* (New York: Braziller, 1962),
88ff., with earlier bibliography.

25
Karl von Frisch, *Aus dem Leben der Bienen* (Berlin:
Springer, 1953), 159.

## 3
SHELLS

1
D'Arcy Wentworth Thompson, *On Growth and Form,*
complete rev. ed. (1942; reprint, New York: Dover, 1992),
648n.

2
Gert Lindner, *Field Guide to Seashells of the World* (New
York: Van Nostrand Reinhold, 1978), 11ff., and with bib-
liography, 252ff.

3
A. P. P. Bonanni, *Ricreatione dell'occhio e della mente,
nell'osservatione delle chiocciole* (Rome, 1681), discusses
shell geometry. In 1685 appeared the first systematic
modern study of conchology, by Martin Lister, *Historiae
conchyliorum bivalium . . .* (London: sumptibus auctoris impressa, 1696).

4
Thompson, *On Growth and Form,* 754. Thompson
reports that Sir Christopher Wren plotted the equiangular spiral of a snail shell logarithmically (785). But (I will
add) he does not seem to have used such spirals in his
architecture.

5
I thank Michael Frame for help here.

6
Lindner, *Seashells,* color plate 37.12.

7
Lindner, *Seashells,* 28.

8
Theodore Andrea Cook, *Spirals in Art and Nature: A
Study of Spiral Formations Based on the Manuscripts of*

*Leonardo da Vinci, with Special Reference to the Architecture of the Open Staircase at Blois* (London: J. Murray, 1903).

9
For the Palazzo Contarini del Bovolo, see Elena Bassi, *Palazzi di Venezia: Admiranda Urbis Venetiae* (Venice: Stamperia di Venezia, 1976), 32. The stairs, dated before 1500, are thought to be the work of Giovanni Candi.

10
Carlo Pedretti, *Leonardo architetto* (New York: Rizzoli, 1978), 263; Cook, *Spirals.*

11
The smaller chambers have another purpose, too: the animal fills or empties them with gas or fluid so as to adjust its level of buoyancy. See Lindner, *Seashells,* 120.

12
Eugène-Emmanuel Viollet-le-Duc, *Dictionnaire raisonné de l'architecture française du xi au xvi siècle* (Paris: B. Bance, 1861), 5:306. For shells as protective devices, see Lindner, *Seashells,* 19. Not only is the shell itself protective, so are the spines, tubercles (bumps), and lamellae (scales).

13
They are left-handed, however, only because in the original drawing for the etching they were right-handed. The spirals print out as left-handed because prints are mirror images of the drawings on which they are based.

14
See also Norbert Miller, *Archäologie eines Traumes: Versuch über Giovanni Battista Piranesi* (Munich: Hauser, 1979), 384ff. Coleridge's account appears secondhand in Thomas De Quincey's *Confessions of an English Opium-Eater* (1820).

15
Ian Stewart and Martin Golubitsky, *Fearful Symmetry: Is God a Geometer?* (Oxford, Blackwell, 1992). For lattices, see 91ff.; spirals, 138ff.

16
Cf. G. B. Pozzo, *Rules and Examples of Perspective* (London, 1707; originally published Rome, 1693); also Alberto Pérez-Gómez and Louise Pelletier, *Architectural Representation and the Perspective Hinge* (Cambridge, Mass.: MIT Press, 1997). Serlio printed exactly Borromini's coffer pattern, albeit in flattened form, in 1619. Sebastiano Serlio, *Tutte l'opere d'architettura et prospettiva* (1540; reprint, Venice: Giacomo de'

Franceschi, 1619), book 3, 58r. The source is the Early Christian church of Santa Costanza, Rome (misidentified by Serlio as Sant'Agnese fuori le mura).

17
The most recent analysis of the spire is Joseph Connors, "The Spire of Sant'Ivo," *Burlington Magazine* 138 (October 1996), 668ff., with earlier bibliography. For Borromini's own shell collection, see Marcello Del Piazzo, *Ragguagli borrominiani* (Rome: Ministero dell'Interno, 1968), 163ff.; also John Beldon Scott, "Sant'Ivo alla Sapienza and Borromini's Symbolic Language," *Journal of the Society of Architectural Historians* 41 (1982), 310ff., which links the shape of the spire to a shell appropriately called *Mitra papalis.*

18
See R. Mortier and H. Hasquin, eds., *Rocaille, Rococo,* exhibition catalogue, Etudes sur le XVIIIe siècle (Brussels: Ed. de l'Université de Bruxelles, 1991); William Park, *The Idea of the Rococo* (Newark: University of Delaware Press, 1992); Hermann Bauer, *Rocaille: Zur Herkunft und zum Wesen eines Ornament-Motivs* (Berlin: De Gruyter, 1962); and Jonathan Prown and Richard Miller, "The Rococo, the Grotto, and the Philadelphia High Chest," in Luke Beckerdite, ed., *American Furniture 1996* (Hanover, N.H.: Chipstone Foundation, 1996), 105ff.

19
Previous writings (listed in Martin Kemp, *Leonardo da Vinci: The Marvelous Works of Nature and Man,* exhibition catalogue [Cambridge, Mass.: Harvard University Press, 1981], 314ff.), are superseded by Stephen Jay Gould, "Leonardo's Living Earth," *Natural History,* May 1997, 18ff.

20
See *Bernard Palissy, mythe et réalité,* exhibition catalogue (n.p.: Musées d'Agen-Niort-Saintes, 1990), and Leonard Amico, *Bernard Palissy: In Pursuit of the Earthly Paradise* (New York: Flammarion, 1996), both with earlier bibliography.

21
Hugo Schnell et al., *Die Wies: Wallfahrtskirche zum gegeisselten Heiland* (Munich: Schnell und Steiner, 1979).

22
Olaf Lind and Annemarie Lund, *Copenhagen Architecture Guide* (Copenhagen: Arkitektens Forlag, 1996), 138.

23
Tokutoshi Torii, *El mundo enigmático de Gaudí* (Madrid: Instituto de España, 1983), 1:53ff.

24
Clovis Prévost and Robert Ducharnes, *The Artistic Vision of Antonio Gaudí* (New York: Viking, 1971), 145.

25
The other possible sources are the conical towers of Lower Egypt and Pere Joan's altar for the church in Castellón de Ampurias near Gerona. See Torii, *El mundo,* 1:53ff.

26
Lindner, *Seashells,* 17.

27
Julius Posener, *Hans Poelzig: Reflections on His Life and Work* (New York: Architectural History Foundation; Cambridge, Mass.: MIT Press, 1992), 119ff. For true concrete freestanding shells, see Alfred Mehmel, "Eisenbetonhallenbauten," in Deutschen Beton-Verein, ed., *Neues Bauen in Eisenbeton* (Berlin: Zementverlag, 1938), 40ff. That a seashell inspiration might have prompted Poelzig in these concert hall designs is suggested, too, by some shells' age-old associations with sound. Conch shells are often made into trumpets, blown for example by tritons, while their openings, as most children know, resound with the roar of the waves.

## 4

### INSECTS

1
Robert Hooke, *Micrographia, or Some Physiological Descriptions of Minute Bodies Made by Magnifying Glasses . . .* (London: J. Martyn and J. Allestry, 1665); Antoni van Leeuwenhoek, *Anatomia seu interiora rerum . . .* (Leyden: Boutesteyn, 1687). See also Marian Fournier, *The Fabric of Life: Microscopy in the Seventeenth Century* (Baltimore: Johns Hopkins University Press, 1996).

2
"Porphyry: The Cave of the Nymphs in the *Odyssey,*" *Arethusa* 2 (1969), 19.

3
James Gould and Carol Grant Gould, *The Honey Bee* (New York: Scientific American Library, 1995), 3. The Goulds describe the sarcophagi of the first four earls of Southampton, whose honey lasted some 400 years.

4
T. F. Boyds, *The Beasts, Birds, and Bees of Virgil* (Oxford: Oxford University Press, 1914); hives, 61ff.

5
Michael C. J. Putnam, *Virgil's Poem of the Earth: Studies in the Georgics* (Princeton: Princeton University Press, 1979), 241ff.

6
It was not until the observations of Jan Swammerdam in the 1680s that these rulers of the hive were properly identified as queens, not kings. Jan Swammerdam, *The Book of Nature; or, the History of Insects . . .* (London: Seyffert, 1748), 159ff.

7
Milton does the same in *Paradise Lost* 1.772.

8
Gino Scarfone, "Ex-Voto borrominiane (?) nella basilica di San Pietro in Vaticano," *Strenna dei romanisti,* 1977, 372ff.; Francis Haskell, *Patrons and Painters: Art and Society in Baroque Italy* (New Haven: Yale University Press, 1980), 24ff.; Philipp Fehl, "The *Stemme* on Bernini's Baldacchino," *Burlington Magazine* 98 (1976), 484ff.; Howard McP. Davis, "Bees on the Tomb of Urban VIII," *Source: Notes on the History of Art,* nos. 8–9 (Fall 1989), 40ff.; and John Beldon Scott, *Images of Nepotism: The Painted Ceilings of the Palazzo Barberini* (Princeton: Princeton University Press, 1991).

9
Joseph Connors, "S. Ivo alla Sapienza: The First Three Minutes," *Journal of the Society of Architectural Historians* 55 (1996), 38ff., with full earlier bibliography. For the question of the bee plan, see 49ff.

10
See Karl von Frisch, *Aus dem Leben der Bienen* (Berlin: Springer, 1953), and Mark L. Winston, *Biology of the Honey Bee* (Cambridge, Mass.: Harvard University Press, 1987), 72ff. Also see Ilkka Teräs, "Bee and Wasp Cells," in *Animal Architecture,* exhibition catalogue (Helsinki: Museum of Finnish Architecture, 1995), 101ff.

11
Winston, *Honey Bee,* 72ff.

12
Giovanni Battista Ferrari, *Flos, seu De florum cultura,* new ed. (Amsterdam: Johannes Janson, 1646), pl. 25. (First published Rome, 1633.)

**13**
Richard Joncas, "Pedagogy and 'Reflex': Frank Lloyd Wright's Hanna House Revisited," *Journal of the Society of Architectural Historians* 52 (1993), 319.

**14**
Wright's first design for a hexagonal building seems to have been the floating summerhouse for Lake Tahoe, California, of 1922. Anthony Alofsin, *Frank Lloyd Wright: The Lost Years, 1910–1922* (Chicago: University of Chicago Press, 1993), fig. 294, 285ff.; Joncas, "Pedagogy and 'Reflex,'" with earlier bibliography.

**15**
Wright is quoted by Joncas, "Pedagogy and 'Reflex,'" 319.

**16**
For the history and influence of the Dymaxion House, see Richard Buckminster Fuller and Robert W. Marks, *The Dymaxion World of Buckminster Fuller* (New York: Anchor Books, 1973).

**17**
Note the erasures in the rendering, which show either that this spire was to have been located elsewhere or that there were to be more than one. In another of the drawings the spire is labeled "carillon and television."

**18**
Johannes Kepler, *On the Six-Cornered Snowflake* (1611), ed. L. L. Whyte (Oxford: Clarendon Press, 1966), 9, makes more or less the same observation.

**19**
D'Arcy Wentworth Thompson, *On Growth and Form,* complete rev. ed. (1942; reprint, New York: Dover, 1992), 526ff. But see also L. Fejes Tóth, "What the Bees Know and What They Do Not Know," *Bulletin of the American Mathematical Society* 70 (1964), 468ff.

**20**
Thompson, *On Growth and Form,* 525ff. Swammerdam, *The Book of Nature,* pl. 23, also publishes these observations.

**21**
Arthur Evans, *The Shaft Graves and Bee-Hive Tombs of Mycenae and Their Interrelation* (London: Macmillan, 1929); he doesn't explain his term.

**22**
Rowland J. Mainstone, *Developments in Structural Form* (Cambridge, Mass.: MIT Press, 1983), fig. 7.17, 123ff. See also Howard Saalman, *Filippo Brunelleschi: The Cupola of Santa Maria del Fiore* (London: Zwemmer, 1980), 71, and Robert Mark and E. C. Robison, "Vaults and Domes," in Robert Mark, ed., *Architectural Technology up to the Scientific Revolution* (Cambridge, Mass.: MIT Press, 1993), 169ff.

**23**
That is the ratio in the executed building. Saalman, *Cupola,* 71, says "4/5" but that is clearly impossible.

**24**
Giorgio Vasari, *The Lives of the Painters, Sculptors, and Architects* (1550), trans. A. B. Hinds (1927; reprint, London: Dent, 1980), 1:288ff.

**25**
J. G. Wood, *Homes without Hands* (New York: Harper and Brothers, 1866), 144, 147.

**26**
Bert Hölldobler and E. O. Wilson, *Journey to the Ants* (Cambridge, Mass.: Harvard University Press, 1994), 130. For the mounds of the wood ants, see 193.

On the development of human territoriality, see e.g. Peter J. Wilson, *The Domestication of the Human Species* (New Haven: Yale University Press, 1988).

**27**
See Hölldobler and Wilson, *Journey to the Ants,* 2–3. One could argue that the pyramid illustrated does not look today as it originally did, for it was built flat-sided. But even so we could still call the pyramid a squared-off, smooth-sided anthill at human scale. The anthills, like the pyramids, were designed to have hard, smooth cladding.

**28**
Karl von Frisch, with the collaboration of Otto von Frisch, *Animal Architecture,* trans. Lisbeth Gombrich (New York: Harcourt Brace Jovanovich, 1974), 129, 149. In Harare, Zimbabwe, Mick Pearce of Pearce Partnership Architects has designed an office building complex, Eastgate, that without air conditioning and central heating borrows its forced-draft temperature control from the termitary (Donald G. McNeil, Jr., "In Africa, Making Offices out of an Anthill," *New York Times,* 13 February 1997, C4).

**29**
Jules Michelet, *The Insect* (London: T. Nelson, 1883), 238ff. The first edition was published (in French) in 1858.

30
Terence Riley, ed., *Frank Lloyd Wright, Architect,* exhibition catalogue (New York: Museum of Modern Art, 1994), 281; Neil Levine, *The Architecture of Frank Lloyd Wright* (Princeton: Princeton University Press, 1996).

31
Von Frisch, *Animal Architecture,* 148ff.

# 5
BIRDS

1
See now Kevin Padian and Luis M. Chiappe, "The Origin of Birds and Their Flight," *Scientific American,* February 1998, 38ff., as well as P. Altangerel, M. A. Norell, L. M. Chiappe, and J. M. Clark, "Flightless Bird from the Cretaceous of Mongolia . . . ," *Nature* 362, no. 6241 (1993), 623ff. See also Edwin Harris Colbert, *A Primitive Ornithischian Dinosaur from the Kayenta Formation of Arizona* (Flagstaff: Museum of Northern Arizona Press, 1981), and M. A. Norell, J. M. Clark, L. M. Chiappe, and D. Dashzeveg, "A Nesting Dinosaur," *Nature* 378, no. 6559 (1995), 774ff.

2
D'Arcy Wentworth Thompson, *On Growth and Form,* complete rev. ed. (1942; reprint, New York: Dover, 1992), 1006.

3
See now Henry Petroski, *Engineers of Dreams: Great Bridge Builders and the Spanning of America* (New York: Knopf, 1995), 234, 244, 254. For mammal skeletons as bridges, see also William K. Gregory, "The Bridge-That-Walks," *Natural History* 46 (1937), 33ff.

4
Karl von Frisch, with the collaboration of Otto von Frisch, *Animal Architecture,* trans. Lisbeth Gombrich (New York: Harcourt Brace Jovanovich, 1974), 210.

5
David Hancocks, *Master Builders of the Animal World* (New York: Harper and Row, 1973), 17.

6
Harry Francis Mallgrave, *Gottfried Semper: Architect of the Nineteenth Century* (New Haven: Yale University Press, 1996), 290ff.

7
Indra Kagis McEwen, "Instrumentality and the Organic Assistance of Looms," *Chora* 1 (1994), 124ff., and esp. 134ff.

8
Jared Diamond, *The Third Chimpanzee: The Evolution and Future of the Human Animal* (New York: HarperCollins, 1992), 173.

9
Paul A. Johnsgard, *Arena Birds: Sexual Selection and Behavior* (Washington, D.C.: Smithsonian Institution Press, 1994), 213.

10
Johnsgard, *Arena Birds,* 215.

11
Johnsgard, *Arena Birds,* 204ff. See also G. Borgia, "Bower Quality, Number of Decorations, and Mating Success of the Male Satin Bowerbirds (*Ptilonorynchus violaceus*): An Experimental Analysis," *Animal Behaviour* 33 (1985), 266ff., and idem, "Bower Destruction and Sexual Competition in the Satin Bowerbird (*Ptilonorynchus violaceus*)," *Behavioral Ecology and Sociobiology* 18 (1985), 91ff. Also Jared Diamond, "Bower Building and Decoration by the Bowerbird *Amblyornis inornatus*," *Ethology* 74 (1987), 177ff.

12
Von Frisch, *Animal Architecture,* 238.

13
Johnsgard, *Arena Birds,* 209.

14
Diamond, "Bower Building," 177ff.

15
Charles Darwin, *The Descent of Man and Selection in Relation to Sex* (1871), in *The Works of Charles Darwin,* ed. Paul H. Barrett and R. B. Freeman (New York: New York University Press, 1989), 22:395. For a recent description of these dances, see Johnsgard, *Arena Birds,* 221, and Diamond, *Third Chimpanzee,* 173ff.

16
Indra Kagis McEwen, *Socrates' Ancestor: An Essay on Architectural Beginnings* (Cambridge, Mass.: MIT Press, 1991).

17
Von Frisch, *Animal Architecture,* 202. Johnsgard, *Arena Birds,* gives several other examples of bird species in

which the males build or adapt theaters for their seduction dances (pp. 141ff., 152ff.). Other species of birds, such as the sociable weaver and the mallee fowl, engage in similar sexually selective building activities.

18
Johnsgard, *Arena Birds,* 228, paraphrasing D. W. Frith and C. B. Frith, "Courtship Display and Mating of the Superb Bird of Paradise *Lophorina superba,*" *Emu* 88 (1988), 183ff.

19
Johnsgard, *Arena Birds,* 132.

20
In the museum at Perge, Greece, is an ancient Greek relief representing a tympanum with a trophy to a slain warrior in the foreground. An eagle perches on the dead man's shield, its spread wings filling the tympanum's upper triangle. On Korkyra, see Manfred Gruben, *Die Tempel der Griechen* (Munich: Hirmer, 1986), 108ff.

21
Mrs. [Anna] Jameson, *Legends of the Monastic Orders as Represented in the Fine Arts* (New York: Longmans, Green, 1900), 261ff. For Gaudí in these respects, see Tokutoshi Torii, *El mundo enigmático de Gaudí* (Madrid: Instituto de España, 1983), vol. 1, passim.

22
Full bibliography on bird architecture is in Peter Nabokov and Robert Easton, *Native American Architecture* (New York: Oxford University Press, 1989), 226ff. See also Aldona Jonaitis, *From the Land of the Totem Poles: The Northwest Coast Indian Art Collection at the American Museum of Natural History* (New York: American Museum of Natural History; Seattle: University of Washington Press, 1989).

23
Nabokov and Easton, *Native American Architecture,* 226ff. See also Marius Barbeau, *Totem Poles According to Crests and Topics* (1950; reprint, Hull, Quebec: Canadian Museum of Civilization, 1990).

24
Franz Boas, "The Decorative Art of the Indians of the North Pacific Coast," *Bulletin of the American Museum of Natural History* 9 (1897), 123ff., 144ff.

25
Claude Lévi-Strauss, *The Way of the Masks,* trans. Sylvia Modleski (Seattle: University of Washington Press, 1988).

# 6
## MAMMALS: TERRITORY AND REPRODUCTIVE RIGHTS

1
Marius Barbeau, *Totem Poles According to Crests and Topics* (1950; reprint, Hull, Quebec: Canadian Museum of Civilization, 1990), passim.

2
John Bettum, "An Evolutionary Architecture," *AA Files,* no. 30 (Autumn 1995), 70ff. See also introduction, note 1.

3
Irenäus Eibl-Eibesfeldt and Christa Sütterlin, *Im Banne der Angst: zur Natur- und Kunstgeschichte menschlicher Abwehrsymbolik* (Munich: Piper, 1992); Irenäus Eibl-Eibesfeldt, "The Biological Foundation of Aesthetics," in Ingo Rentscher, Barbara Hertzberger, and David Epstein, eds., *Beauty and the Brain: Biological Aspects of Aesthetics* (Basel: Birkhaüser, 1989), 19ff.

4
Here I draw on J. G. Fleagle, *Primate Adaptation and Evolution* (San Diego: Academic Press, 1988).

5
Some of these ideas, as they affect human architecture, are trenchantly developed in Aaron Betsky, *Building Sex: Men, Women, Architecture, and the Construction of Sexuality* (New York: Morrow, 1995).

6
Peter J. Wilson, *The Domestication of the Human Species* (New Haven: Yale University Press, 1988), 29.

7
Tim Ingold, "Territoriality and Tenure: The Appropriation of Space in Hunting and Gathering Societies," paper presented at the Third Annual International Conference on Hunter-Gatherers, Bad Homburg, West Germany, 1983, 21.

8
Walter Burkert, *Creation of the Sacred: Tracks of Biology in Early Religions* (Cambridge, Mass.: Harvard University Press, 1996), 165ff.

9
Jay Appleton, *The Experience of Landscape,* rev. ed. (Chichester: Wiley, 1996); idem, *The Symbolism of Habitat: An Interpretation of Landscape and the Arts* (Seattle: University of Washington Press, 1990). See also the essays in Jerome H. Barkow, Leda Cosmides, and John Tooby, eds., *The Adapted Mind* (Oxford: Oxford

196

University Press, 1992), passim, especially Gordon H. Orions and Judith Heerwagen, "Evolved Responses to Landscape," 555ff.

10

W. D. Hamilton, "Geometry for the Selfish Herd," *Journal of Theoretical Biology* 31 (1971), 295ff.

11

David Solkin, *Richard Wilson and the Landscape of Reaction,* exhibition catalogue (London: Tate Gallery, 1982). Other recent writings in this vein are Chris Fitter, *Poetry, Space, Landscape: Toward a New Theory* (Cambridge: Cambridge University Press, 1995); W. J. T. Mitchell, ed., *Landscape and Power* (Chicago: University of Chicago Press, 1994); and Eric Hirsch and Michael O'Hanlon, eds., *The Anthropology of Landscape: Perspectives on Place and Space* (Oxford: Clarendon Press, 1995).

12

Appleton, *Experience of Landscape,* 64.

13

See *Antelopes: Global Survey and Regional Action Plans* (Gland, Switzerland: IUCN, 1988–). For the animal capitals, see Donald Wilber, *Persepolis: The Archaeology of Parsa, Seat of the Persian Kings,* rev. ed. (Princeton: Darwin Press, 1989), 40ff.

14

François de Polignac, *Cults, Territory, and the Origin of the Greek City-State* (Chicago: University of Chicago Press, 1995), esp. 33ff.

15

Polignac, *Cults,* 144, 149.

16

Wilson, *Domestication,* 67ff.

17

See William M. Krogman, "The Scars of Human Evolution," *Scientific American,* December 1951, 54ff. I thank Jonathan Marks for this reference.

18

Wilhelm Heinrich Roscher, ed., *Ausführliches Lexikon der griechischen und römischen Mythologie,* 6 vols. (Leipzig: Teubner, 1884–1937), s.v. "Helios," col. 2012. Herbert Maryon, "The Colossus of Rhodes," *Journal of the Hellenic Society* 76 (1956), 68ff., restores the figure as an unarmed nude looking out to sea, shielding his gaze with his right hand. He does not bestride the harbor

entrance. This conjecture is based on an existing ancient relief fragment said to depict the colossus.

19

Barbara Mikoda-Hüttel, "Der Colossus der Fischer von Erlach auf dem Hohern Markt zu Wien: Ein Beitrag zur Entwurfs- und Planungsgeschichte," in Friedrich Polleross, ed., *Fischer von Erlach und der Wiener Barocktradition* (Cologne: Böhlau, 1955).

20

That the Statue of Liberty was seen as a second colossus of Rhodes is made clear by Lazarus's poem, "The New Colossus," inscribed at the entrance to the pedestal.

21

Dirk Hoerder and Horst Rässler, eds., *Distant Magnets: Expectations and Realities in the Immigrant Experience, 1840–1930* (New York: Holmes and Meier, 1993), 211ff.

22

Pointed out by Marvin Trachtenberg, *The Statue of Liberty* (New York: Penguin Books, 1977), 196.

23

Strabo, Pliny, and Plutarch tell other versions of the story. See *Paulys Realencyclopädie der classischen Altertumswissenschaft,* s.v. "Deinokrates." See also Werner Oechslin, "Dinokrates-legende und Mythos megalomaner Architekturstiftung," *Daidalos,* no. 47–26 (June 1982), 7ff. (the best thing ever written on Deinocrates), and Simon Schama's extraordinary "Dinocrates and the Shaman" in his *Landscape and Memory* (New York: Knopf, 1995), 385ff.

24

Francesco di Giorgio Martini, *Trattati di architettura ingegneria e arte militare,* ed. C. Maltese (Milan: Polifilo, 1967), 362. In 1672 Michel Anguier revived this idea in a lecture for the French Academy titled "The Human Body, Represented as a Strong Citadel," printed in André Fontaine, ed., *Conférances inédites de l'Académie royale de peinture et de sculpture* (Paris: Fontemoing, 1903), 152ff. The teeth are guard towers, the tongue the long-robed keeper of the library (the brain), the eyes windows, the ears portals, etc.

25

Rudolf Wittkower, "A Counter-Project to Bernini's Piazza di San Pietro," *Journal of the Warburg and Courtauld Institutes* 8 (1939–1940), 88ff.; reprinted in idem, *Studies in the Italian Baroque* (London: Thames and Hudson, 1975), 61ff.

26
Bernini is quoted by Timothy K. Kitao, *Circle and Oval in the Square of St. Peter's: Bernini's Art of Planning* (New York: New York University Press for the College Art Association of America, 1974), 90 n. 40.

27
Paul Fréart de Chantelou, *Journal du voyage en France du Chevalier Bernin par Chantelou* (Paris: Stock: 1930), 58f.

28
Howard Morphy, *Ancestral Connections: Art and an Aboriginal System of Knowledge* (Chicago: University of Chicago Press, 1991), 233ff.; Christopher Tilley, *A Phenomenology of Landscape: Places, Paths, and Monuments* (Oxford: Berg, 1994), 35ff.

29
R. Porro, in *L'Architecture d'Aujourd'hui* 41 (1970), 84. For a stimulating interpretation of cities as living human-like bodies, with circulatory systems, traffic management, etc., see Richard Sennett, *Flesh and Stone: The Body and the City in Western Civilization* (New York: Norton, 1994).

30
Wilson, *Domestication,* 157ff.

31
The eastern and southern ranges of the main inner square, which would have completed the complex, remained unbuilt. See L. M. Delaporte, *Voyage au Cambodge: L'Architecture Khmer* (Paris: C. Delagrave, 1880).

32
For mandala plans in Cambodia, see Eleanor Mannikka, *Angkor Wat: Time, Space, and Kingship* (Honolulu: University of Hawai'i Press, 1996), 55ff. Hindus also saw the earth itself as a colossal recumbent god or goddess. See David Smith, *The Dance of Shiva: Religion, Art, and Poetry in South India* (Cambridge: Cambridge University Press, 1996), 81, 97.

33
Pre Rup's symmetry is, however, marred by the unequal number of small temples just behind the main gate (lower part of plan) and by the high placement of the lateral axis and its buildings.

34
See Udo Kultermann, "Die himmlische Stadt Ch'ang-an," *Die alte Stadt,* January 1993. Also Nancy Steinhardt,

*Chinese Imperial City Planning* (Honolulu: University of Hawai'i Press, 1990), 4ff., with earlier bibliography.

35
The inscription is quoted in Jean Vassiliou, *Angkor,* trans. Maximo Portassi (Paris: Morancé, 1971), 136.

# 7
## PENIS PARADIGMS

1
A. Lima-de-Faria, *Evolution without Selection: Form and Function by Autoevolution* (Amsterdam: Elzevier, 1988), 225. See also R. Robin Baker and Mark A. Bellis, *Human Sperm Competition* (London: Chapman and Hall, 1995), 34 and passim.

2
William G. Eberhard, *Sexual Selection and Animal Genitalia* (Cambridge, Mass.: Harvard University Press, 1985), passim; see also idem, *Female Control: Sexual Selection by Cryptic Female Choice* (Princeton: Princeton University Press, 1996), 349ff.; Baker and Bellis, *Sperm Competition,* 168, 174.

3
But larger penises have not always been considered attractive. Aristophanes, *Clouds* 1011–1013, contrasts the warriors of Marathon ("big-assed and small-pricked") with degenerate contemporary Athenians ("small-assed and huge-pricked"). I thank Andrew Stewart for the reference.

4
Richard Payne Knight, *A Discourse on the Worship of Priapus* . . . (1786) (Secaucus, N.J.: University Books, 1974), 67ff.

5
See Simon Schama, *Landscape and Memory* (New York: Knopf, 1995), 252ff.

6
Dolores Hayden, "Skyscraper Seduction, Skyscraper Rape," *Heresies* 2 (May 1977), 108ff., with earlier bibliography; for Trump, see Robin Pogrebin, "52-Story Comeback Is So Very Trump," *New York Times,* 25 April 1996, B4. For penis lore, see Kit Schwartz, *The Male Member* (New York: St. Martin's, 1985).

7
Jutta Gassner, *Phallos: Fruchtbarkeitssymbol oder*

198

*Abwehrzauber?* (Vienna: Böhlau, 1993), with earlier bibliography.

8

John Boardman and Eugenio La Rocca, *Eros in Greece* (London: Murray, 1978).

9

There were other penis-gods—Phallos, Ithyphallos, Min (an Egyptian), Mutinus, and Pan among them. See Hans Herter, *De Priapo,* Religionsgeschichtliche Versuche und Vorarbeiten 23 (Giessen: A. Topelmann, 1932), 13ff.

10

Gassner, *Phallos,* 76ff.; Dietrich Drost, "Tönerne Dachaufsätze in Afrika," *Jahrbuch des Museums für Völkerkunde zu Leipzig* (Berlin DDR) 15 (1956, 1957).

11

Adolf E. Jensen, "Die Banna/Die Hammar," in Ad. E. Jensen, ed., *Altvölker Südäthiopiens* (Stuttgart: W. Kohlhammer, 1959), 313ff. For the penis as a weapon and, alternatively, as a boundary marker, see Wolfgang Wickler, "Ursprung und biologische Deutung des Genitalpräsentierens männlicher Primaten," *Zeitschrift für Tierpsychologie* 23 (1966), 422ff.; idem, "Socio-Sexual Signals and Their Intraspecific Imitation among Primates," in Desmond Morris, ed., *Primate Ethology* (Chicago: Aldine Publishing, 1967), 89ff.; and idem, *The Sexual Code* (Garden City, N.Y.: Doubleday, 1972), with bibliography.

12

Paraphrased from Robin Baker, *Sperm Wars: The Science of Sex* (New York: Basic Books, 1996), 41.

13

For the importance of sperm size, see Baker and Bellis, *Sperm Competition,* 23ff.

14

Scott Pitnick et al., "How Long Is a Giant Sperm?" *Nature,* 11 May 1995, 109.

15

A. F. Dixson, "Observations on the Evolution of the Genitalia and Copulatory Behaviour in Male Primates," *Journal of Zoology* 213 (1978), 423ff.

16

See now Clara Pinto-Correia, *The Ovary of Eve: Egg and Sperm and Preformation* (Chicago: University of Chicago Press, 1997), esp. 211ff.

17

Correia-Pinto, *Ovary of Eve,* 103.

18

Felix Cleve, *The Giants of Pre-Sophistic Greek Philosophy* (The Hague: Nijhoff, 1969), 1, xxix. Antoni van Leeuwenhoek, *Anatomia seu interiora rerum . . .* (Leyden: Boutesteyn, 1687), 175, however, denies that he personally ever saw preformed humans in sperm, a misconception he attributes to one Cornelius Boutekoe.

19

Chonosoke Okamura of the Okamura Fossil Laboratory in Nagoya, Japan, an Ig-Nobel laureate, claims to have discovered microscopic fossils of princesses, dragons, and a thousand other extinct homunculi and animalculi. See *Scientific American,* December 1996, 32.

20

Hans Herter's article "Phallos" in *Paulys Realencyclopädie der classischen Altertumswissenschaft* is still the best essay on these.

21

*Inscriptiones graecae* 2.45.13; Herodotus 2.48, 49; Aristophanes, *Acharnians* 243. At a temple of Bacchus described by Lucian (*Dea Syria* 16.28.9) there were two large columns shaped like penises outside the gate, identified as those of the god. At certain seasons men climbed up and meditated on their glanses. One thinks once again of homunculi.

22

Vincenzo Re, *Narrazione delle solenni reali feste fatte celebrare in Napoli da Sua Maestà il re delle Due Sicilie, infante di Spagna . . .* (Naples, 1749), 14ff.

23

Knight, *Priapus,* 5ff. See also Gassner, *Phallos,* 60.

24

Ledoux made two such projects, one of them for a site on Montmartre in Paris. See Anthony Vidler, *Claude-Nicolas Ledoux* (Cambridge, Mass.: MIT Press, 1990), 8, 244, 356ff.

25

Claude-Nicolas Ledoux, *L'Architecture considérée sous le rapport de l'art, des moeurs, et de la législation* (1804; reprint, Paris, 1847), 2: pls. 238–241.

26

Erik Iversen, *Obelisks in Exile* (Copenhagen: Gad, 1968), 1:16ff., with earlier bibliography.

27
R. B. Onians, *The Origins of European Thought about the Body, the Mind, the Soul, the World, Time, and Fate* (1951; reprint, Cambridge: Cambridge University Press, 1988), 109 n. 2.

28
Horst Beinlich, *Die "Osirisreliquien": zum Motiv der Körperzergliederung in der Altägyptischen Religion* (Wiesbaden: Harrassowitz, 1984), 22off. See also John Gwyn Griffiths, *The Origins of Osiris and His Cult* (Leiden: Brill, 1980); Walter Burkert, *Ancient Mystery Cults* (Cambridge, Mass.: Harvard University Press, 1987), 82ff.

29
Labib Habachi, *The Obelisks of Egypt* (New York: Scribner's, 1977); E. A. Wallis Budge, *Cleopatra's Needles and Other Egyptian Obelisks* (1926; reprint, New York: Dover, 1990), 21ff., 100ff., 112, 260.

30
James P. Allen, personal communication, 1997. See also Henri Frankfort, *Kingship and the Gods: A Study of Ancient Near Eastern Religion as the Integration of Society and Nature* (Chicago: University of Chicago Press, 1948), 153.

31
Frankfort, *Kingship,* 66, 156, fig. 35.

32
Allen, personal communication.

33
Pinto-Correia, *Ovary of Eve,* 83.

34
Allen, personal communication.

35
Frankfort, *Kingship,* 169; Wickler, *Sexual Code,* passim. For the sperm-competitive basis of such ideas, see Baker and Bellis, *Sperm Competition,* 19ff.

36
This discussion of the obelisks of Rome rests on Michele Mercati, *Gli obelischi di Roma* (1589), ed. Gianfranco Centelli (Bologna: Cappelli, 1981), esp. 94. See also Schama, *Landscape and Memory,* 282ff.

37
Iversen, *Obelisks,* 1:65ff.

38
Stefano De Fiores and Salvatore Meo, eds., *Nuovo dizionario de mariologia* (Milan: Edizioni paoline, 1985), 687; Roberto Luciani, *Santa Maria dei Miracoli e Santa Maria di Montesanto* (Rome: Fratelli Palumbo, 1990); and Daniela del Pesco, *L'Architettura del Seicento* (Turin: UTET, 1998), 88ff.

39
Iversen, *Obelisks,* 1:65ff. For the seed cults of the Immaculate Conception, see de Fiores and Meo, *Dizionario,* 1114ff.

40
Iversen, *Obelisks,* 1:76ff.

41
Norbert Huse, "La Fontaine des Fleuves du Bernin," *Revue de l'art* 7 (1970), 6ff.; R. Preimesberger, "Obeliskus Pamphilius," *Münchner Jahrbuch der Bildenden Künste* [or *für Kunstgeschichte*] (1974), 77ff.; T. A. Marder, *Bernini and the Art of Architecture* (New York: Abbeville, 1998), 93ff.

42
Habachi, *Obelisks,* 11.

43
Iversen, *Obelisks,* 1:19ff.

44
The best book on skyscraper anatomy as engineering is Karl Sabbagh, *Skyscraper* (London: Macmillan, 1989), a blow-by-blow account of the design and construction of Skidmore, Owings, and Merrill's Worldwide Plaza, New York, 1989. (Sabbagh does not, however, make the penis comparison.)

45
Frederick C. Luebke, ed., *A Harmony of the Arts: The Nebraska State Capitol* (Lincoln: University of Nebraska Press, 1990). For Lee Lawrie, see 49ff.

46
Baker, *Sperm Wars,* 79.

47
Richard H. Davis, *Ritual in an Oscillating Universe: Worshipping Shiva in Medieval India* (Princeton: Princeton University Press, 1991), 123, 149; David Smith, *The Dance of Shiva: Religion, Art, and Ritual in South India* (Cambridge: Cambridge University Press, 1996), 72.

48
Andreas Volwahsen, *Living Architecture: Indian* (New

York: Grosset and Dunlap, 1969), 43ff.; T. A. Gopinatha Rao, *Elements of Hindu Iconography,* 2nd ed. (Varanasi: Indological Book House, 1971), 2:75ff. (on lingas). See also Stella Kramrisch, *Manifestations of Shiva,* exhibition catalogue (Philadelphia: Philadelphia Museum of Art, 1981).

49
Volwahsen, *Living Architecture,* 44.

50
Davis, *Ritual,* 119.

51
Volwahsen, *Living Architecture,* 51.

52
Davis, *Ritual,* 60.

53
Wendy Doniger O'Flaherty, *Asceticism and Eroticism in the Mythology of Shiva* (London: Oxford University Press, 1973), 256ff., 90ff.

54
See Gritli von Mitterwallner, "Evolution of the Linga," in Michael W. Meister, ed., *Discourses on Siva: Proceedings of a Symposium on the Nature of Religious Imagery* (Philadelphia: University of Pennsylvania Press, 1984), 12ff., with earlier bibliography; I. Karthikeye Sarma, "New Light on Art through Archaeological Conservation," *Journal of the Indian Society of Oriental Art,* n.s. 10 (1978–1979), 50ff.; and idem, *Parasuramesvara Temple at Gudmallam: A Probe into Its Origins* (Nagpur: Dattsuns, 1994). I am grateful to Professor Phillip Wagoner for these references.

55
O'Flaherty, *Asceticism and Eroticism,* 144. Or he could be Death, on whom Shiva tramples when he bursts from his linga; see Smith, *Dance of Shiva,* 201.

56
Davis, *Ritual,* 4ff., on the great temple of Rajaraja in Thanjavur, erected beginning in 1003, which had one of the largest lingas in existence.

57
Devangana Desai, *Erotic Sculpture of India: A Socio-Cultural Study* (New Delhi: Tata McGraw-Hill, 1975), 114.

58
O'Flaherty, *Asceticism and Eroticism,* 131. See also Smith, *Dance of Shiva,* 67.

59
O'Flaherty, *Asceticism and Eroticism,* 256ff.

60
E.g., see John Noble Wilford, "Scientists Use Radar to Chart Cambodia's Ancient Ruins," *New York Times,* 13 February 1998, A6.

61
Jacques Dumarçay, *Le Bayon: Histoire architecturale du temple* (Paris, 1967–), and Jean Vassiliou, *Angkor,* trans. Maximo Portassi (Paris: Morancé, 1971), 139ff.

62
Davis, *Ritual,* 120.

63
O'Flaherty, *Asceticism and Eroticism,* 11. In some mukhalingas the head is not Shiva's but Brahma's, cut off by Shiva (Brahma, however, had other heads); Smith, *Dance of Shiva,* 89, 95.

64
Bodo Ebhardt, *Die Bürgen Italiens,* 6 vols. (Berlin: Wasmuth, 1907–1927).

65
For Northwest Coast marriage and birth totemism, see Franz Boas, *Contributions to the Ethnology of the Kwakiutl* (New York: Columbia University Press, 1925), 56ff. (inheritance), 112ff. (newborns), 236ff. (marriage).

66
Rosa Maria Malet, *Joan Miró* (New York: Rizzoli, 1983), 29ff., and figs. 117, 128, 141 (*Woman and Bird*).

# 8

## THE FEMALE GENITAL PALACE

1
De la Valle Poussin, "Buddhist Tantrism," in *Encyclopedia of Religion and Ethics,* 12:196.

2
André Leroi-Gourhan, *L'Art pariétal: Langage de la préhistoire* (Grenoble: Millon, 1992), especialy the article by Marc Groenen, "L'Art pariétal: Un art structuré," 92ff., and, by Leroi-Gourhan, "La Caverne," 197ff., esp. 364ff.

3
Jean-Marie Chauvet, Eliette Brunel Deschamps, and Christian Hillaire, *La Grotte Chauvet à Vallon-Pont-d'Arc* (Paris: Seuil, 1995).

4
For the most recent studies on the value of complexity in the female genital architecture, see William G. Eberhard, *Female Control: Sexual Selection and Cryptic Female Choice* (Princeton: Princeton University Press, 1996), esp. 5ff., 37ff., and Robin Baker, *Sperm Wars: The Science of Sex* (New York: Basic Books, 1996). The best account of the analogies I make in this chapter between eggs, breasts, and various artificial extended phenotypes is in Clara Pinto-Correia, *The Ovary of Eve: Egg and Sperm and Preformation* (Chicago: University of Chicago Press, 1997). As to eggs being the source of all things, notice the frontispiece of William Harvey's *Exercitationes de generatione animalium* (1651), which shows Zeus liberating all living things from a single egg (Pinto-Correia, 2).

5
Vassos Karageorghis, *Cyprus from the Stone Age to the Romans* (London: Thames and Hudson, 1982), 33ff., with earlier bibliography.

6
Aubrey Burl, *Rings of Stone: The Prehistoric Stone Circles of Britain and Ireland* (New Haven: Ticknor and Fields, 1979), 268ff., with earlier bibliography.

7
Jan Assmann, "Death and Initiation in the Funerary Religion of Ancient Egypt," in William Kelly Simpson, ed., *Religion and Philosophy in Ancient Egypt* (New Haven: Yale Egyptological Seminar, Department of Near Eastern Languages and Civilizations, The Graduate School, Yale University, 1989), esp. 137ff.

8
James P. Allen, "The Cosmology of the Pyramid Texts," in Simpson, *Religion and Philosophy,* 1ff., and esp. 26.

9
James P. Allen, personal communication, 1997.

10
Text quoted by Allen, "Cosmology," 20.

11
David S. Goodsell, *Our Molecular Nature: The Body's Motors, Machines, and Messages* (New York: Copernicus, 1996), 107.

12
Baker, *Sperm Wars,* 29.

13
R. Robin Baker and Mark A. Bellis, *Human Sperm Competition* (London: Chapman and Hall, 1995), 38ff., 71ff.

14
See bibliography above in chapter 3, note 18. Also Jan Swammerdam, *Miraculum naturae . . .* (London: Sollers, 1680) (on the uterus).

15
See Rem Koolhaas, *Delirious New York* (New York: Oxford University Press, 1978), 68ff., quotation, 98.

16
See Catharine Johns, *Sex or Symbol? Erotic Images of Greece and Rome* (Austin: University of Texas Press, 1982), figs. 10, 11, color plate 13, figs. 51, 55, etc. See also, in this book, the phalloi that are composed of tight-packed vulvas.

17
Sanjukta Gupta, Dirk Jan Hoens, and Teun Goudriaan, *Hindu Tantrism* (Leiden: Brill, 1979); Philip Rawson, *Tantra: The Indian Cult of Ecstasy* (Greenwich, Conn.: New York Graphic Society, 1973); Douglas Renfrew Brooks, *The Secret of the Three Cities: An Introduction to Hindu Sakta Tantrism* (Chicago: University of Chicago Press, 1990), 69ff.

18
Helmut Uhlig, *Tantrische Kunst des Buddhismus* (Berlin: Kunstamt Berlin-Tempelhof, 1981).

19
Richard H. Davis, *Ritual in an Oscillating Universe: Worshiping Shiva in Medieval India* (Princeton: Princeton University Press, 1991), 63. For more on Hindu erotic art, see Devangana Desai, *Erotic Sculpture of India: A Socio-Cultural Study* (New Delhi: Tata McGraw-Hill, 1975); Gerd Kreisel, *Die Siva-Bildwerke der Mathura-Kunst* (Stuttgart: F. Steiner, 1986), 44ff. (on lingas and yonis); Lakshinarayana Pacauri, *The Erotic Sculpture of Khajuraho* (Calcutta: Naya Prokash, 1989); Mulk Raj Anand, *Homage to Khajuraho* (Bombay: Marg Publications, 1962).

20
George Michell, *The Hindu Temple: An Introduction to Its Meaning and Forms* (1977; reprint, Chicago, 1988), 24, with earlier bibliography. For *bodhichitta,* see Desai, *Erotic Sculpture,* 114.

21
Desai, *Erotic Sculpture,* 40ff.; Eliky Zannas and Jeannine
Auboyer, *Khajuraho* (The Hague: Mouton, 1960), glossary.

22
Desai, *Erotic Sculpture,* 115. See also Mircea Eliade,
*Yoga: Immortality and Freedom,* trans. Willard R. Trask
(Princeton: Princeton University Press, 1948), 248. On
the link to yoga, see Wendy Doniger O'Flaherty,
*Asceticism and Eroticism in the Mythology of Shiva*
(London: Oxford University Press, 1973), 10.

23
For the ceremony as practiced today, see Nik Douglas,
*Tantra Yoga* (New Delhi: Munshiram Manoharlal, 1971),
83ff.

24
Desai, *Erotic Sculpture,* 114ff. See also Davis, *Ritual,*
97ff.

25
O'Flaherty, *Asceticism and Eroticism,* 107ff.

26
Martin Nilsson, "Das Ei im Totenkult der Alten," *Archiv
für Religionsgewissenschaft* 11 (1908), 530ff.

27
Giorgio Vasari, *The Lives of the Painters, Sculptors and
Architects* (1550), trans. A. B. Hinds (1927; reprint,
London: Dent, 1980), 1:280.

28
But see now Mary Garrard, "Brunelleschi's Egg: Nature,
Art, and Gender Ideology in the Making of the
Renaissance," paper presented at the conference on
Classicism and Sexuality in the Italian Renaissance,
UCLA, Los Angeles, March 1995.

29
Rowland J. Mainstone, *Developments in Structural Form*
(Cambridge, Mass.: MIT Press, 1983), 123ff.; Robert Mark
and E. C. Robison, "Vaults and Domes," in Robert Mark,
ed., *Architectural Technology up to the Scientific
Revolution* (Cambridge, Mass.: MIT Press, 1993), 169ff.;
Howard Saalman, *Filippo Brunelleschi: The Cupola of
Santa Maria del Fiore* (London: Zwemmer, 1980).

30
Eve Blau and Edward Kaufman, eds., *Architecture and Its
Image,* exhibition catalogue (Montreal: Canadian Centre

for Architecture, 1989), 123, 346 (entry by Hannes
Mayer).

31
E. Baldwin Smith, *The Dome: A Study in the History of
Ideas* (Princeton: Princeton University Press, 1950).

32
Smith, *The Dome,* 5, 77ff. For domes in the United
States, see Eric Oxendorf, *Domes of America* (San
Francisco: Pomegranate Artbooks, 1994). On the Taj
Mahal, see W. E. Begley and Z. A. Desai, *Taj Mahal, the
Illumined Tomb: An Anthology of Seventeenth-Century
Mughal and European Documentary Sources* (Seattle:
University of Washington Press, 1989), 66.

33
Zuccaro is quoted by Wolfgang Lotz, "Die ovalen
Kirchenräume des Cinquecento," *Römisches Jahrbuch für
Kunstgeschichte* 7 (1955), 87ff.

34
Stefano De Fiores and Salvatore Meo, eds., *Nuovo
dizionario di mariologia* (Milan: Edizioni paoline, 1985),
687.

35
First published in Tycho Brahe, *Astronomiae instauratae
progymnasmata,* ed. Johannes Kepler (Prague,
1602–1603); see also Fernand Hallyn, *The Poetic
Structure of the World: Copernicus and Kepler,* trans.
Donald M. Leslie (New York: Zone; Cambridge, Mass.:
distributed by MIT Press, 1990), 204ff.; and Alexandre
Koyré, *The Astronomical Revolution: Copernicus, Kepler,
Borelli,* trans. R. E. W. Maddison (1973; reprint, New
York: Dover, 1992), 225ff.

36
Bernard Campbell, *Human Evolution: An Introduction to
Man's Adaptations,* 3rd ed. (New York: Aldine, 1985),
303.

37
Marilyn Yalom, *A History of the Breast* (New York: Knopf,
1997), passim.

38
Begley and Desai, *Taj Mahal,* 11ff.

39
Begley and Desai, *Taj Mahal,* 17, 38, 44, 50, 135.

# 9

## THE BIOLOGY OF ARCHITECTURAL REPRODUCTION

**1**

Such experiments go back to the work of A. H. Sturtevant, "Experiments on Sex Recognition and the Problem of Sexual Selection in *Drosophila*" (1915), reprinted in *Genetics and Evolution: Selected Papers of A. H. Sturtevant,* ed. E. B. Lewis (San Francisco: Freeman, 1961), 24ff. See now William Safer, *Introduction to Genetic Engineering* (Boston: Butterworth-Heinemann, 1991).

**2**

J.-N.-L. Durand's main book for reproductive techniques was *Précis des leçons d'architecture données à l'Ecole royale polytechnique,* 2 vols. (Paris: Bernard, 1802–1805). See Werner Szambien, *Jean-Nicolas Durand, 1760–1834: De l'imitation à la norme* (Paris: Picard, 1984), 56ff., and Sergio Villari, *J.-N.-L. Durand (1764–1834): Art and Science of Architecture* (New York: Rizzoli, 1990).

**3**

Anthony J. F. Griffiths et al., *An Introduction to Genetic Analysis,* 5th ed. (New York: Freeman, 1993), 58ff.

**4**

Hans Sedlmayr, *Die Architektur Borrominis* (Berlin: Frankfurter Verlags-Anstalt, 1930), 39ff. ("Genetische Beschreibungen"). See now Marco Pogacnik, ed., *L'architettura di Borromini: La figura e l'opera con un'appendice storico-stilistica* (Milan: Electa, 1996).

**5**

Griffiths et al., *Genetic Analysis,* 20ff.

**6**

Sedlmayr, *Architektur Borrominis,* 42.

**7**

On fractal architecture, see Michael Batty and Paul Longley, *Fractal Cities: A Geometry of Form and Function* (London: Academic Press, 1994), and Carl Bovill, *Fractal Geometry in Architecture and Design* (Cambridge, Mass.: Birkhäuser Boston, 1996).

**8**

David Peak and Michael Frame, *Chaos under Control: The Art and Science of Complexity* (New York: Freeman, 1994), 66ff. The first person to make this approach to DNA data was H. Noel Jeffrey; see "Chaos and the

Visualization of Sequences," *Computers and Graphics* 16 (1992), 25ff.

**9**

To achieve that outcome, however, the computer's rules could not again be randomly applied. To reconvert, the computer would have to remember and retrace its earlier "random" steps exactly.

**10**

Sebastiano Serlio, *Tutte l'opere d'architettura et prospettiva di Sebastiano Serlio* (Venice: de' Franceschi, 1619), f. 122.

**11**

Fritz Schreiber, *Die französische Renaissance-Architektur und die Poggio-Reale Variationen des Sebastian Serlio* (Halle, 1938). For more recent bibliography on Poggioreale itself, see my "Poggioreale," *Architectura,* January 1973, 13ff., to which can be added Ulrike Kiby, "Poggioreale: Das erste Nymphaeum der Renaissance," *Gartenkunst* 7 (1995), 68ff.

**12**

Gülru Necipoglu, *The Topkapi Scroll: Geometry and Ornament in Islamic Architecture* (Santa Monica, Calif.: Getty Center for the History of Art and the Humanities, 1995).

**13**

Discussed by Szambien, *Durand,* 64ff. See also Jacques Guillerme, "Notes pour l'histoire de la régularité," *Revue de l'esthétique,* no. 3 (1971), 383ff., and idem, *La figurazione in architettura,* trans. Laura Agnesi (Milan: F. Angeli, 1982), 81ff.

**14**

The best review of the literature is Thomas Seebohm, "A Response to William J. Mitchell's Review of *Possible Palladian Villas* by George Hersey and Richard Freedman," *AA Files,* no. 30 (Autumn 1995), 109ff.

**15**

Hans Lauwerier, *Fractals: Endlessly Repeated Geometrical Figures,* trans. Sophia Gill-Hoffstadt (Princeton: Princeton University Press, 1992), 166.

**16**

Lauwerier, *Fractals,* 138ff.

**17**

James Gleick, *Chaos: Making a New Science* (New York: Viking, 1988), 99.

204

18

Benoit B. Mandelbrot, *The Fractal Geometry of Nature,* new ed. (New York: Freeman, 1983), 31ff.

19

Lauwerier, *Fractals,* 36.

20

George L. Hersey, *High Renaissance Art in St. Peter's and the Vatican* (Chicago: University of Chicago Press, 1993), 89ff.

21

Lauwerier, *Fractals,* 72ff., 166ff., 200.

22

Hersey, *High Renaissance Art,* 71.

23

For more on the biological aspects of this idea, see Rupert Riedl, *Order in Living Organisms: A Systems Analysis of Evolution* (Chichester: Wiley, 1978), 97ff.

24

Bramante's plan has no scale. Franz Wolff Graf von Metternich attempts to arrive at the intended dimensions in his "Über die Massgrundlagen des Kuppelentwürfes Bramantes für Peterskirche in Rom," in Douglas Fraser, Howard Hibbard, and Milton Lewine, eds., *Essays in the History of Architecture Presented to Rudolf Wittkower* (London: Phaidon, 1967), 40ff.; see esp. fig. VI.1, which displays Wolff Metternich's scale. He estimates the main dome as 160 Roman *palmi* in diameter, or about 36 meters.

25

E. O. Wiley et al., *The Compleat Cladist: A Primer of Phylogenetic Procedures* (Lawrence Kan.: Museum of Natural History, University of Kansas, 1991), and P. L. Forey et al., *Cladistics: A Practical Course in Systematics* (Oxford: Clarendon Press, 1992), both with earlier bibliography. H. Don Cameron's paper, "The Upside-Down Cladogram: Problems in Manuscript Affiliation," in Henry M. Hoenigswald and Linda F. Wiener, eds., *Biological Metaphor and Cladistic Classification* (Philadelphia: University of Pennsylvania Press, 1987), 227ff., is especially appropriate for art history. For a cladistic critique of Haeckel's tree, see Jane M. Oppenheimer, "Haeckel's Variations on Darwin," in the same volume, 123ff.

26

See Darrell J. Siebert, "Tree Statistics . . . ," in Forey et al., *Cladistics.*

27

Recently a fossil snake apparently with hind legs has been discovered. See Charles Arthur in *The Independent* (London), 17 April 1997.

28

See S. Bonde, R. Mark, and E. C. Robison, "Walls and Other Vertical Elements," in Robert Mark, ed., *Architectural Technology up to the Scientific Revolution* (Cambridge, Mass.: MIT Press, 1993), 108.

29

See Robert Mark and E. C. Robison, "Vaults and Domes," in Mark, *Architectural Technology,* 138ff. They have a good earlier bibliography.

# 40
## WHERE TO NOW?

1

A good, breezy introduction to this idea is Delta Willis, *The Sand Dollar and the Slide Rule: Drawing Blueprints from Nature* (Reading, Mass.: Addison-Wesley, 1995). Though without visual analysis, this book also proposes many ways in which nature has inspired architecture. On morphology, see also S. A. Wainwright, W. D. Biggs, J. D. Currey, and J. M. Gasline, *Mechanical Design in Organisms* (Princeton: Princeton University Press, 1982); and Thomas A. McMahon and John Tyler Bonner, *On Size and Life* (New York: Freeman, 1983). See also D'Arcy Wentworth Thompson, *On Growth and Form,* complete rev. ed. (1942; reprint, New York: Dover, 1992); Norbert Schmidt Kittler and Klaus Vogel, eds., *Constructional Morphology and Evolution* (Berlin: Springer, 1991); R. McNeill Alexander, *Optima for Animals* (London: Arnold, 1982); and idem, *Size and Shape* (London: Arnold, 1971).

2

Louis Sullivan's *System of Architectural Ornament, According with a Philosophy of Man's Powers* (1924; reprint, New York: Eakins Press, 1967) is still available.

3

See also P. B. Tomlinson, "Tree Architecture," *American Scientist* 71 (1983), 141ff.

4

Benoit B. Mandelbrot, *The Fractal Geometry of Nature,* new ed. (New York: Freeman, 1983).

5

Stephen Jay Gould and R. C. Lewontin, "The Spandrels of San Marco and the Panglossian Paradigm: A Critique of the Adaptationist Programme," *Proceedings of the Royal Society* B205 (1979), 581ff. Of all the many who have written on this article, only Robert Mark, "Architecture and Evolution," *American Scientist,* July–August 1996, 383ff., calls attention to the correct definitions, and actual architectural roles, of spandrels and pendentives. But see also Ellen Dissanayake, "Chimera, Spandrel, or Adaptation: Conceptualizing Art in Human Evolution," *Human Nature* 6/2 (1995).

6

See Jack Cohen and Ian Stewart, *The Collapse of Chaos: Discovering Simplicity in a Complex World* (New York: Penguin, 1994), 114ff.; on the interesting question of parasitism and an orgnaism's visual character, see Randy Thornhill and Steven Gangestad, "Human Facial Beauty: Averageness, Symmetry, and Parasite Resistance," *Proceedings of the Royal Society of London* B261 (1994), 111ff.

7

Scott Robinson et al., "Regional Forest Fragmentation and the Nesting Success of Migratory Birds," *Science,* 1 April 1995, 1987ff.

8

Karl von Frisch, with the collaboration of Otto von Frisch, *Animal Architecture,* trans. Lisbeth Gombrich (New York: Harcourt Brace Jovanovich, 1974), 71.

9

On animal consciousness, see Marian Stamp Dawkins, *Through Our Eyes Only? The Search for Animal Consciousness* (New York: W. H. Freeman, 1993); Daisie Radner and Michael Radner, *Animal Consciousness* (Buffalo, N.Y.: Prometheus Books, 1989).

# Bibliography

Abbott, R. Tucker. *The Kingdom of the Seashell.* 1972. Reprint, New York: Bonanza Books, 1982.

Adams, Ann Jensen. "Competing Communities in 'the Great Bog of Europe': Identity of Seventeenth-Century Dutch Landscape Painting." In W. J. T. Mitchell, ed., *Landscape and Power.* Chicago: University of Chicago Press, 1994.

Alberti, Leone Battista. *L'Architettura* [*De re aedificatoria,* 1485]. Ed. G. Orlandi. Milan: Polifilo, 1966.

Alberti, Leone Battista. *De re aedificatoria.* Florence: Alemani, 1485.

Alföldy, Géza. *Der Obelisk auf dem Petersplatz in Rom: Ein historisches Monument der Antike.* Heidelberg: C. Winter, 1990.

Alexander, R. McNeill. *Optima for Animals.* London: Arnold, 1982.

Alexander, R. McNeill. *Size and Shape.* London: Arnold, 1971.

Alland, Alexander. *The Artistic Animal: An Inquiry into the Biological Roots of Art.* Garden City, N.Y.: Anchor Books, 1977.

Allen, James P. "The Cosmology of the Pyramid Texts." In William Kelly Simpson, ed., *Religion and Philosophy in Ancient Egypt.* New Haven: Yale Egyptological Seminar, Department of Near Eastern Languages and Civilizations, the Graduate School, Yale University, 1989.

Alofsin, Anthony. *Frank Lloyd Wright: The Lost Years, 1910–1922.* Chicago: University of Chicago Press, 1993.

Alofsin, Anthony. "Frank Lloyd Wright and Modernism." In Terence Riley, ed., *Frank Lloyd Wright, Architect.* New York: Museum of Modern Art, 1994.

Altangerel P., M. A. Norell, L. M. Chiappe, and J. M. Clark. "Flightless Bird from the Cretaceous of Mongolia. . . ." *Nature* 362, no. 6241 (1993), 623ff.

Amico, Leonard. *Bernard Palissy: In Pursuit of the Earthly Paradise.* New York: Flammarion, 1996.

Anand, Mulk Raj. *Homage to Khajuraho.* Bombay: Marg Publications, 1962.

Anderson, O. Roger. *Radiolaria.* New York: Springer, 1983.

Anguier, Michel. "The Human Body, Represented as a Strong Citadel." In André Fontaine, ed., *Conférances inédites de l'Académie royale de peinture et de sculpture.* Paris: Fontemoing, 1903.

*Antelopes: Global Survey and Regional Action Plans.* Gland, Switzerland: IUCN, 1988–.

Appleton, Jay. *The Experience of Landscape.* Rev. ed. Chichester: Wiley, 1996.

Appleton, Jay. *The Symbolism of Habitat: An Interpretation of Landscape and the Arts.* Seattle: University of Washington Press, 1990.

Arbeiter, Achim. *Alt-St. Peter in Geschichte und Wissenschaft.* Berlin: Gebr. Mann, 1988.

Arslan, Edoardo. *Gothic Architecture in Venice.* New York: Phaidon, 1972.

Assmann, Jan. "Death and Initiation in the Funerary Religion of Ancient Egypt." In William Kelly Simpson, ed., *Religion and Philosophy in Ancient Egypt.* New Haven: Yale Egyptological Seminar, Department of Near Eastern Languages and Civilizations, the Graduate School, Yale University, 1989.

Baker, Robin. *Sperm Wars: The Science of Sex.* New York: Basic Books, 1996.

Baker, R. Robin, and Mark A. Bellis. *Human Sperm Competition.* London: Chapman and Hall, 1995.

Balas, Edith. "The Unbuilt Architecture of the Early Modern Sculptors." *Gazette des Beaux-Arts,* ser. 6, 110, no. 1426 (1987), 181ff.

Ball, Philip. *Designing the Molecular World: Chemistry at the Frontier.* Princeton: Princeton University Press, 1994.

Baltrušaitis, Jurgis. *Le Stylistique ornementale dans la sculpture romane.* Paris: E. Leroux, 1931.

Barbeau, Marius. *Totem Poles According to Crests and Topics,* 1950. Hull, Quebec: Canadian Museum of Civilization, 1990.

Barkow, Jerome H., Leda Cosmides, and John Tooby, eds. *The Adapted Mind.* Oxford: Oxford University Press, 1992.

Barni, G. L. *Il tempo delle torri.* Milan: n.p., 1969.

Bassi, Elena. *Palazzi di Venezia: Admiranda Urbis Venetiae.* Venice: Stamperia di Venezia, 1976.

Batty, Michael, and Paul Longley. *Fractal Cities: A Geometry of Form and Function.* London: Academic Press, 1994.

Bauer, Herman. *Rocaille: Zur Herkunft und zum Wesen eines Ornament-Motivs.* Berlin: De Gruyter, 1962.

Baumann, Hellmut. *Die griechische Pflanzenwelt in Mythos, Kunst, und Literatur.* Munich: Hirmer, 1982.

Begley, W. E., and Z. A. Desai. *Taj Mahal, the Illumined Tomb: An Anthology of Seventeenth-Century Mughal and European Documentary Sources.* Seattle: University of Washington Press, 1989.

Beinlich, Horst. *Die "Osirisreliquien": Zum Motiv der Körperzergliederung in der Altägyptischen Religion* Wiesbaden: Harrassowitz, 1984.

Betsky, Aaron. *Building Sex: Men, Women, Architecture, and the Construction of Sexuality.* New York: Morrow, 1995.

Bettum, Johan. "An Evolutionary Architecture." *AA Files,* no. 30 (Autumn 1995), 70ff.

Bierhorst, John. *The Mythology of North America.* New York: Morrow, 1985.

Biotti, Alessandro, ed. and comm. *Georgica Liber 4,* by Virgil. Bologna: Patron editore, 1994.

Birch, S. "Notes on Obelisks." In E. Falkner, *Museum of Classical Antiquity, 2,* ch. xiii, xvi, 203ff.

Birindelli, Massimo. *La machina heroica: Il disegno di Gianlorenzo Bernini per piazza San Pietro.* Rome: Istituto di fondamenti dell'architettura, Università degli studi di Roma, 1980.

Blau, Eve, and Edward Kaufman, eds. *Architecture and Its Image.* Exhibition catalogue. Montreal: Canadian Centre for Architecture, 1989.

Boardman, John, and Eugenio La Rocca. *Eros in Greece.* London: Murray, 1978.

Boas, Franz. *Contributions to the Ethnology of the Kwakiutl.* New York: Columbia University Press, 1925.

Boas, Franz. "The Decorative Art of the Indians of the North Pacific Coast." *Bulletin of the American Museum of Natural History* 9 (1897), 123ff., 144ff.

Boas, Franz. "Kwakiutl Culture as Reflected in Mythology." *Memoirs of the American Folk-Lore Society* 28 (1935).

Bonanni, A. P. P. *Ricreatione dell'occhio e della mente, nell'osservatione delle chiocciole.* Rome, 1681.

Bonde, S., R. Mark, and E. C. Robison. "Walls and Other Vertical Elements." In Robert Mark, ed., *Architectural Technology up to the Scientific Revolution.* Cambridge, Mass.: MIT Press, 1993.

Borgia, G. "Bower Destruction and Sexual Competition in the Satin Bowerbird (*Ptilonorynchus violaceus*)." *Behavioral Ecology and Sociobiology* 18 (1985), 91ff.

Borgia, G. "Bower Quality, Number of Decorations, and Mating Success of the Male Satin Bowerbirds (*Ptilonorynchus violaceus*): An Experimental Analysis." *Animal Behaviour* 33 (1985), 266ff.

Borsi, Franco, and Ezio Godoli. *Paris 1900*. Trans. J. C. Palmes. New York: Rizzoli, 1977.

Bottineau, Yves. *L'Art baroque*. Paris: Editions Mazenod, 1986.

Bovill, Carl. *Fractal Geometry in Architecture and Design*. Cambridge, Mass.: Birkhäuser Boston, 1996.

Boyds, T. F. *The Beasts, Birds, and Bees of Virgil*. Oxford: Oxford University Press, 1914.

Brahe, Tycho. *Astronomiae instauratae progymnasmata*. Ed. Johannes Kepler. Prague, 1602–1603.

Brooks, Douglas Renfrew. *The Secret of the Three Cities: An Introduction to Hindu Sakta Tantrism*. Chicago: University of Chicago Press, 1990.

Budge, E. A. Wallis. *Cleopatra's Needle and Other Egyptian Obelisks*. 1926. Reprint, New York: Dover, 1990.

Burkert, Walter. *Ancient Mystery Cults*. Cambridge, Mass.: Harvard University Press, 1987.

Burkert, Walter. *Creation of the Sacred: Tracks of Biology in Early Religions*. Cambridge, Mass.: Harvard University Press, 1996.

Burl, Aubrey. *Rings of Stone: The Prehistoric Stone Circles of Britain and Ireland*. New Haven: Ticknor and Fields, 1979.

Buschor, Ernst. "Ein choregisches Denkmal." *Mitteilungen des deutschen archäologischen Instituts,* Abteilung 53 (1928).

Cairns-Smith, A. G. Graham. *Seven Clues to the Origin of Life*. Cambridge: Cambridge University Press, 1990.

*Cambridge Encyclopedia of Human Evolution*. Ed. Steve Jones, Robert Martin, and David Pilbeam. Cambridge: Cambridge University Press, 1992.

Cameron, H. Don. "The Upside-Down Cladogram: Problems in Manuscript Affiliation." In Henry M. Hoenigswald and Linda F. Wiener, eds., *Biological Metaphor and Cladistic Classification*. Philadelphia: University of Pennsylvania Press, 1987.

Campbell, Bernard. *Human Evolution: An Introduction to Man's Adaptations*. 3rd ed. New York: Aldine, 1985.

Castriota, David. *The Ara Pacis Augustae and the Imagery of Abundance in Later Greek and Early Roman Imperial Art*. Princeton: Princeton University Press, 1996.

Cesariano, Cesare. *Vitruvius, de Architectura*. Como: Gottardus de Ponte, 1521.

Chantelou, Paul Fréart de. *Journal du voyage en France du Chevalier Bernin par Chantelou.* Paris: Stock: 1930.

Chauvet, Jean-Marie, Eliette Brunel Deschamps, and Christian Hillaire. *La Grotte Chauvet à Vallon-Pont-d'Arc.* Paris: Seuil, 1995.

Cipriani, Giovanni. *Gli obelischi egizi: oolitica e cultura nella Roma barocca.* Florence: Olschki, 1993.

Cleve, Felix. *The Giants of Pre-sophistic Greek Philosophy.* The Hague: Nijhoff, 1969.

Cohen, Jack, and Ian Stewart. *The Collapse of Chaos: Discovering Simplicity in a Complex World.* New York: Penguin, 1994.

Cohen, Ronald E., and Lars Stixrude. "High Pressure Elasticity of Iron and Anistropy of Earth's Inner Core." *Science,* 31 March 1995, 1972ff.

Colbert, Edwin Harris. *A Primitive Ornithischian Dinosaur from the Kayenta Formation of Arizona.* Flagstaff: Museum of Northern Arizona Press, 1981.

Colonna, Francesco. *Hypnerotomachia Poliphili.* New York: Garland, 1976. Facsimile ed. (Venice: Manutius, 1499).

Conklin, William A. *Nature's Art: The Inner and Outer Dimensions of the Shell.* Columbia: University of South Carolina Press, 1985.

Connors, Joseph. "S. Ivo alla Sapienza: The First Three Minutes." *Journal of the Society of Architectural Historians* 55 (1996), 38ff.

Connors, Joseph. "The Spire of Sant'Ivo." *Burlington Magazine* 138 (October 1996), 668ff.

Conrads, Ulrich, and Hans G. Sperlich. *The Architecture of Fantasy.* New York: Praeger, 1962.

Cook, Theodore Andrea. *Spirals in Nature and Art: A Study of Spiral Formations Based on the Manuscripts of Leonardo Da Vinci, with Special Reference to the Architecture of the Open Staircase at Blois.* London: J. Murray, 1903.

Cortis, Michael. "The Form, Function, and Synthesis of the Molluskan Shell." In István Hargittai and Clifford A. Pickover, eds., *Spiral Symmetry.* Singapore: World Scientific, 1992.

Cronin, Helena. *The Ant and the Peacock: Altruism and Sexual Selection from Darwin to Today.* Cambridge: Cambridge University Press, 1991.

"Daniel Libeskind: Architect of the V & A's Proposed Extension." *Country Life,* 13 June 1996, 154ff.

Darwin, Charles. *The Descent of Man and Selection in Relation to Sex* (1871). In *The Works of Charles Darwin,* ed. Paul H. Barrett and R. B. Freeman. vols. 21–22. New York: New York University Press, 1989.

Davis, Howard McP. "Bees on the Tomb of Urban VIII." *Source: Notes on the History of Art,* nos. 8–9 (Fall 1989), 40ff.

Davis, Richard H. *Ritual in an Oscillating Universe: Worshiping Shiva in Medieval India.* Princeton: Princeton University Press, 1991.

Dawkins, Marian Stamp. *Through Our Eyes Only? The Search for Animal Consciousness.* New York: W. H. Freeman, 1993.

Dawkins, Richard. *The Extended Phenotype: The Gene as the Unit of Selection.* Oxford: Oxford University Press, 1982.

De Fiores, Stefano, and Salvatore Meo, eds. *Nuovo dizionario di mariologia.* Milan: Edizione paoline, 1985.

Delaporte, L. M. *Voyage au Cambodge: L'Architecture Khmer.* Paris: C. Delagrave, 1880.

Del Pesco, Daniela. *L'architettura del Seicento.* Turin: UTET, 1998.

Del Piazzo, Marcello. *Ragguagli borrominiani.* Rome: Ministero dell'Interno, 1968.

Desai, Devangana. *Erotic Sculpture of India: A Socio-Cultural Study.* New Delhi: Tata McGraw-Hill, 1975.

Descharnes, Robert, and Clovis Prévost. *The Artistic Vision of Antoni Gaudí.* New York: Viking, 1982.

De Solá-Morales, Ignasi. *Gaudí.* New York: Rizzoli, 1984.

Diamond, Jared. "Bower Building and Decoration by the Bowerbird *Amblyornis inornatus.*" *Ethology.* 74 (1987), 177ff.

Diamond, Jared. *The Third Chimpanzee: The Evolution and Future of the Human Animal.* New York: HarperCollins, 1992.

Dissanayake, Ellen. "Chimera, Spandrel, or Adaptation: Conceptualizing Art in Human Evolution." *Human Nature* 6/2 (1995).

Dissanayake, Ellen. *Homo Aestheticus: Where Art Comes from and Why.* New York: Free Press, 1992.

Dixson, A. F. "Observations on the Evolution of the Genitalia and Copulatory Behaviour in Male Primates." *Journal of Zoology* 213 (1978), 423ff.

D'Onofrio, Cesare. *Gli obelischi di Roma: storia e urbanistica di una città dall'età antica al XX secolo.* 3d ed. Rome: Romana Società Editrice, 1992.

Douady, S., and Y. Couder. "Phyllotaxis as a Dynamical Self-Organization Process." *Journal of Theoretical Biology* 178, no. 3 (1996), 255ff., 275ff., 295ff.

Douglas, Nik. *Tantra Yoga.* New Delhi: Munshiram Manoharlal, 1971.

Drost, Dietrich. "Tönerne Dachaufsätze in Afrika." *Jahrbuch des Museums für Völkerkunde zu Leipzig* (Berlin DDR) 15 (1956, 1957).

Dumarçay, Jacques. *Le Bayon: Histoire architecturale du temple.* Paris, 1967–.

Dunning, Joan. *Secrets of the Nest.* Boston: Houghton Mifflin, 1994.

Durand, J.-N.-L. *Précis des leçons d'architecture données à l'Ecole royale polytechnique.* 2 vols. Paris: Bernard, 1802–1805.

Eberhard, William G. *Female Control: Sexual Selection and Cryptic Female Choice.* Princeton: Princeton University Press, 1996.

Eberhard, William G. *Sexual Selection and Animal Genitalia.* Cambridge, Mass.: Harvard University Press, 1985.

Ebhardt, Bodo. *Die Bürgen Italiens.* 6 vols. Berlin: Wasmuth, 1907–1927.

Eibl-Eibesfeldt, Irenäus. "The Biological Foundation of Aesthetics." In Ingo Rentscher, Barbara Herzberger, and David Epstein, eds., *Beauty and the Brain: Biological Aspects of Aesthetics.* Basel: Birkhaüser, 1989.

Eibl-Eibesfeldt, Irenäus, and Christa Sütterlin. *Im Banne der Angst: zur Natur- und Kunstgeschichte menschlicher Abwehrsymbolik.* Munich: Piper, 1992.

Eigen, Manfred. "Self-Replication and Molecular Evolution." In D. S. Bendall, ed., *Evolution from Molecules to Men.* Cambridge: Cambridge University Press, 1983

Eigen, Manfred. *Steps towards Life.* Trans. Paul Woolley. Oxford: Oxford University Press, 1992.

Eigen, Manfred. "Wie entsteht Information? Prinzipien der Selbstorganisation in der Biologie." *Berichtete der Bunsengesellschaft für Physikalische Chemie* 80 (1976), 1059ff.

Eliade, Mircea. *Yoga: Immortality and Freedom.* Trans. Willard R. Trask. Princeton: Princeton University Press, 1948.

Emmeche, Claus. *The Garden in the Machine: The Emerging Science of Artificial Life.* Trans. Steven Sampson. Princton: Princeton University Press, 1994.

Evans, Arthur. *The Shaft Graves and Bee-Hive Tombs of Mycenae and Their Interrelation.* London: Macmillan, 1929.

Evans, Robin. *The Projective Cast: Architecture and Its Three Geometries.* Cambridge, Mass.: MIT Press, 1995.

Fagan, Paul J., and Michael D. Ward. "Building Molecular Crystals." *Scientific American*, July 1992, 48ff.

Fagiolo dell'Arco, Maurizio, ed. *The Art of the Popes: From the Vatican Collection: How Pontiffs, Architects, Painters, and Sculptors Created the Vatican.* New York: Greenwich House, 1982.

Faulkner, R. O., ed. *The Ancient Egyptian Pyramid Texts.* Oxford: Clarendon Press, 1969.

Fehl, Philipp. "The *Stemme* on Bernini's Baldacchino." *Burlington Magazine* 98 (1976), 484ff.

Fejes Tóth, L. "Symmetry Induced by Economy." In István Hargittai, ed., *Symmetry: Unifying Human Understanding.* New York: Pergamon Press, 1983.

Fejes Tóth, L. "What the Bees Know and What They Do Not Know." *Bulletin of the American Mathematical Society* 70 (1964), 468ff.

Ferrari, Giovanni Battista. *Flos, seu De florum cultura.* New ed. Amsterdam: Johannes Janson, 1646. First published Rome, 1633.

Fibonacci, Leonardo. *The Book of Squares* (1225). Trans. and ed. L. E. Sigler. Boston: Academic Press, 1987.

Fischer von Erlach, Johann Bernhard. *Entwurff einer historische Architektur in Abbildung.* Vienna, 1721.

Fitter, Chris. *Poetry, Space, Landscape: Toward a New Theory.* Cambridge: Cambridge University Press, 1995.

Flaker, Aleksander. "Die Spiral als optimate Projektion." In Jürgen Harten, ed., *Vladimir Tatlin: Leben Werk Werkung: Ein internationale Symposium.* Cologne: Dumont, 1993.

Fleagle, J. G. *Primate Adaptation and Evolution.* San Diego: Academic Press, 1988.

Fleming, R. M., et al. "Crystalline Fullerenes." In George S. Hammond and Valerie J. Kuck, eds., *Fullerenes: Synthesis, Properties, and Chemistry of Large Carbon Clusters.* Washington, D.C.: American Chemical Society, 1992.

Fletcher, Banister. *A History of Architecture on the Comparative Method.* 15th ed. New York: Scribner's, 1950.

Fontana, Domenico. *Della trasportazione dell'obelisco vaticano. . . .* Rome: Domenico Basa, 1590.

Forey, P. L., et al. *Cladistics: A Practical Course in Systematics.* Oxford: Clarendon Press, 1992.

Fournier, Marian. *The Fabric of Life: Microscopy in the Seventeenth Century.* Baltimore: Johns Hopkins University Press, 1996.

Fowler, P. W., and D. E. Manopoulos. *An Atlas of Fullerenes*. Oxford: Clarendon Press, 1995.

Francesco di Giorgio Martini. *Trattati di architettura ingegneria e arte militare*. Ed. C. Maltese. Milan: Polifilo, 1967.

Francia, Ennio. *1506–1606: Storia della costruzione del nuovo San Pietro*. Rome: De Luca, 1989.

Frankfort, Henri. *Kingship and the Gods: A Study of Ancient Near Eastern Religion as the Integration of Society and Nature*. Chicago: University of Chicago Press, 1948.

Frazer, John. *An Evolutionary Architecture*. London: Architectural Association, 1995.

Frazer, John, et al. "The Interactivator." In *Architects in Cyberspace*. Special issue, *Architectural Design* 65, nos. 11–12 (1995), 79ff.

Friedman, Dawn. "Determination of Spiral Symmetry in Plants and Polymers." In István Hargittai and Clifford A. Pickover, eds., *Spiral Symmetry*. Singapore: World Scientific, 1992.

Frith, D. W., and C. B. Frith. "Courtship Display and Mating of the Superb Bird of Paradise *Lophorina superba*." *Emu* 88 (1988), 183ff.

Fuller, Richard Buckminster (in collaboration with E. J. Applewhite). *Synergetics: Explorations in Geometry and Thinking*. New York: Macmillan, 1975.

Fuller, Richard Buckminster, and Robert W. Marks. *The Dymaxion World of Buckminster Fuller*. New York: Anchor Books, 1973.

Gardner, Alan. *Egyptian Grammar*. 2nd ed. London: Oxford University Press, 1950.

Gardner, Martin. *The Ambidextrous Universe*. New York: Basic Books, 1964.

Garrard, Mary. "Brunelleschi's Egg: Nature, Art, and Gender Ideology in the Making of the Renaissance." Paper presented at the conference on Classicism and Sexuality in the Italian Renaissance, UCLA, Los Angeles, March 1995.

Gassner, Jutta. *Phallos: Fruchtbarkeitssymbol oder Abwehrzauber?* Vienna: Böhlau, 1993.

Gaudin, Marc-Antoine. *L'Architecture du monde des atomes*. Paris: Gaulthier-Villars, 1873.

Glaeser, Ludwig. *The Work of Frei Otto*. New York: Museum of Modern Art, 1972.

Gleick, James. *Chaos: Making a New Science*. New York: Viking, 1988.

Goodsell, David S. *Our Molecular Nature: The Body's Motors, Machines, and Messages*. New York: Copernicus, 1996.

Gopinatha Rao, T. A. *Elements of Hindu Iconography*. 2nd ed. Varanasi: Indological Book House, 1971.

Gorum Sergiu M., et al. "Low Resolution Single-Crystal X-Ray Structure of Solvated Fullerenes. . . ." In George S. Hammond and Valerie J. Kuck, eds., *Fullerenes: Synthesis, Properties, and Chemistry of Large Carbon Clusters.* Washington, D.C.: American Chemical Society, 1992.

Gould, James L., and Carol Grant Gould. *The Animal Mind.* New York: Scientific American Library, 1994.

Gould, James, and Carol Grant Gould. *The Honey Bee.* New York: Scientific American Library, 1995.

Gould, James L., and Carol Grant Gould. *Sexual Selection.* New York: Scientific American Library, 1989.

Gould, Stephen Jay. "Common Pathways of Illumination." *Natural History,* December 1994, 14.

Gould, Stephen Jay. "Leonardo's Living Earth." *Natural History,* May 1997, 18ff.

Gould, Stephen Jay, and R. C. Lewontin. "The Spandrels of San Marco and the Panglossian Paradigm: A Critique of the Adaptationist Programme." *Proceedings of the Royal Society* B205 (1979), 581ff.

Gregory, William K. "The Bridge-That-Walks." *Natural History* 46 (1937), 33ff.

Griffiths, Anthony J. F., et al. *Introduction to Genetic Analysis.* 5th ed. New York: Freeman, 1993.

Griffiths, John Gwyn. *The Origins of Osiris and His Cult.* Leiden: Brill, 1980.

Groenen, Marc. "L'Art pariétal: Un art structuré." In André Leroi-Gourhan, *L'Art pariétal: Langage de la préhistoire.* Grenoble: Millon, 1992.

Gruben, Gottfried. *Die Tempel der Griechen.* Munich: Hirmer, 1986.

Guillaume, Jean. "Léonard de Vinci et l'architecture française, 1. Le Problème de Chambord." *Revue de l'art,* no. 25 (1974), 71ff.

Guillerme, Jacques. *La figurazione in architettura.* Trans. Laura Agnesi. Milan: F. Angeli, 1982.

Guillerme, Jacques. "Notes pour l'histoire de la régularité." *Revue de l'esthétique,* no. 3 (1971), 383ff.

Gupta, Sanjukta, Dirk Jan Hoens, and Teun Goudriaan. *Hindu Tantrism.* Leiden: Brill, 1979.

Habachi, Labib. *The Obelisks of Egypt.* New York: Scribner's, 1977.

Haeckel, Ernst. *Anthropogenie oder Entwicklungsgeschichte des Menschen: Gemein verständliche wissenschaftliche Vortrage über die Grundzuge der menschlichen Keimes- und Stammes-Geschichte.* Leipzig: Wilhelm Engelmann, 1874.

Haeckel, Ernst. *Art Forms in Nature.* New York: Dover, 1974.

Haeckel, Ernst. *The Evolution of Man: A Popular Exposition of the Principal Points of Human Ontogeny and Phylogeny.* 2 vols. New York: Appleton, 1879.

Haeckel, Ernst. *Die Radiolarien.* 3 vols. Berlin: G. Reimer, 1862–1888.

Hallyn, Fernand. *The Poetic Structure of the World: Copernicus and Kepler.* Trans. Donald M. Leslie. New York: Zone; Cambridge, Mass.: distributed by MIT Press, 1990.

Hamilton, W. D. "Geometry for the Selfish Herd." *Journal of Theoretical Biology* 31 (1971), 295ff.

Hancocks, David. *Master Builders of the Animal World.* New York: Harper and Brothers, 1973.

Hansell, Michael H. *Animal Architecture and Building Behaviour.* London: Longmans, 1984.

Harries, Karsten. *The Bavarian Rococo Church: Between Faith and Aestheticism.* New Haven: Yale University Press, 1983.

Harten, Jürgen, ed. *Vladimir Tatlin: Leben Werk Werkung: Ein internationale Symposium.* Cologne: Dumont, 1993.

Hartsoeker, Nicolas. *Essai de dioptrique.* Paris: Jean Anisson, 1694.

Haskell, Francis. *Patrons and Painters: Art and Society in Baroque Italy.* New Haven: Yale University Press, 1980.

Hayden, Dolores. "Skyscraper Seduction, Skyscraper Rape." *Heresies* 2 (May 1977), 108ff.

Henderson, Linda Dalrymple. *The Fourth Dimension and Non-Euclidean Geometry in Modern Art.* Princeton: Princeton University Press, 1983.

Hersey, George L. "Alberti e il tempio etrusco: Postille a Richard Krautheimer." In Joseph Rykwert and Anne Engel, eds., *Leone Battista Alberti.* Mantua: Olivetti/Electa, 1994.

Hersey, George L. *High Renaissance Art in St. Peter's and the Vatican.* Chicago: University of Chicago Press, 1993.

Hersey, George L. "Poggioreale." *Architectura,* January 1973, 13ff.

Herter, Hans. *De Priapo.* Religionsgeschichtliche Versuche und Vorarbeiten 23. Giessen: A. Topelmann, 1932.

Hirsch, Eric, and Michael O'Hanlon, eds. *The Anthropology of Landscape: Perspectives on Place and Space.* Oxford: Clarendon Press, 1995.

Hoenigswald, Henry M., and Linda F. Wiener, eds. *Biological Metaphor and Cladistic Classification.* Philadelphia: University of Pennsylvania Press, 1987.

Hoerder, Dirk, and Horst Rässler, eds. *Distant Magnets: Expectations and Realities in the Immigrant Experience, 1840–1930.* New York: Holmes and Meier, 1993.

Hölldobler, Bert, and E. O. Wilson. *Journey to the Ants.* Cambridge, Mass.: Harvard University Press, 1994.

Hooke, Robert. *Micrographia, or Some Physiological Descriptions of Minute Bodies Made by Magnifying Glasses. . . .* London: J. Martyn and J. Allestry, 1665.

Huse, Norbert. "La Fontaine des Fleuves du Bernin." *Revue de l'art* 7 (1970), 6ff.

Ingber, Donald E. "The Architecture of Life." *Scientific American,* January 1998, 48ff.

Ingold, Tim. "Territoriality and Tenure: The Appopriation of Space in Hunting and Gathering Society." Paper presented at the Third Annual International Conference on Hunter-Gatherers, Bad Homburg, West Germany, 1983.

Ingold, Tim, David Riches, and James Woodburn, eds. *Hunters and Gatherers.* Oxford: Oxford University Press, 1988.

Iversen, Erik. *Obelisks in Exile.* 2 vols. Copenhagen: Gad, 1968.

Jacob, François. "Molecules: Tinkering in Evolution." In D. S. Bendall, ed., *Evolution from Molecules to Men.* Cambridge: Cambridge University Press, 1983.

James, T. G. H. *Ancient Egypt: The Land and Its Legacy.* Austin: University of Texas Press, 1988.

Jameson, Mrs. [Anna]. *Legends of the Monastic Orders as Represented in the Fine Arts.* New York: Longmans, Green, 1900.

Janson, H. W. *History of Art.* New York: Abrams, 1985.

Jean, Roger V. "On the Origins of Spiral Symmetry in Plants." In István Hargittai and Clifford A. Pickover, eds., *Spiral Symmetry.* Singapore: World Scientific, 1992.

Jean, Roger V. *Phyllotaxis: A Systematic Study of Plant Morphogenesis.* Cambridge: Cambridge University Press, 1994.

Jeffrey, H. Noel. "Chaos and the Visualization of Sequences." *Computers and Graphics* 16 (1992), 25ff.

Jensen, Ad. E. "Die Banna/Die Hammar." In Ad. E. Jensen, ed., *Altvölker Südädthiopiens.* Stuttgart: W. Kohlhammer, 1959.

Jobst, W. "Das 'öffentliche Freudenhaus' in Ephesos." *Österreichische Jahreshafte* 51 (1976).

Johns, Catherine. *Sex or Symbol? Erotic Images of Greece and Rome.* Austin: University of Texas Press, 1982.

Johnsgard, Paul A. *Arena Birds: Sexual Selection and Behavior.* Washington, D.C.: Smithsonian Institution Press, 1994.

Jonaitis, Aldona. *Chiefly Feasts: The Enduring Kwakiutl Potlatch.* Seattle: University of Washington Press, 1991.

Jonaitis, Aldona. *From the Land of the Totem Poles: The Northwest Coast Indian Art Collection at the American Museum of Natural History.* New York: American Museum of Natural History; Seattle: University of Washington Press, 1991.

Joncas, Richard. "Pedagogy and 'Reflex': Frank Lloyd Wright's Hanna House Revisited." *Journal of the Society of Architectural Historians* 52 (1993), 319ff.

Karageorghis, Vassos. *Cyprus from the Stone Age to the Romans.* London: Thames and Hudson, 1982.

Kelly, Kevin. *Out of Control: The Rise of Neo-Biological Civilization.* Reading, Mass.: Addison-Wesley, 1994.

Kemp, Martin. *Leonardo da Vinci: The Marvelous Works of Nature and Man.* Cambridge, Mass.: Harvard University Press, 1981.

Kemp, Martin. "The Vortex." In *Leonardo da Vinci.* Exhibition catalogue. [New Haven]: Yale University Press in association with the South Bank Centre, 1989.

Kennon, Noel F. *Patterns in Crystals.* New York: Wiley, 1978.

Kepler, Johannes. *On the Six-Cornered Snowflake* (1611). Ed. L. L. Whyte. Oxford: Clarendon Press, 1966.

Kiby, Ulrike. "Poggioreale: Das erste Nymphaeum der Renaissance." *Gartenkunst* 7 (1995), 68ff.

Kircher, Athanasius. *Obeliscus Pamphilius.* Rome, 1650.

Kirwin, William Chandler. *Powers Matchless: The Pontificate of Urban VIII, the Baldachin, and Gian Lorenzo Bernini.* New York: Lang, 1997.

Kitao, Timothy K. *Circle and Oval in the Square of St. Peter's: Bernini's Art of Planning.* New York: New York University Press for the College Art Association of America, 1974.

Knight, Richard Payne. *A Discourse on the Worship of Priapus. . . .* (1786). Secaucus, N.J.: University Books, 1974.

Koolhaas, Rem. *Delirious New York.* New York: Oxford University Press, 1978.

Kostof, Spiro. *A History of Architecture: Settings and Rituals.* New York: Oxford University Press, 1985.

Kowitz, Vera. *La Tour Eiffel.* Essen: Die blaue Eule, 1989.

Koyré, Alexandre. *The Astronomical Revolution: Copernicus, Kepler, Borelli.* Trans. R. E. W. Maddison. 1973. Reprint, New York: Dover, 1992.

Kramrisch, Stella. *Manifestations of Shiva.* Exhibition catalogue. Philadelphia: Philadelphia Museum of Art, 1981.

Krause, Erika. "L'Influence de Ernst Haeckel sur l'art nouveau." In Jean Clair, ed., *L'Ame au corps: Arts et sciences 1793–1993.* Exhibition catalogue. Paris: Grand Palais, 1993.

Krautheimer, Richard. "Alberti's *Templum Etruscum.*" *Kunstchronik* 13 (1960), 364ff.

Krautheimer, Richard. *The Rome of Alexander VII.* Princeton: Princeton University Press, 1985.

Kreisel, Gerd. *Die Siva-Bildwerke der Mathura-Kunst.* Stuttgart: F. Steiner, 1986.

Krogman, William M. "The Scars of Human Evolution." *Scientific American,* December 1951, 54ff.

Kruft, Hanno-Walter. "The Origins of Bernini's Oval." *Burlington Magazine* 121 (1979), 796.

Kultermann, Udo. *Architecture in the Twentieth Century.* New York: Van Nostrand-Reinhold, 1993.

Kultermann, Udo. "Die himmlische Stadt Ch'ang-an." *Die alte Stadt,* January 1993.

Kultermann, Udo. *Die Maxentius-Basilika: Ein Schlüsselwerk spätantiker Architektur.* Architektur der Welt 1. Weimar: VDG, 1996.

Lauer, Jean-Philippe. *Fouilles à Saqqarah: La Pyramide à degrés, L'Architecture.* Cairo: Institut Français, 1936.

Lauwerier, Hans. *Fractals: Endlessly Repeated Geometrical Figures.* Trans. Sophia Gill-Hoffstadt. Princeton: Princeton University Press, 1992.

Lavin, Irving. *Bernini and the Crossing of St. Peter's.* New York: New York University Press, 1968.

Le Corbusier. *Le Modulor: A Harmonious Measure to the Human Scale Universally Applicable to Architecture and Mechanics.* 2nd ed. Trans. Peter de Francia and Anna Bostock. Cambridge, Mass.: Harvard University Press, 1954.

Ledoux, Claude-Nicolas. *L'Architecture considérée sous le rapport de l'art, des moeurs, et de la législation.* 2 vols. 1804. Reprint, Paris, 1847.

Leeuwenhoek, Antoni van. *Anatomia seu interiora rerum. . . .* Leyden: Boutesteyn, 1687.

Lemoine, Bertrand. *Gustave Eiffel.* Paris: Hazan, 1984.

Leonardo da Vinci. *The Literary Works of Leonardo da Vinci.* 2nd ed., enl. and rev. Jean Paul Richter and Irma A. Richter.

*Leonardo da Vinci.* Exhibition catalogue. [New Haven]: Yale University Press in association with the South Bank Centre, 1989.

Leroi-Gourhan, André. *L'Art pariétal: Langage de la préhistoire.* Grenoble: Millon, 1992.

Lévi-Strauss, Claude. *The Way of the Masks.* Trans. Sylvia Modleski. Seattle: University of Washington Press, 1988.

Levine, Arnold J. *Viruses.* New York: Scientific American Library, 1992.

Levine, Neil. *The Architecture of Frank Lloyd Wright.* Princeton: Princeton University Press, 1996.

Lima-de-Faria, A. *Evolution without Selection: Form and Function by Auto-Evolution.* Amsterdam: Elsevier 1988.

Lind, Olaf, and Annemarie Lund. *Copenhagen Architecture Guide.* Copenhagen: Arkitektens Forlag, 1996.

Lindner, Gert. *Field Guide to Seashells of the World.* New York: Van Nostrand Reinhold, 1978.

Lister, Martin. *Historiae conchyliorum bivalvium. . . .* London: sumptibus auctoris impressa, 1696.

Lodder, Christina. *Russian Constructivism.* New Haven: Yale University Press, 1983.

Lotz, Wolfgang. "Die ovalen Kirchenräume des Cinquecento." *Römisches Jahrbuch für Kunstgeschichte* 7 (1955), 87ff.

Luciano, Roberto. *Santa Maria dei Miracoli e Santa Maria di Montesanto.* Rome: Fratelli Palumbo, 1990.

Luebke, Frederick C., ed. *A Harmony of the Arts: The Nebraska State Capitol.* Lincoln: University of Nebraska Press, 1990.

Mainstone, Rowland J. *Developments in Structural Form.* 1975. Reprint, Cambridge, Mass.: MIT Press, 1983.

Malet, Rosa Maria. *Joan Miró.* New York, Rizzoli, 1983.

Mallgrave, Harry Francis. *Gottfried Semper: Architect of the Nineteenth Century.* New Haven: Yale University Press, 1996.

Mandelbrot, Benoit B. *The Fractal Geometry of Nature.* New ed. New York: Freeman, 1983.

Mannikka, Eleanor. *Angkor Wat: Time, Space, and Kingship.* Honolulu: University of Hawai'i Press, 1996.

Marder, T. A. *Bernini and the Art of Architecture.* New York: Abbeville, 1998.

Mark, Robert. "Architecture and Evolution." *American Scientist,* July–August 1996, 383ff.

Mark, Robert, and E. C. Robison. "Vaults and Domes." In Robert Mark, ed., *Architectural Technology up to the Scientific Revolution.* Cambridge, Mass.: MIT Press, 1993.

Maryon, Herbert. "The Colossus of Rhodes." *Journal of the Hellenic Society* 76 (1956), 68ff.

Mathieu, Caroline, and Françoise Cachin. *1889: La Tour Eiffel et l'Exposition Universelle.* Exhibition catalogue. Paris: Musée d'Orsay, 1989.

Mauceri, Enrico. "Colonne tortili così dette del Tempio de Salomone." *L'Arte* 1 (1898), 377ff.

McEwen, Indra Kagis. "Instrumentality and the Organic Assistance of Looms." *Chora* 1 (1994), 124ff.

McEwen, Indra Kagis. *Socrates' Ancestor: An Essay on Architectural Beginnings.* Cambridge, Mass.: MIT Press, 1993.

McMahon, Thomas A., and John Tyler Bonner. *On Size and Life.* New York: Freeman, 1983.

Meeks, Carroll L. V. *Italian Architecture, 1750–1914.* New Haven: Yale University Press, 1966.

Meeks, Dimitri, and Christine Favard-Meeks. *Daily Life of the Egyptian Gods.* Ithaca: Cornell University Press, 1996.

Mehmel, Alfred. "Eisenbetonhallenbauten." In Deutschen Beton-Verein, ed., *Neues Bauen in Eisenbeton.* Berlin: Zementverlag, 1938.

Mendell, Elizabeth Lawrence. *Romanesque Sculpture in Santonge.* New Haven: Yale University Press, 1940.

Mercati, Michele. *Gli obelischi di Roma* (1589). Ed. Gianfranco Centelli. Bologna: Cappelli, 1981.

Meyen, S. V. "Plant Morphology in Its Nomothetical Aspects." *Botanical Review* 39, no. 3 (1974), 205ff.

Michelet, Jules. *The Insect.* London: T. Nelson, 1883.

Michell. George. *The Hindu Temple: An Introduction to Its Meaning and Forms.* 1977. Reprint, Chicago: University of Chicago Press, 1988.

Mikoda-Hüttel, Barbara. "Der *Colossus* der Fischer von Erlach auf dem Hohern Markt zu Wien: ein Beitrag zur Entwurfs- und Planungsgeschichte." In Friedrich Polleross, ed., *Fischer von Erlach und die Winer Barocktradition.* Cologne: Böhlau, 1955.

Miller, Norbert. *Archäologie eines Traumes: Versuch über Giovanni Battista Piranesi.* Munich: Hauser, 1979.

Milner, John. *Vladimir Tatlin and the Russian Avant-Garde.* New Haven: Yale University Press, 1983.

Mitchell, W. J. T., ed. *Landscape and Power.* Chicago: University of Chicago Press, 1994.

Morgan, Elaine. *The Descent of Woman.* New York: Stein and Day, 1972.

Morolli, Gabriele. "I 'templa' Albertiani: Dal trattato alle fabbriche." In Joseph Rykwert and Anne Engel, eds., *Leone Battista Alberti.* Mantua: Olivetti/Electa, 1994.

Morphy, Howard. *Ancestral Connections: Art and an Aboriginal System of Knowledge.* Chicago: University of Chicago Press, 1991.

Mortier R., and H. Hasquin, eds. *Rocaille, Rococo.* Exhibition catalogue. Etudes dur le XVIIIe siècle 18. Brussels: l'Université de Bruxelles, 1991.

Mugan, I., ed. *Domes from Antiquity to the Present.* Istanbul: Mimar Sinan Universitesi, 1988.

Müller, Johann Heinrich. "Das regulierte Oval." PhD diss. (Marburg), Bremen, 1967.

Munro, Thomas. *Evolution and the Arts.* Cleveland: Cleveland Museum of Art, 1957.

Nabokov, Peter, and Robert Easton. *Native American Architecture.* New York: Oxford University Press, 1989.

Napler, David. "Bernini's Anthropology: A 'Key' to the Piazza San Pietro." *Res* 16 (Autumn 1988), 17ff.

Necipoglu, Gülru. *The Topkapi Scroll: Geometry and Ornament in Islamic Architecture.* Santa Monica, Calif.: Getty Center for the History of Art and the Humanities, 1995.

Neri Lusanna, Enrica. "L'atelier del 'Maestro dei mesi' nella scultura medievale della Cattedrale di Ferrara." In *La Cattedrale di Ferrara.* Ferrara: Belriguardo, 1982.

Netter, Frank H. *Atlas of Human Anatomy.* Summit, N.J.: Ciba Geigy, 1989.

Neufforge, Jean François de. *Receuil elementaire d'architecture. . . .* 8 vols. Paris: chez l'auteur, 1757–1768.

Nilsson, Martin. "Das Ei im Totenkult der Alten." *Archiv für Religionsgewissenschaft* 11 (1908), 530ff.

Nonell, Juan Bassegoda. *El gran Gaudí.* Barcelona: Ausa, 1989.

Norell, M. A., J. M. Clark, L. M. Chiappe, and D. Dashzeveg. "A Nesting Dinosaur." *Nature* 378, no. 6559 (1995), 774ff.

Oeschslin, Werner. "Dinokrates-legende und Mythos megalomaner Architeckturstiftung." *Daidalos,* no. 47-26 (June 1982), 7ff.

O'Flaherty, Wendy Doniger. *Asceticism and Eroticism in the Mythology of Shiva.* London: Oxford University Press, 1973.

Olby, Robert. *The Path to the Double Helix.* Seattle: University of Washington Press, 1974.

Onians, Richard Broxton. *The Origins of European Thought about the Body, the Mind, the Soul, the World, Time, and Fate.* 1951. Reprint, Cambridge: Cambridge University Press, 1988.

Oppenheimer, Jane M. "Haeckel's Variations on Darwin." In Henry M. Hoenigswald and Linda F. Wiener, eds., *Biological Metaphor and Cladistic Classification.* Philadelphia: University of Pennsylvania Press, 1987.

Orgel, Leslie E. "The Origin of Life on Earth." *Scientific American,* October 1994, 76ff.

Orions, Gordon H., and Judith Heerwagen. "Evolved Responses to Landscape." In Jerome H. Barkow, Leda Cosmides, and John Tooby, eds., *The Adapted Mind.* Oxford: Oxford University Press, 1992.

Oxendorf, Eric. *Domes of America.* San Francisco: Artbooks, 1994.

Pacuari, Lakshinarayana. *The Erotic Sculpture of Khajuraho.* Calcutta: Naya Prokash, 1989.

Padian, Kevin, and Luis M. Chiappe. "The Origin of Birds and Their Flight." *Scientific American,* February 1998, 38ff.

Palissy, Bernard. *Bernard Palissy, mythe et réalité.* Exhibition catalogue. N.p.: Musées d'Agen-Niort-Saintes, 1990.

[Pallasmaa, Juhani]. *Animal Architecture.* Exhibition catalogue. Helsinki: Museum of Finnish Architecture, 1992.

Papadopoulo, Alexandre. *Islam and Muslim Art.* Trans. Robert Erich Wolf. New York: Abrams, 1976.

Park, William. *The Idea of the Rococo.* Newark: University of Delaware Press, 1992.

Peak, David, and Michael Frame. *Chaos under Control: The Art and Science of Complexity.* New York: Freeman, 1994.

Pedretti, Carlo. *A Chronology of Leonardo da Vinci's Architectural Studies after 1500.* Geneva: Droz, 1962.

Pedretti, Carlo. *Leonardo architetto.* New York: Rizzoli, 1978.

Pérez-Gomez, Alberto, and Louise Pelletier. *Architectural Representation and the Perspective Hinge.* Cambridge, Mass.: MIT Press, 1997.

Peterson, Roger Tory. *The Birds.* New York: Time-Life Books, 1963.

Petroski, Henry. *Engineers of Dreams: Great Bridge Builders and the Spanning of America.* New York: Knopf, 1995.

Pevsner, Nikolaus. *Outline of European Architecture.* 1942. Reprint, Harmondsworth: Penguin, 1944.

*Piemonte.* Milan: Touring Club Italiano, 1961.

Pinto, John. *Italian Baroque Architecture.* New York: Oxford University Press.

Pinto-Carreia, Clara. *The Ovary of Eve: Egg and Sperm and Preformation.* Chicago: University of Chicago Press, 1997.

Piranesi, Giovanni Battista. *Carceri.* Rome, 1761.

Piranesi, Giovanni Battista. *Piranesi: Rome Recorded, A Complete Edition of Giovanni Battista Piranesi's "Vedute di Roma" from the Collection of the Arthur Ross Foundation.* Rev. 2nd ed. New York: Arthur Ross Foundation, 1990.

Pitnick, Scott, et al. "How Long Is a Giant Sperm?" *Nature,* 11 May 1995, 109.

Polignac, François de. *Cults, Territory, and the Origin of the Greek City-State.* Chicago: University of Chicago Press, 1995.

Posener, Julius. *Hans Poelzig: Reflections on His Life and Work.* New York: Architectural History Foundation; Cambridge, Mass.: MIT Press, 1992.

Pozzo, G. B. *Rules and Examples of Perspective . . .* London, 1707. First published in Rome, 1693.

Preimesberger, R. "Obeliskus Pamphilius." *Münchner Jahrbuch der bildenden Künste* (1974), 77ff.

Prévost, Clovis, and Robert Ducharnes. *The Artistic Vision of Antonio Gaudí.* New York: Viking, 1971.

Prown, Jonathan, and Richard Miller. "The Rococo, the Grotto, and the Philadelphia High Chest." In Luke Beckerdite, ed., *American Furniture 1996.* Hanover, N.H.: Chipstone Foundation, 1996.

Putnam, Michael C. J. *Virgil's Poem of the Earth: Studies in the Georgics.* Princeton: Princeton University Press, 1979.

Radner, Daisie, and Michael Radner. *Animal Consciousness.* Buffalo, N.Y.: Prometheus Books, 1989.

Raj Anand, Mulk. *Homage to Khajuraho.* Bombay: Marg Publications, 1962.

Ramírez, Juan Antonio. "Guarino Guarini, Fray Juan Ricci, and the Complete Solomonic Orders." *Art History* 4 (June 1981), 175ff.

Ramírez, Juan Antonio. "Sinédoque: Columnas Salomonicas." In Juan Antonio Ramírez, René Taylor, André Corboz, Robert Jan van Pelt, and Antonio Martinez Ripoll, *Dios, Arquitecto: J. B. Villalpando y el templo de Salomón*. Madrid: Siruela, 1991.

Ramírez, Juan Antonio, René Taylor, André Corboz, Robert Jan van Pelt, and Antonio Martinez Ripoll. *Dios, Arquitecto: J. B. Villalpando y el Templo de Salomón*. Madrid: Siruela, 1991.

Rawson, Philip. *Tantra: The Indian Cult of Ecstasy*. Greenwich, Conn.: New York Graphic Society, 1973.

Re, Vincenzo. *Narrazione delle solenni reali feste fatte celebrare in Napoli da Sua Maestà il re delle Due Sicilie, infante di Spagna . . .* Naples, 1749.

Rea, John. *Flora seu de florum cultura*. London: Marriott, 1665.

Rebek, Julius, Jr. "Synthetic Self-Replicating Molecules." *Scientific American,* July 1994, 48ff.

Remane, A. *Die Grundlagen des natürlichen Systems der vergleichenden Anatomie und der Phylogenetik*. 2nd ed. Leipzig: Akademische Verlagsgesellschaft Geest und Portig, 1956.

Renyi, Alfred. *Tagebuch über die Informationstheorie*. Basel: Birkhaüser, 1982.

Ridley, Mark. *Evolution*. Boston: Blackwell, 1993.

Riedl, Rupert. *Order in Living Organisms: A Systems Analysis of Evolution*. Chichester: Wiley, 1978.

Riedl, Rupert. "A Systems-Analytical Approach to Macro-Evolutionary Phenomena." *Quarterly Review of Biology* 52 (1977), 351ff.

Riegl, Alois. *Problems of Style: Foundations for a History of Ornament*. Trans. Evelyn Kain. Princeton: Princeton University Press, 1992. First published as *Stilfragen: Grundlegungen zu einer Geschichte der Ornamentik* (Berlin: Georg Siemens, 1893).

Riley, Terence, ed. *Frank Lloyd Wright, Architect*. Exhibition catalogue. New York: Museum of Modern Art, 1994.

Robinson, Scott, et al. "Regional Forest Fragmentation and the Nesting Success of Migratory Birds." *Science,* 1 April 1995, 1987ff.

Romano, Elisa. *La capanna e il tempio: Vitruvio o dell'architettura*. Palermo: Palumbo, 1987.

Rossi, Paolo. *The Dark Abyss of Time: The History of the Earth and the History of Nations from Hooke to Vico*. Chicago: University of Chicago Press, 1984.

Rothman James E., and Lelio Orci. "Budding Vesicles in Living Cells." *Scientific American,* March 1996, 70ff.

Ruelle, David. *Chance and Chaos.* Princeton: Princeton University Press, 1991.

Ruskin, John. *The Seven Lamps of Architecture.* 1849. Reprint, London: Everyman's Library, 1956.

Rykwert, Joseph. *The Dancing Column: On Order in Architecture.* Cambridge, Mass.: MIT Press, 1996.

Rykwert, Joseph. *On Adam's House in Paradise: The Idea of the Primitive Hut in Architectural History.* New York: Museum of Modern Art, 1972.

Rykwert, Joseph, et al., eds. *Leone Battista Alberti.* Mantua: Olivetti/Electa, 1994.

Saalman, Howard. *Filippo Brunelleschi: The Cupola of Santa Maria del Fiore.* London: Zwemmer, 1980.

Sabbagh, Karl. *Skyscraper.* London: Macmillan, 1989.

Safer, William. *Introduction to Genetic Engineering.* Boston: Butterworth-Heinemann, 1991.

Sands, Donald E. *Introduction to Crystallography.* New York: Dover, 1975.

Sarma, I. Karthikeya. "New Light on Art through Archaeological Conservation." *Journal of the Indian Society of Oriental Art,* n.s. 10 (1978–1979), 50ff.

Sarma, I. Karthikeya. *Parasuramesvara Temple at Gudmallam: A Probe into Its Origins.* Nagpur: Dattsuns, 1994.

Scarfone, Gino. "Ex-Voto borrominiane (?) nella basilica di San Pietro in Vaticano." *Strenna dei romanisti* (1977), 372ff.

Schama, Simon. *Landscape and Memory.* New York: Knopf, 1995.

Scheiper, Renate. *Bildpropaganda der römischen Kaiserszeit.* Bonn: R. Habell, 1982.

Schiebinger, Londa. "The Loves of the Plants." *Scientific American,* February 1996, 110ff.

Schmidt Kittler, Norbert, and Klaus Vogel, eds. *Constructional Morphology and Evolution.* Berlin: Springer, 1991.

Schnell, Hugo, et al. *Die Wies: Wallfahrtskirche zum gegeisselten Heiland.* Munich: Schnell und Steiner, 1979.

Schreiber, Fritz. *Die französische Renaissance-Architektur und die Poggio-Reale Variationen des Sebastian Serlio.* Halle University, 1938.

Schwartz, Kit. *The Male Member.* New York: St. Martin's, 1985.

Scott, John Beldon. *Images of Nepotism: The Painted Ceilings of the Palazzo Barberini.* Princeton: Princeton University Press, 1991.

Scott, John Beldon. "Sant'Ivo alla Sapienza and Borromini's Symbolic Language." *Journal of the Society of Architectural Historians* 41 (1982), 310ff.

Sedlmayr, Hans. *Die Architektur Borrominis.* Berlin: Frankfurter Verlags-Anstalt, 1930. Italian translation by Marco Pogacnik, *L'architettura di Borromini.* Milan: Electa, 1996.

Seebohm, Thomas. "A Response to William J. Mitchell's Review of *Possible Palladian Villas* by George Hersey and Richard Freedman." *AA Files,* no. 30 (Autumn 1995), 109ff.

Seilacher, A. "Arbeitskonzepte zur Konstructionsmorphologie." *Lethaia* 5 (1972), 325ff.

Selzer, Jack, ed. *Understanding Scientific Prose.* Madison: University of Wisconsin Press, 1993.

Semper, Gottfried. *The Four Elements of Architecture* (1863). Cambridge: Cambridge University Press, 1989.

Sennett, Richard. *Flesh and Stone: The Body and the City in Western Civilization.* New York: Norton, 1994.

Serlio, Sebastiano. *Tutte l'opere d'architettura et prospettiva di Sebastiano Serlio.* Venice: de' Franceschi, 1619.

Siebert, Darrell J. "Tree Statistics. . . ." In P. L. Forey et al., *Cladistics: A Practical Course in Systematics.* Oxford: Clarendon Press, 1992.

Smith, David. *The Dance of Shiva: Religion, Art, and Poetry in South India.* Cambridge: Cambridge University Press, 1996.

Smith, E. Baldwin. *The Dome: A Study in the History of Ideas.* Princeton: Princeton University Press, 1950.

Soler, Juan José, Anders Pape Møller, and Manuel Soler. "Nest Building, Sexual Selection, and Parental Investment." *Evolutionary Ecology.* In press 1997.

Solkin, David. *Richard Wilson and the Landscape of Reaction.* Exhibition catalogue. London: Tate Gallery, 1982.

Staski, Edward, and Jonathan Marks. *Evolutionary Anthropology.* New York: Harcourt Brace Jovanovich, 1992.

Steadman, Philip. *The Evolution of Designs: The Biological Analogy in Architecture and the Applied Arts.* Cambridge: Cambridge University Press, 1979.

Steinhardt, Nancy. *Chinese Imperial City Planning.* Honolulu: University of Hawai'i Press, 1990.

Stevens, Peter S. *Patterns in Nature.* Boston: Little, Brown, 1974.

Stewart, Ian, and Martin Golubitsky. *Fearful Symmetry: Is God a Geometer?* Oxford: Blackwell, 1994.

Storer, William Allin. *The Frank Lloyd Wright Companion.* Chicago: University of Chicago Press, 1994.

Sturtevant, A. H. "Experiments on Sex Recognition and the Problem of Sexual Selection in *Drosophila*" (1915). In E. B. Lewis, ed., *Genetics and Evolution: Selected Papers of A. H. Sturtevant.* San Francisco: Freeman, 1961.

Sullivan, Louis. *A System of Architectural Ornament, According with a Philosophy of Man's Powers.* 1924. Reprint, New York: Eakins Press, 1967.

Swammerdam, Jan. *The Book of Nature; or, the History of Insects. . . .* London: Seyffert, 1748.

Swammerdam, Jan. *The Letters of Jan Swammerdam to Melchisedek Thévenet.* Amsterdam: Swets and Zeitlinger, 1975.

Swammerdam, Jan. *Miraculum naturae sive uteri muliebris fabrica.* London: Sollers, 1680.

Szambien, Werner. *Jean-Nicolas Durand, 1760–1834: De l'imitation à la norme.* Paris: Picard, 1984.

Tempko, Allan. *Eero Saarinen.* New York: Braziller, 1962.

Templer, John. *The Staircase: History and Theories.* Cambridge, Mass.: MIT Press.

Teräs, Ilkka. "Bee and Wasp Cells." In *Animal Architecture.* Exhibition catalogue. Helsinki: Museum of Finnish Architecture, 1995.

Thompson, D'Arcy Wentworth. *On Growth and Form.* Complete rev. ed. 1942. Reprint, New York: Dover, 1992. First ed. published 1917.

Thornhill, Randy, and Steven Gangestad. "Human Facial Beauty: Averageness, Symmetry, and Parasite Resistance." *Proceedings of the Royal Society of London* B261 (1994), 111ff.

Tilley, Christopher. *A Phenomenology of Landscape: Places, Paths, and Monuments.* Oxford: Berg, 1994.

Tomlinson, P. B. "Tree Architecture." *American Scientist* 71 (1983), 141ff.

Torii, Tokutoshi. *El mundo enigmático de Gaudí.* 2 vols. Madrid: Instituto de España, 1983.

Toulmin, Stephen, and June Goodfield. *The Architecture of Matter.* New York: Harper and Row, 1962.

Trachtenberg, Marvin. *The Statue of Liberty.* New York: Penguin Books, 1977.

Uhlig, Helmut. *Tantrische Kunst des Buddhismus.* Berlin: Kunstamt Berlin-Tempelhof, 1981.

Vannini, Vannio, and Giuliano Pogliani. *The Color Atlas of Human Anatomy.* New York: Harmony Books, 1980.

Varriano, John. *Italian Baroque and Rococo Architecture*. New York: Oxford University Press, 1986.

Vasari, Giorgio. *The Lives of the Painters, Sculptors, and Architects* (1550). Trans. A. B. Hinds, 4 vols. 1927. Reprint, London: Dent, 1980.

Vassiliou, Jean. *Angkor*. Translated by Maximo Portassi. Paris: Morancé, 1971.

Vidler, Anthony. *Claude-Nicolas Ledoux: Architecture and Social Reform at the End of the Ancien Regime*. Cambridge, Mass.: MIT Press, 1990.

Vidmann, Ladislao. *Isis und Serapis* [Osiris] *bei den Griechen und Römern. Epigraphische Studien*. . . . Religionsgeschichtliche Versuche und Vorarbeiten, n.s. 29. Giessen: A. Topelmann, 1970.

Villalpando, Juan Bautista. *In Ezechielem explanationes . . .* (1604). Madrid: Ediciones Siruela, 1991.

Villari, Sergio. *J.-N.-L. Durand (1764–1834): Art and Science of Architecture*. New York: Rizzoli, 1990.

Viollet-le-Duc, Eugène-Emmanuel. *Dictionnaire raisonné de l'architecture française du xi au xvi siècle*. 10 vols. Paris: B. Bance, 1861.

Volwahsen, Andreas. *Living Architecture: Indian*. New York: Grosset and Dunlap, 1969.

von Frisch, Karl. *Aus dem Leben der Bienen*. Berlin: Springer, 1953.

von Frisch, Karl, with the collaboration of Otto von Frisch. *Animal Architecture*. Trans. Lisbeth Gombrich. New York: Harcourt Brace Jovanovich, 1974.

von Mitterwallner, Gritli. "Evolution of the Linga." In Michael W. Meister, ed., *Discourses on Siva: Proceedings of a Symposium on the Nature of Religious Imagery*. Philadelphia: University of Pennsylvania Press, 1984.

Wachsmann, Konrad. *Wendepunkt im Bauen*. Wiesbaden: Krausskopf, 1959.

Wainwright, Stephen A. *Axis and Circumference: The Cylindrical Shape of Plants and Animals*. Cambridge, Mass.: Harvard University Press, 1988.

Wainwright, S. A., W. D. Biggs, J. D. Currey, and J. M. Gasline. *Mechanical Change in Organisms*. Princeton: Princeton University Press, 1982.

Watkin, David. *History of Western Architecture*. London: Thames and Hudson, 1986.

Watson, James D. *The Double Helix: A Personal Account of the Structure of DNA*. New York: Atheneum, 1968.

Weiner, Jonathan. *The Beak of the Finch: A Story of Evolution in Our Time*. New York: Knopf, 1994.

Weyl, Hermann. *Symmetry.* Princeton: Princeton University Press, 1951.

Whitesides, George M. "Self-Assembling Materials." *Scientific American,* September 1995, 146ff.

Whyte, Iain Boyd, ed. *The Crystal Chain Letters: Architectural Fantasies by Bruno Taut and His Circle.* Cambridge, Mass.: MIT Press, 1985.

Wickler, Wolfgang. *The Sexual Code.* Garden City, N.Y.: Doubleday, 1972.

Wickler, Wolfgang. "Socio-Sexual Signals and Their Intraspecific Imitation among Primates." In Desmond Morris, ed., *Primate Ethology.* Chicago: Aldine, 1967.

Wickler, Wolfgang. "Ursprung und biologische Deutung des Genitalpräsentierens männlicher Primaten." *Zeitschrift für Tierpsychologie* 23 (1966), 422ff.

Wilber, Donald. *Persepolis: The Archaeology of Parsa, Seat of the Persian Kings.* Rev. ed. Princeton: Darwin Press, 1989.

Wiley, E. O., et al. *The Compleat Cladist: A Primer of Phylogenetic Procedures.* Lawrence, Kan.: Museum of Natural History, University of Kansas, 1991.

Willis, Delta. *The Sand Dollar and the Slide Rule: Drawing Blueprints from Nature.* Reading, Mass.: Addison-Wesley, 1995.

Wilson, P. I. "The Geometry of Golden Section Phyllotaxis." *Journal of Theoretical Biology* 177, no. 4 (1995), 315ff.

Wilson, Peter J. *The Domestication of the Human Species.* New Haven: Yale University Press, 1988.

Winston, Mark L. *Biology of the Honey Bee.* Cambridge, Mass.: Harvard University Press, 1987.

Wiseman, Carter. *I. M. Pei: A Profile in American Architecture.* New York: Abrams, 1990.

Wittkower, Rudolf. "A Counter-Project to Bernini's Piazza di San Pietro." *Journal of the Warburg and Courtauld Institutes* 8 (1939–1940), 88ff.

Wittkower, Rudolf. *Studies in the Italian Baroque.* London: Thames and Hudson, 1975.

Wittkower, Rudolf, and Irma B. Jaffe, eds. *Baroque Art: The Jesuit Contribution.* New York: Fordham University Press, 1972.

Wolff Metternich, Franz, Graf. *Die frühen St.-Peter-Entwürfe, 1505–1514.* Tübingen: Wasmuth, 1987.

Wolff Metternich, Franz, Graf. "Über die Massgrundlagen des Kuppelentwürfes Bramantes für Peterskirche in Rom." In Douglas Fraser, Howard Hibbard, and Milton Lewine, eds., *Essays in the History of Architecture Presented to Rudolf Wittkower.* London: Phaidon, 1967.

Wood, J. G. *Homes without Hands*. New York: Harper and Brothers, 1866.

Yalom, Marilyn. *A History of the Breast*. New York: HarperCollins, 1996.

Zagorska-Marek, B. "Phyllotaxis Diversity in Magnolia Flowers." *Acta Societatis Botanicorum Poloniae* 63, no. 2 (1994), 117ff.

Zannas, Eliky, and Jeannine Auboyer. *Khajuraho*. The Hague: Mouton, 1960.

Zocca, Mario. *La Cupola di San Giacomo in Augusta e le cupole ellitiche in Roma*. Il Volto di Roma dei secoli 4. Rome: Istituto di studi romani, 1945.

Zoega Dano, Georg. *De Origine et usu obeliscorum*. Rome, 1797.

# INDEX

Distychous pairs, 27
Dixson, A. F., 120
DNA molecules, 5, 10, 48, 119, 180
  and architecture, 162–164
  and spiral stairs, 7
  as twisted columns, 30
Dogfish, xvii, xviii
Domains of danger, 101
Domes, xiii, 149–155, 172
  as breasts, 154
  as eggs, 153
  geodesic, 16
  guava, 152
  as vegetal growths, 22
Doric order, plant origins of, 287
Dormice, 98
*Drosophila bifurca*, 119
Durand, J.-N.-L.
  genetic formulas in architecture, 159–160, 162
  possible plans by, 166
  prison plan by, 165

Eagle
  fern, 27
  as gable, 90
  god, 95
Eberhard, William G., 116, 118
Echinoi, 28
Ecouen, France
  château, 54
Egg-and-dart moldings, 149
Eggs, xiii, 149–154, 158, 181
  albuminous corridors of, 150
  as cell containers, 18
  chalazae, 150
  cosmic, 152
  fertilization of, 119
  as fortresses, 143
  as nests, 139
  as sacrifices, 150
  uterine journeys of, 143
  vitelline membrane of, 151
Egypt, xii, 117, 125, 141, 152
  cosmos, as reproductive system, 141
  floral ornament, 28
  Old and Middle Kingdoms, 141
  woman-centeredness in, 141
Eiffel, Gustave, 12–13
Ejaculatory duct, in penis, 116
Eliot, George, xii
Embalming, Egyptian, 141

Embryo, 142
  human-shaped (homunculus), 120
Eos, 106
Epidauros, Greece, 27
Ethiopia, 118
Europa, 109, 112
Evans, Sir Arthur, 70
Evolution, in inanimate objects, 2
Extended phenotypes, 84, 93
Eyes, evolution of, xvii, xviii
Ezekiel, prophet, 8

Fallopian tubes, 144
Fascias, penis, 117, 130
Ferrara, cathedral, 30
Ferrari, Giovanni Battista, 66
Ferriss, Hugh, 146
Fetal membranes, 140
*Fibonacci Quarterly*, 36
Fibonacci sequence, 35–38, 180
Finials, 183
Finsterlin, Hermann, 18
Fischer von Erlach, Johann Bernhard, 106
Fish, 173
Flash Gordon, 69
Fleagle, J. G., 98–99
Fletcher, Banister, xiv, xvii, 47, 87, 172, 173
Fleurs-de-lis, 32
Flora, 180
Floreale, 22
Florence, Italy
  as city of towers, 135
  Santa Maria del Fiore (Duomo), 71–72, 150
Fontana, Domenico, 128
*Formica fusca*, 72
*Formica polyctena*, 73
Fossae, in human uterus, 142
Fountains, 121, 127
Fractals, 18, 162–164, 183
  defined, 167
  reproduction, 167–172
*Fragaria*, 26
Frame, Michael, 163
France, 110
Francesco di Giorgio Martini, 108, 109
  church plan by, 19
Francis, Saint, 92
Frankfort, Henri, 124
*Frauenkirchen*, 153
Fruit, 149, 154, 158

Uterus, 145
Utricle, 129

Vaginas, 105, 145, 158
    and fountains, 145
Vallon-Pont-d'Arc, France
    Grotte Chauvet, 138–139
Valves, in architecture, 42
Vancouver, 92
Vasari, Giorgio, 72, 150
Vastu Purusha, 130
Vatican. *See* Rome
Vaults, 175, 182
Vela Luca (former Yugoslavia), 111
Venae cavae, 142
Venice
    Palazzo Contarini del Bovolo, 48, 49, 51
    San Marco, 170
Vertebral column, 105
Vertebrates, xviii
Vertical condensation, 22
Vesicles, 19, 21
Vienna, 161
Vignola, Giacomo, 160
Villa books, Victorian, 181
Villages, prehistoric, 19
Viollet-le-Duc, Eugène-Emmanuel, 50
Virgil, 27, 72, 117
    *Aeneid*, 63
    *Georgics*, 63
Viruses, xx, 15–16
    rhinovirus, 16
    T4 bacteriophage, 15
Vistas, in territories, 101
Vitelline membrane, egg, 143
Vitreous humor, xvii
Vitruvius Pollio, xiii, xix, 27, 68, 82, 87
    temple recipes of, 158–159
Vittozzi, Ascanio, 152–153
Volutes, 44
Von Frisch, Karl, 65, 74
Voussoirs, 175
Vriesendorp, Madelon, 146–147
Vulcan, 63
Vulvas, 116, 145, 158

Wachsmann, Konrad, 15–16
Wallpaper, ant, 73
Washington (D.C.)
    White House, Oval Office, 149
Weaverbirds, 82–83, 140, 183

Weaving, as origin of architecture, 83, 180
Whelk shells, xiii, 43, 44
Whorls and hyperwhorls, 8–10
Wies, die, Church of, Austria, 54, 55
Wilson, E. O., 73
Wilson, Peter J., xix–xx, 99, 112
Wings, architectural, 91
Wittkower, Rudolf, 108
Wittwer, Hans, 151
Woman-centeredness, Egyptian, 141
Womb, 139, 141
    chambers, 130–131
Wood, Rev. J. G., 72
Wright, Frank Lloyd, xiii, xix, 11, 48
    Arizona State Capitol project, 68
    Hanna House, 67–68
    and hexagons, 67–69
    Mile High Skyscraper, 74, 76
    Steel Cathedral, 5
    Usonian houses, 67

Yoga, 148
Yoingu colossus, 111
Yonis, 130–133, 144, 147, 149

Zebras, 180
Zeus, 110
Zimmermann, Domenikus, 54, 55, 183
Zona, egg, 143
Zophos, 106
Zoroaster, 7
Zuccaro, Federigo, 152, 153
Zygotes, 123